ENGRAVED UPON THE HEART

"A fine practical theological study combining liturgical studies, religious education and developmental psychology. Moon makes a convincing argument that liturgical participation is a primary means of formation of persons for the Christian life. Weaving care for persons and justice, he demonstrates that inclusion of the young in ritual participation is theologically warranted and pedagogically astute. This study helpfully extends conversations about children, worship and sacraments."

—JACK L. SEYMOUR
Professor of Religious Education, Garrett-Evangelical Theological Seminary; editor, *Religious Education*

ENGRAVED UPON THE HEART

Children, the Cognitively Challenged,
and Liturgy's Influence on Faith Formation

Hwarang Moon

WIPF & STOCK · Eugene, Oregon

ENGRAVED UPON THE HEART
Children, the Cognitively Challenged, and Liturgy's Influence on Faith Formation

Copyright © 2015 Hwarang Moon. All rights reserved. Except for brief quotations in critical publications or reviews, no part of this book may be reproduced in any manner without prior written permission from the publisher. Write: Permissions, Wipf and Stock Publishers, 199 W. 8th Ave., Suite 3, Eugene, OR 97401.

Wipf & Stock
An Imprint of Wipf and Stock Publishers
199 W. 8th Ave., Suite 3
Eugene, OR 97401

www.wipfandstock.com

ISBN 13: 978-1-4982-2012-5

Manufactured in the U.S.A.   07/09/2015

Contents

Acknowledgments | vii
Introduction | ix

1 The Role of Liturgy and Ritual in Public Worship | 1
2 John Calvin's Thoughts on Liturgy and Faith Formation | 23
3 Liturgy as a Tool for Christian Faith Formation and Learning | 56
4 Participation of Children and Persons with Cognitive Challenges in Church Life | 96
5 Cognitive Ability and Religious Concepts | 123
6 Why Children and Cognitively Challenged Individuals Should Fully Participate in the Sacraments | 151
7 What are the Benefits for Children and Cognitively Challenged Individuals? | 189

Conclusion | 208
Bibliography | 213
Index | 237

Acknowledgments

THANKS TO GOD, WHO has led my way and protected all my family while I have been studying in United States. I wish to specially thank Dr. E. Byron Anderson, who taught me liturgical studies at Garrett Evangelical Theological Seminary. Without his warm heart, scholarly wisdom, and guidance, I could not write this book. I am so proud to be his student. Also, there are many other scholars who have helped me on my way to becoming a liturgical theologian and Christian Educator: Dr. Ruth Duck, Frank C. Senn, Dr. Jack Seymour, Dr. Karen-Marie Yust, Dr. John Witvliet, Dr. Brett Webb-Mitchell, Dr. David Hogue, Dr. Darwin K. Glassford, and others.

I owe a special debt of thanks to Rev. Jangoun Youn (Seongan Presbyterian Church), Rev. Seogu Cho (Busan Buk Church), and their church members for their steadfast support and prayer for my studies.

In addition, there are some friends and institutes who have helped my research and book writings: United Library at Garrett Theological Evangelical Seminary, Hekman Library at Calvin Seminary, Kathleen Kordesh, Paul Fields, Lugene Schemper, Meredith Carey Asher, Tammy Wiens, and Marguerite Westbrook.

I wish to dedicate my work to my lovely parents, Jonggyu Moon and Sangyoung Chang, and Seogu Cho and Soondeuk Han, who supported and prayed for my studies in America. Also, my wife Kyungmok Cho and lovely daughters Sujung and Susie Moon, who have patiently endured and helped my studies for 7 years. Soli Deo gloria.

Introduction

HOW DOES LITURGY INFLUENCE FAITH FORMATION?

How do we know God? How do people acquire faith? Is faith a confession that comes merely from the cognitive dimension? In other words, is it only a matter of the mental ability? Does having faith require the ability to explain faith logically? Or do only those who can explain faith logically have real faith? Does it mean that very young children and the cognitively challenged cannot have faith?[1] How do they learn? If people consider these people's faith to be somewhat more deficient than adults, is adult faith different from a child's faith? And, what of children and adults with cognitive challenges?

---

1. Generally, when naming people with cognitive disabilities, the terms "mental retardation," "intellectual disability," and "learning disability" have been frequently used. Luckasson and Reeve say, "Terminology in the field of mental retardation is almost always a topic that precipitates a lively discussion. The term mental retardation, used for more than 50 years, is most often used in the United States. Worldwide, the term intellectual disability is the preferred designation." See Beirne-Smith, et al., *Mental Retardation*, 44. John Swinton points out that in England, the term "learning disability" has been favored. See Swinton and Mowat, *Practical Theology*, 253. However, some people misunderstand the difference between intellectual disability and mental disability or illness, which are distinct in that intellectual disability "refers to cognitive impairment rather than conditions of mental illness." See Reinders, *Receiving the Gift of Friendship*. According to the American Association on Intellectual and Developmental Disabilities, the two main characteristics of mental retardation are limitation of intellect and lack of adaptive behavior. See Ibid., 61. In general, "range of severity is typically defined as mild (IQ 50–55 to 70), moderate (IQ 35–40 to 50–55), severe (IQ 20–25 to 35–40), and profound (IQ below 20–25)." See Rojahn and Meier, "Epidemiology of Mental Illness," 241. I think the terms "retarded" and "disabled" convey negative images; so I will use the term "cognitively challenged" in this work.

If there are many methods of communication, can bodily action and expression be the confessional expression of a person?[2]

From their beginning, Reformed churches have placed significant emphasis on the cognitive knowledge in faith formation. In contrast to the Roman Catholic Church, which emphasized sacrament and liturgy, the Reformed churches have emphasized preaching and catechesis, which reinforced the idea that belief comes from hearing (Rom 10:17).[3] To the Reformed churches, orthodox faith could be gained from the proper exegesis and knowledge of the Bible.[4] Therefore, reformers such as Zwingli, Bucer, and Calvin stressed church education, especially catechetical instruction for children from an early age, and published many catechisms and directories for them.

However, many reformers had little concern about the possibility of learning through doing liturgical practice or participating in public worship, including the sacraments.[5] According to their concepts of faith formation, the Reformers believed that preparation and discernment before participation in worship were very necessary because of their emphasis on God's holiness; emphasizing preaching and catechetical instruction, they looked down on the possibility of learning and the transformation of believers through Christian worship. In the case of Bucer's and Calvin's faith formation systems, the emphasis was on parents' educational duties; catechism services for the younger generations were arranged as afterthoughts to Sunday public worship, to make young children qualified participants of the worship.[6]

Since the 1971 Conference of the Faith and Order Commission of the World Council of Churches, the Reformed churches in North America have begun giving attention to the function and merit of liturgy. In particular, Reformed scholars, such as Nicholas Wolterstorff, John Witvliet, and James

---

2. These questions have a close relationship with the work of reformed theologian Jean-Jacques von Allmen and United Methodist theologian Don Saliers's work. See Saliers, *Worship and Spirituality*, 47–66 and von Allmen, *Celebrer le Salut*, 122–53.

3. Robert Webber says, "The positive feature of the catechism is that it teaches the Christian faith, a matter neglected in the medieval era. The negative feature of the catechism is that children become subject to intellectual faith and lose the spirit of being a creative and mystical Christian." Webber, *Ancient-Future Evangelism*, 29.

4. To teach the Bible, Reformers emphasized humanistic education in the public schools, and, through education in family and church, they intended catechetical instruction from the early ages. See Wandel, "Zwingli and Reformed Practice," 270–87.

5. Wolterstorff, "Reformed Liturgy," 274.

6. Regarding the family's educational duty in Calvin's thought, see Calvin, "Commentaries on the First Book of Moses," 481. Regarding detailed explanation of catechism worship for children in Geneva at that time, see Spieling, *Infant Baptism*.

K. Smith, have tried to explore the formative function of liturgy and ritual based on Reformed theology and tradition. Even though they stand firmly in the Reformed tradition, they feel the necessity of using liturgy for helping people's understanding and memory in making faithful Christians.[7] My book lies in the same vein with them.

In this book, I will start from the idea that faith includes not only cognition, but also emotion and volition. As Calvin insisted, without *pietas*, there is no knowledge of God.[8] Even though Calvin emphasized cognition and knowledge in defining faith, his commentary and later edition of the *Institutes* considered *fiducia*, which is another dimension of faith.[9] Generally, many Calvin scholars have insisted on the supremacy of intellect in the matter of faith.[10] However, Richard Muller insists,

> Calvin does say that faith is frequently called *agnitio* (recognition) in Scripture and is called *scientia* (knowledge) by John—but in the same passage, he cites Eph 3:18–19, drawing the conclusion that faith is far beyond understanding (*esse omni intelligentia longe sublimius*) and that the knowledge of faith (*fidei notitiam*) consists of assurance (*certitudine*) rather than apprehension (*apprehension*).[11]

Muller shows Calvin's consideration that faith is not just a matter of cognition or accumulating knowledge about God, but that it is more profound than the matter of understanding and intelligence. To proceed, Muller demonstrates that knowledge itself, in Calvin's theology, has a character of experiential and not abstract: seems to emphasize "certainty than in comprehension."[12] In other words, Calvin did not pursue "a purely cerebral meaning of faith when he identifies faith as *cognitio* (knowledge)." According to Muller, "Calvin speaks of a 'sense of the divine' engraved not on the mind or brain but upon the heart."[13] For Calvin, the interrelationship between intellect and human will is very important for getting faith.[14]

While knowledge of God is an important concept in Calvin's thought on faith, this knowledge can be gained by participation in the Triune God

---

7. See Wolterstorff, *Until Justice and Peace Embrace*, chapter 7; Witvliet, *Worship Seeking Understanding*; Smith, *Desiring the Kingdom*.

8. Calvin, *Institutes*, I.ii.1.

9. Muller, *Unaccommodated Calvin*, 159.

10. Ibid., 255.

11. Ibid., 160.

12. Ibid., 161.

13. Ibid., 168.

14. Ibid., 171.

and gives assurance to the mind of participants in worship; therefore, it can be called experiential. I argue that faith, while closely related to the knowledge of God, is not merely a matter of accumulation of knowledge but can be enhanced by participation in public worship composed of the Word and sacraments. This assertion does not devalue the necessity of studying the Bible and Christian doctrine, but recognizes the merit of knowledge from experience. People learn while participating in the Christian worship. They may be unable to clearly explain how knowledge was delivered to their minds and hearts, but it is certain that participation in worship and using liturgy can take a great role in learning about God and developing their faith. Knowledge gained from experience is a tacit dimension of knowledge.

Michael Polanyi, scientist and philosopher, insists that "the premises underlying a major intellectual process are never formulated and transmitted in the form of definite precepts. When children learn to think naturalistically, they do not acquire any explicit knowledge of the principles of causation."[15] Epistemology is neither objectivity nor subjectivity; it should be personal.[16] By "personal," Polanyi means the necessity of a person's "participation through indwelling."[17] This repudiates excessive objectivism or subjectivism, a question to which we return in chapter 3. Knowledge does not need to be attained through distancing from the object; rather, people who participate in the event and interact with other people will get personal knowledge composed of tacit knowing.

What, then, is the meaning of *tacit knowing*? Different from "explicit knowing," tacit knowing can be best understood by the motto: "We can know more than we can tell."[18] By indwelling in reality, while interacting with other object or people, "the process of immersing oneself in the particulars of subsidiary awareness by means of embodied activity," people come to know.[19] This means a person can identify with the object of knowledge.[20] However, indwelling is a sort of participation, not merely empathy.[21] Therefore, "we participate in them [all comprehensive entities] as if their subsidiaries were parts of our body."[22] So, according to Polanyi, meaning

---

15. Polanyi, *Science, Faith and Society*, 42.
16. See Polanyi, *Personal Knowledge*, 300.
17. Polanyi and Prosch, *Meaning*, 44.
18. Polanyi, *Tacit Dimension*, 4.
19. Gill, *Tacit Mode*, 52.
20. Polanyi, *Meaning*, 44.
21. Polanyi, *Tacit Dimension*, 16–17.
22. Ibid., 138.

can be gotten by interaction among simultaneous and interpenetrating dimensions of reality.[23]

Polanyi's thought can be an important point in supporting the validity of participation in worship and sacrament for children and persons with cognitive challenges. Along with Reformed philosopher James Smith, I argue that liturgy forms the *habitus* (simply defined here as "the set of habitual dispositions through which people 'give shape and form to social conventions,'"[24]) of people, and this *habitus* forms the character of faith in the mind. By participating in the liturgy, people can understand more than by merely listening to the preaching; by doing, people can better understand and remember; and these are the processes that transform the people.[25]

To create a basis for inclusion of children and cognitively challenged individuals in the liturgy, we must define what liturgy is, especially the meaning and usage of liturgy in the Bible. This is particularly applicable to Reformed churches, which still resist use of liturgy. If we understand the essence and necessity of liturgy, the Protestant church can rethink the formative function of liturgy in the process of faith formation.

We must also study John Calvin, who had a great impact on the formation of the Reformed church's worship, liturgy, rituals, and faith education. Even though Calvin emphasized God's Word, preaching and catechetical instruction in his Strasbourg French liturgy of 1540 and his Geneva liturgy of 1542, he discussed deep liturgical considerations and ideas as he tried to enhance the Reformed spirit while balancing the Word and liturgy. His insistence on the weekly observance of the Lord's Supper, insertion of the epiclesis, introduction of psalms and hymns, and the value of confession and absolution show his positive stance on the use of liturgy.[26]

To Calvin, as Bousma points out, faith is a matter of "the heart rather than the head and the affections rather than the understanding."[27] Of course, Bousma also recognizes the other possible interpretation—that Calvin emphasized reason and understanding in the medieval scholastic philosophical tradition.[28] Lee Wandel notes that Calvin's *Institutes* start not from God's on-

---

23. See Gill, *Tacit Mode*, 34.

24. Bell, *Ritual Theory, Ritual Practice*, 79.

25. See Smith, *Desiring the Kingdom*, 26–27.

26. van de Poll, *Martin Bucer's Liturgical Idea*, 111–17; Thompson, *Liturgies of the Western Church*, 159–224.

27. Bousma, *John Calvin*, 158. However, some scholars believe Calvin emphasized intellectualism in defining the faith. For example, Kendall's analysis of Calvin emphasized the priority of intellect in the matter of faith, based on Calvin's use of terms like "*scientia, agnitio, illuminatio,* and *cognitio.*" See Muller, *Unaccommodated Calvin*, 160.

28. Bousma, *John Calvin*, 230.

tology, but from the "human capacity to recognize God."[29] Calvin's concern was in the *episteme*, especially the interrelationship between knowledge of God and knowledge of people. However, Calvin does not devalue experience itself. He says, "There are two kinds of knowledge: the knowledge of faith, and what they call experimental knowledge."[30]

That is to say, Calvin affirms human experience. To Calvin, the worldly signs and elements serve to bridge "human blindness and divine revelation."[31] These factors provide a "cognitive bridge, between the corporeality of human intelligence and God's speaking."[32] Experience through signs is not worthless to Calvin.[33]

Traditionally, the Church has upheld dualistic opinions of humans, so that the soul was considered good and the body considered evil—the body has been considered the origin of human sin.[34] However, the Bible does not support this opinion. A human being is a whole person who has a body and a spirit, and the incarnation of God is the powerful proof that God affirmed human bodiliness.[35] In addition, the Bible promises the resurrection of the body.[36] Not only the human soul, but also the human body, is the object of salvation; liturgy can be the means of disciplining human learning and faith. In the learning process, the human body is important in that it receives information and forms perception. While doing liturgy and rituals in the church, participants fortify their memory; they can then remember God's Word more vividly and efficiently. While practicing liturgy, people become active participants, and the minds of the worshippers are transformed by the encoded messages of the liturgy. This leads to a consideration of ritual knowing. Recently, anthropologists and liturgical scholars have been exploring the ways in which ritual provides a kind knowledge in the symbolic dimension.[37] Ritual knowing can arouse not only cognition, but also emotions; through ritual in Christian worship, people can learn more efficiently. Even the Reformed Church has had negative feelings about rituals, but I believe that rituals have been used in Christian worship, in not

29. Wandel, *Eucharist in the Reformation*, 148.
30. Calvin, "Commentaries on Zechariah," 73.
31. Wandel, *Eucharist in the Reformation*, 157.
32. Ibid.
33. Wandel says, "The project of the *Institutes* was to teach the faithful how to read God's marks and signs." See Ibid., 159.
34. Moltmann-Wendel, *I am My Body*, 36, 42.
35. Bavinck, *Reformed Dogmatics*, 2:554–62.
36. See 1 Cor 15:42–44.
37. Saliers, *Worship as Theology*, 209–13.

only the Roman Catholic Church, but also the Protestant Church, and can impact human memory in the brain and in the body. The possibility of ritual knowing is the most important reason to include children and cognitively challenged individuals. In particular, James K. A. Smith's model of moving "from cognitive to affective" by "bodily participation" and "habit forming rituals" would be great tools for this.[38] Also, the works of Roy Rappaport, Ronald Grimes, Catherine Bell, and Paul Connerton show that memory is not only personal but also communal.[39] The human act is not meaningless but makes the space of memory in the human brain.[40]

In the work of Augustine, Aquinas, and Martin Luther, we find how the church has (or has not) endeavored to include cognitively challenged persons into the life of the church throughout history. Similarly, North American churches' denominational documents, reports, and constitutions illustrate how North American churches theologically reflect to include children and the cognitively challenged in public worship. A look at the Korean Presbyterian Church's current practices regarding inclusion of cognitively challenged persons in public worship and sacrament also shows that more concern and cooperation is necessary before the church can truly be one for all people.

It is very difficult to even find mention of the cognitively challenged in the confessions and historical documents throughout church history.[41] More recently, many scholars insist that even though cognitively challenged persons have limited abilities for expression, they still have religious abilities in the practice of worship services.[42] In his books, Brett Webb-Mitchell reports many examples from his experiences with cognitively challenged people. He shows that persons labeled as mentally handicapped, autistic, or as having Down syndrome sometimes show deep religious response and potential while participating in the public worship, regardless of their "intelligence" as it is seen by society and the church ministry.[43] He demonstrates

38. See Smith, *Desiring the Kingdom*, 64; 69.

39. Bell, *Ritual*. See also Rappaport, *Ritual and Religion* and Grimes, *Deeply into the Bone*.

40. Connerton, *How Societies Remember*. See also Atkins, *Memory and Liturgy*.

41. The only Reformed confession that mentions the participation of persons with cognitive challenges is Micron's Shorter Catechism (1552). It was made for the Dutch refugee church of London. See van't Spijker, *Church's Book of Comfort*, 142.

42. Regarding a child's religious potential, see Cavalletti, *Religious Potential*; Hay and Nye, *Spirit of the Child*. Regarding persons who are cognitively challenged, see Webb-Mitchell, *Christly Gestures*; Yong, *Theology and Down Syndrome*; Eiesland, *Disabled God*; Swinton, *Critical Reflections*.

43. Regarding many examples in Webb-Mitchell's studies, see Webb-Mitchell, *Dancing with Disabilities*, 20–22. After spending a week with Rachel, a mentally retarded

that faith formation does not depend merely on cognitive development. However, in studying children and the cognitively challenged, the similarities and differences between them should be noted; I particular, learning power, learning strategies, and communication methods as well as the level of ease with which children and the cognitively challenged appropriate the verbal content of worship, and the differences in how each accesses and expresses their emotional engagement through worship.[44] Recently, cognitive developmental theory and cognitive psychology have contributed to our understanding of children's thinking ability and religious development.[45] According to Daniel Stern, infants can show surprising perception and reaction.[46] Through an experience, the young child gathers information, then the self is emergent. Developmental psychologists insist that children do not have abstract thinking power like adults; but this does not mean they do not have religious abilities, or that they cannot know God.[47] As Calvin says, "a sense of deity is inscribed on every heart."[48] The spiritual senses of children can recognize the existence of God, and can proceed to God with perhaps more open minds than adults do.

Like children, persons who are cognitively challenged are also able to do more than merely assent to faith. Even though they may encounter difficulty learning and accepting knowledge, they can in fact learn and have potential to develop. Even though their expressions do not show their ability and potential, their learning and memory can be enhanced by experience and participation in study groups, not only by verbal means, but also through communication methods such as music, painting, body movement,

---

five-year-old, as well as other families with cognitively challenged kids, Webb-Mitchell began to take note of their religious abilities. While worshipping together, especially at the Lord's Supper, which was performed with intention, Rachel showed her voluntary wish to join the ritual act. Webb-Mitchell also tells George's story. He was 19 years old; however, because of autism, his mental age was that of a toddler. However, by typing, he could express his inner mind, and showed his desire to be Christian. See *God Plays Piano*, 135–41. Also, Webb-Mitchell tells a story from the United Methodist Church in Wilmington, Delaware. During the vacation Bible School, an 8-year-old boy who had severe mental retardation showed his desire to participate in the worship while holding the Bible. See Webb-Mitchell, *Unexpected Guests*, 173–74.

44. Even Vygotsky insists that young children and the cognitively challenged have the same learning structures. See Vygotsky, *Mind in Society*, 90.

45. For a detailed study, see Goswami, *Cognitive Development*.

46. Stern, *Interpersonal World*.

47. See Fowler, *Stages of Faith*, 128–31.

48. See Calvin, *Institutes*, I.iii.1. Regarding recent studies, see Yust, *Real Kids, Real Faith*, and Hay and Nye, *Spirit of the Child*.

and gestures, all of which can represent their thoughts and reveal their inner minds.

While the church agrees that worship forms the faith of believers, it has nonetheless restricted the participation of children and persons with cognitive challenges in public worship and the sacraments because of both groups' lack of cognitive ability. The assumption is that these two group's cognitive disadvantages will lead to noisy or disruptive behavior in church, and thereby destroy the calm the church considers necessary for showing holiness.[49] Because liturgy has a formative power that reaches beyond cognitive knowledge, children and the cognitively challenged must be allowed to participate in worship. These two groups of people can have full participation in public worship, and they will reap the benefits of participation from an early age.

Like you and me, children and cognitively challenged individuals are born in the image of God (Gen 1:27). Though this image of God has been distorted by human degeneration, the Bible says "for all of you who were baptized into Christ have clothed yourselves with Christ. There is neither Jew nor Greek, slave nor free, male nor female, for you are all one in Christ Jesus" (Gal 3:26–27). This does not merely mean equality that can be seen in the world, but the promise of God. As Bavinck points out, "the whole human being is [the] image and likeness of God, in soul and body, in all human faculties, powers, and gifts. Nothing in humanity is excluded from God's image."[50]

In the same vein, children and persons who are cognitively challenged can participate in public worship and sacrament because the Triune God encounters them in public worship and invites them into his presence as his people. God's grace and calling has wisdom far beyond any human response. As the Holy Trinity shows hospitality for each hypostasis, God shows this hospitality toward human beings, a significant reason for including all persons in public worship.

The faith of children and persons cognitive challenged can be nurtured by the help of the faith community. Currently, John Westerhoff's work on faith community and the Christian Reformed Church's studies on intergenerational worship show how a church community, by participating in public worship and the sacraments, can have a positive impact on the formation of faith.[51] According to Westerhoff, when a faith community

---

49. Mercer, *Welcoming Children*, 1–2.

50. Bavinck, *Reformed Dogmatics*, 2:561.

51. Westerhoff, *A Faithful Church*; *Bringing up Children*; *Inner Growth, Outer Change*; *Liturgy and Learning*; Vanderwell, ed., *Church of all Ages*.

composed of three generations joins in public worship together—not merely hearing a sermon or instruction, but also experiencing the sacraments and liturgy—faith can be transferred to the next generation. At the same time, the participation of children alters the experience and knowledge of God for all ages. This can be called a process of socialization.[52] The Sunday school system has contributed to church growth and faith formation; however, separation from public worship has led to a generational gap in the church. Children can learn by hearing and seeing; participation and experience increase a child's ability to understand Christian doctrine and adapt themselves to the mood of Christian public worship. This is not to say that children and cognitively challenged merely conform to adult expectations; rather, they should take their rightful place in the church community, in particular through the concept of covenant. The covenant is inclusive, and the covenant community is bigger than the Church, and has included family and posterity from the time of the Old Testament—through God's grace, rather than human effort.[53] Covenant is an expression of God's love for his people; if a person belongs to a covenant community, the person joins the community as a member. Since the covenant community includes children and those who are cognitively challenged, they can be welcomed as active members of the covenant community.

Most importantly, children and the cognitive challenged should be included in the worship based on the work of the Holy Spirit who surpasses human expectation and understanding. The Holy Spirit has sovereignty and freely permits faith according to his will: salvation is not dependent on human action. God gives faith as a gift, regardless of race, gender, age, and ability. The Church prays for the presence of God while calling on the Holy Spirit in worship. Taking this into consideration, is it not stubborn to prohibit children and the cognitively challenged from participating based on the limits of the Church's human understanding of the workings of the Holy Spirit?

The issue of objectivity and subjectivity of sacraments is important to note. Historically, the Reformed Church has emphasized the subjectivity of the sacraments, underscoring the discernment of the individual participant.[54] However, does this not make participation in the sacrament itself a useless thing? If not, does the sacrament itself have an efficacy? Calvin's sacramental theology does not merely insist on the subjectivity of the sacrament; even he emphasizes the necessity of "discernment" before participat-

---

52. See Westerhoff, *Will Our Children have Faith?* xi–xii.
53. Horton, *Christian Faith*, 716–17.
54. Mathison, *Given for You*, 47.

ing in the sacraments. He recognizes the necessity of earthly signs to aid human understanding: "God condescends to lead us to himself even by these earthly elements."[55]

Liturgical worship has great value in forming faith. Even though the cognitive factor is important in the process of faith formation, practicing liturgy can reach a more profound aspect of knowledge, which cannot be achieved by human cognition. Including children and the cognitively challenged in public worship can be a visible act that shows the meaning of Church. Hospitality and inclusiveness for them can also show God's love is not only for members of the Christian family, but also for non-Christians.

Liturgy touches human cognition, emotion, and volition and forms the human character. By practicing it every week, people can remember the contents of Christian faith more effectively. Liturgy is the symbol of God's grace. Even when we recognize the priority of God's Word, we cannot deny the power of liturgy in forming human faith.

LITURGICAL THEOLOGY: PURSUING BALANCED FAITH FORMATION

People can learn the Christian faith by practice, and although practice itself cannot guarantee faith, it has value in enhancing the understanding of the Christian faith in participants. Although doctrinal knowledge and faithful confession are very important, we need to recognize that doctrine came from the practice of worship.[56]

Aidan Kavanagh, in his book *On Liturgical Theology*, separates liturgy and dogmatics as *theologia prima* and *theologia secunda*. To Kavanagh, the primary theology is that theology expressed in the practice of worship: by enacting the liturgy, adjustment and gradual evolution of liturgy occur in assembly, and in this process, deep change among people occurs. Liturgy is formative.[57] Kavanagh goes on to say that "theology is in fact neither primary nor seminal but secondary and derivative: *theologia secunda*."[58] Theology appears through the process of reflecting on the practice of liturgy: Kavanagh rightly evaluates the importance of liturgy in the faith formation. He emphasizes the priority of liturgy over systematic theology. He says,

---

55. Wandel, *Eucharist in the Reformation*, 157.
56. LaCugna, *God for Us*, chapter 9.
57. Kavanagh, *On Liturgical Theology*, 73–75.
58. Ibid., 75.

> It was a Presence, not faith, which drew Moses to the burning bush, and what happened there was a revelation, not a seminar. It was a presence, not faith, which drew the disciples to Jesus, and what happened then was not an educational program but his revelation to them of himself as the long-promised Anointed One, the redeeming because reconciling Messiah-Christos. Their lives, like that of Moses, were changed radically by that encounter with a Presence which upended all their ordinary expectations. Their descendants in faith have been adjusting to that change ever since, drawn into assembly by that same Presence, finding there always the troublesome upset of change in their lives of faith to which they must adjust still. Here is where their lives are regularly being constituted and reconstituted under grace. Which is why *lex supplicandi legem statuat credendi*.[59]

People did not go to God's presence with belief, but, in the presence of God, came to experience God and thus to believe. To Kavanagh, liturgy is essential in faith formation.

Kavanagh understands liturgy as an experience of persons being brought to the brink of chaos in the presence of the living God. It helps people to encounter and have fellowship with God. The transformative power of liturgy can be applied to any person, because liturgy depends on God's grace and fellowship with God, not on human effort and cognitive power itself.

Liturgical participation leads to deep change for its participants because, through participation, the space for transformation is formed in the mind. Participation and repetition are more powerful than intelligence or cognition.

> What results in the first instance from liturgical experience is deep change in the very lives of those who participate in the liturgical act. And deep change will affect their next liturgical act, however slightly. . . . This adjustment causes the next liturgical act to be in some degree different from its predecessor because those who do the next act have been unalterably changed.[60]

The practice of liturgy is formative and assertive, even for children and the cognitively challenged who are often believed to lack reason. While doing liturgy, people learn the Christian faith and are changed. Everyone can experience the formation of faith; anyone can be a theologian and practice theology in the practice of liturgy.

59. Ibid., 92.
60. Ibid., 73–74.

Against the idealized and speculative, Kavanagh insists theology cannot be monopolized by a few special scholars:

> Theology at its genesis is communitarian, even proletarian; that it is aboriginally liturgical in context, partly conscious and partly unconscious; that it stems from an experience of near chaos; that it is long term and dialectical; and that its agents are more likely to be charwomen and shopkeepers than pontiffs and professors.[61]

Theology is not solely for certain educated scholars; in the liturgical context, people participate in making theology. Interestingly, this notion is very similar to the Eastern definitions of theology. In fact, Kavanagh believes Western theology's weak point is that it has emphasized the logic (*-logia*), not the God (*theo-*) in the definition of *theologia*.

> A sense of rite and symbol in the West was breaking down and under siege. And since it now appears that those who sought to repair the breakdown were its products rather than its masters they may be said with greater accuracy to have substituted something in its place that was new and, to them, more relevant to the times. It was a new system of worship which would increasingly bear the burden formerly borne by richly ambiguous corporate actions done with water, oil, food, and the touch of human hands ... liturgy had begun to become worship.... And the primary theological act which the liturgical act had once been now began to be controlled increasingly by practitioners of secondary theology whose concerns lay with correct doctrine in a highly polemical climate.[62]

Emphasizing the logic and academic aspects, Western theology has looked down on rites and symbols in the worship service and has restricted people's understanding of worship. As an alternative idea, liturgy and liturgical theology can help us gain an understanding of the meaning of worship and a more balanced faith formation. Kavanagh points out that by emphasizing divine ethos and God's supremacy, Reformed worship looks down on the human pathos. How, then, can we overcome the Western emphasis on logic in theology?

The practice of worship is not merely a repetitive human act, but that the *ordo* of worship forms the holy *habitus*, and takes on a significant role

---

61. Ibid., 74–75. Kavanagh also says, "*Theologia prima* is not done by private individuals, but publicly, in the community of faith. The liturgical assembly is a theological corporation." Kavanagh, "Response," 309–24.

62. See Kavanagh, *On Liturgical Theology*, 108–09.

in forming the faith of the people. As Don Saliers points out, worship forms the person's faith and spirituality.[63] God does not devalue the human pathos, but considers the human status, and, giving liturgy and Word, forms the divine ethos.[64] To focus on the role of liturgy as a primary factor in faith formation is to overcome Western Protestant churches' unbalanced pursuit of learning the dogma while losing the vitality of worship practice.

I do not absolutize liturgy; if I did, it would be a sort of liturgical Pelagianism. Nonetheless, liturgy can be formative. Liturgy is a sort of tool for communicating with God, and is effective when is guided by Holy Spirit. Throughout church history, the ancestors of faith have prayed to God for help in their worship practices. For example, Eastern liturgy emphasized the epiclesis; the Reformed church prayed for illumination before preaching the Word.[65] The church called on the help of the Holy Spirit in its liturgical actions (prayer, litany, and song). Therefore, we cannot disregard the role of liturgy in the formation of faith.

Even though I argue the importance of liturgy in faith formation, this does not neglect the role of the Holy Spirit in a person's faith formation. However, it is not my aim to discuss liturgical pneumatology here. While remembering that the Holy Spirit uses the human endeavor and liturgical factors for helping people's worship, I put forth a balanced stance in which liturgy can effectively help the process of faith formation and be helping hand for enhancing knowledge of God.

Above all, my emphasis on the role of liturgy in the process of faith formation starts from the current scholarly emphasis on the importance of practice. Don Browning insists that "church and religious communities are simultaneously communities of memory and communities of practical reason."[66] While impacted by Gadamer's thought, Browning does not follow the traditional "theory to practice (text to application)" but instead insists on a "practice-theory-practice model of understanding."[67] This model is helpful for emphasizing the priority of primary theology; however, because primary theology has been displaced by dogmatics, I use Reformed tradition and theology as important conversational partners to understanding liturgy is essential to faith formation.

---

63. Saliers, *Worship and Spirituality*, 42.

64. Saliers, *Worship as Theology*, 21–38.

65. See Schmemann, *For the Life of the World*, 39, and Chapell, *Christ-Centered Worship*, 50–51.

66. Browning, *Fundamental Practical Theology*, 2.

67. Ibid., 39.

1

The Role of Liturgy and Ritual in Public Worship

IN ORDER TO EXPLORE the impact of liturgy on faith formation, it is necessary to define and then study the role of liturgy. What is the meaning of liturgy? Is liturgical action necessary in the worship? Is faithfulness to God's Word enough for worshipping God? Although sincerity or intent of the worshiper has been emphasized, such an emphasis does not consider human nature and God's concern for human weakness.

Reformed worship theologian Jean-Jacques von Allmen says, "The forms in Christian theology are not a necessary evil or altogether regrettable."[1] According to Allmen, "The liturgy must be done because it is an echo of the incarnation."[2] As Jesus humbly accommodated us through the incarnation, God helps human understanding through the forms of liturgy and rituals. If not for the incarnation of God, people could not understand God. Jesus' incarnation is God's gift to help us beyond the limits of human understanding. Likewise, liturgy starts from God's incarnation and accommodation of human needs.[3] The human being possesses a bodily nature; because of this, "we human beings express meaning through our bodies, through external

---

1. von Allmen, *Celebrer le Salut*, 106. "Les forms, en theologie chretienne ne sont pas un mal necessaire et somme toute regrettable."

2. Ibid., 107. "La liturgie doit etre formulae parce qu'elle fait echo a l'incarnation."

3. Smith, *Who's Afraid of Post Modernism?* 136–43.

acts such as words, gestures, and movement."[4] Humans can express their inner minds with bodily gestures and experience the formation of character through embodied actions.

God created humanity "from the dust of the ground and breathed into his nostrils the breath of life, and the man became a living being" (Gen 2:7). In this verse, we can see that God used material and spiritual factors when he created Adam. A human is a whole person, not merely a spiritual existence. Because humans are embodied beings, it is necessary to use the body in worshipping God; at the same time, "liturgical practice is linked to the formation of the self over time and the building of a world of meaning."[5] This is because, as Meeks says, "Our outward activity and our inward activity cannot be separated."[6] In the same vein, Reformed theologian Herman Bavinck says,

> Also the human body belongs integrally to the image of God . . . Man has a spirit, but that spirit is psychically organized and must, by virtue of its nature, inhabit a body. It is of the essence of humanity to be corporeal and sentient . . . The body is not a prison, but a marvelous piece of art from the hand of God Almighty, and just as constitutive for the essence of humanity as the soul.[7]

Liturgy as a bodily action impacts human spirituality. But we must address the dualistic idea of the relationship between body and spirit.

Every human was degenerated by sin; it corrupts not only the body, but the whole of human nature. Jesus Christ did not deny human bodiliness, but was incarnated in a human body. Bavinck says, "The incarnation of God is proof that human beings and not angels are created in the image of God, and that the human body is an essential component of that image."[8] Rather than perpetuating a dualism which considers the body as a organ vulnerable to the enticements of sin, it is necessary to see that human beings need divine accommodation for understanding God's Word, and liturgy can support this human weakness. We need worship that makes use of the signs and symbols that make use of creation because of our own createdness.[9]

In liturgy, there are two interchanges between God and humans. Liturgy's main function is worshipping God, but also, by using liturgy, God

---

4. Weil, *Theology of Worship*, 74.
5. Belcher, *Efficacious Engagement*, 47.
6. Micks, *Joy of Worship*, 43.
7. Bavinck, *Reformed Dogmatics*, 2:559.
8. Ibid., 560.
9. Ratzinger, *Der Geist der Liturgie*, 53–54.

teaches us.[10] God adjusts himself to help human faith and piety; "worship cannot be done in the abstract; actual forms are needed to express our praise and adoration of God by which we offer our prayer and thanksgiving."[11] If people believe in the incarnation of God, they can affirm the bodiliness of being human. With such affirmations, they can then also affirm the role of liturgy and ritual in helping human understanding, memory, and expression. At this point, the question arises of whether the cognitively challenged can truly bear the image of God, considering their inabilities and dysfunctions. However, the human body comes in all shapes, sizes and skills, and the affirmation is of the human body itself, whatever each one of those bodies is like: liturgy as a human embodiment can overcome the lack of human reason, because of its formative function. Therefore, I will study liturgy and rituals, and how they play a role in the process of faith formation.

THE MEANING OF LITURGY

What is the definition of liturgy? As A. G. Martimort points out, "it is hard to find the term 'liturgy' in books before the twentieth century."[12] However, generally, liturgy is now considered "those forms of public corporate worship which follow a set structure or series of rites (procedures required or usual in a solemn celebration)."[13] At a macro level, "liturgy" has been used to refer to the official worship of the faith community, including structure, order, text, music, movement, vestments, ornaments, and vessels. At the micro level, "liturgy" has been used to denote specific forms or sequences of worship and worship as a subject.[14] In fact, among Protestant churches, rather than liturgy, the term "worship" has been used more popularly, because Protestants have emphasized the inner nature of worship which is faithful to the Bible rather than to an "external form."[15] Of course, liturgy sometimes becomes locked into a specific form.[16] However, worship cannot exist without form. A synod report of the Christian Reform Church says, "Liturgy is what people do when they worship . . . every church has a liturgy, whether it worships with set forms inherited from the ages or whether it

---

10. Shepherd, *Worship of the Church*, 64.
11. Senn, *Introduction to Christian Liturgy*, 4.
12. Martimort, *Church at Prayer, Volume 1*, 7.
13. Schaefer, "What is Liturgical Worship?" in *Liturgy and Music*, 5.
14. Harper, *Forms and Orders*, 12.
15. Ibid.
16. Shepherd, *Worship of the Church*, 63.

worships in the freedom of the moment."[17] Every church has already used their own liturgy; Protestants no longer have antipathy towards the term. Many Reformed scholars, such as Robert Rayburn and Brian Chappel, suggest that Isaiah 6 provides an outline for Christian worship, showing the elements and patterns for worship.[18] Chappel insists, "The Christian church has a consistent worship pattern. We have this common pattern because the gospel that stimulates our worship also affects our worship."[19] His intention is not that the sequence of worship cannot be changed, but that liturgy must have certain components if it is to be faithful to the gospel itself. Reformed systematic theologian Michael Horton affirms the necessity of liturgy as form: "Regardless of where we find ourselves on the ecclesiastical map, it can hardly be disputed that all churches have some sort of liturgy."[20] He also believes that liturgy can be adapted to the circumstances of time and place, but the elements must remain intact.[21] Actually, some denominations with a liturgical inclination consider liturgy as the most important part of worship; however, some denominations that pursue only the Word consider liturgical churches as "esthetic and spiritual deviation(s) from the real task of the church."[22] Both these opinions have a problem in understanding the concept of liturgy. Liturgy and worship are not separate things; rather, worship is liturgy, liturgy is worship. These two stances see the tree, not the woods. They do not recognize the original meaning of liturgy.

The term "liturgy" comes from the Greek word "*leitourgia*," a combination of "people" (*leitos*) and "work" (*ergon*). It was used in ancient Greece to refer to public works, such as providing money for festivals and supplying tools for the army.[23] Gradually, liturgy became a term with religious meaning. In the Septuagint, "liturgy" referred to a duty or work enacted by the priests or Levites. As Wolterstorff notes, "In the Septuagint translation of the Old Testament, the word *leitourgia* was regularly borrowed from its Greek civic use and applied, by metaphorical extension, to the kind of service rendered by the priests in the temple."[24]

---

17. Christian Reformed Church, "Liturgical Committee Report," in *Acts of Synod*, 135–36.

18. Rayburn, *O Come, Let Us Worship*, 118–20.

19. Chapell, *Christ-Centered Worship*, 100–01.

20. Horton, *A Better Way*, 141

21. Ibid., 160.

22. See Schmemann, *For the Life of the World*, 25.

23. Harper, *Forms and Orders*, 12.

24. See Wolterstorff, "Reformed Liturgy," in *Major Themes*, 274. Strahmann says, "The modern ecclesiastical use of the word liturgy is quite different from the original meaning of *leitourgia*, which were wholly secular terms. On the other hand, it bears

In the New Testament, "*leitourgia*" was used to mean God's charismatic ministry.[25] Paul confessed himself to be a liturgist (*leitourgon*) of the Gospel for the Gentiles (Rom 15:16). Also, in Acts 13:2, Paul said that "prophets and teachers were performing their ministry (*leitourgia*) to the Lord and fasting."[26] After that time, the term "*leitourgia*" had a constricted definition that points to the church officials' work, which was done by the priest.[27] In the Eastern Church, it denotes the Eucharist.[28]

Currently, in *Sacrosanctum Concilium* (The Constitution on the Sacred Liturgy, promulgated December 4, 1963), the Roman Catholic Church defines liturgy as follows:

> Rightly, then, the liturgy is considered as an exercise of the priestly office of Jesus Christ. In the liturgy, by means of signs perceptible to the senses, human sanctification is signified and brought about in ways proper to each of these signs; in the liturgy the whole public worship is performed by the Mystical Body of Jesus Christ, that is, by the Head and his members.[29]

The Roman Catholic definition points out that the faith community worships God and is sanctified in the liturgy through signs.[30] Through liturgy, the church exercises its priestly ministry, a point that has some resonance with a Reformed understanding of the priesthood of all baptized. Each Christian observes liturgy in the worship and has a role in the liturgy.[31] When the Church prays for the world, proclaims and hears the Gospel, and shares in communion, the Church is acting on behalf of the world.[32]

---

some relation to non-biblical usage. Nevertheless, the only way to understand the change in meaning is by way of the LXX and its almost uniform cultic and priestly use of the words. The ecclesiastical use is the result of a transfer to the Christian *cultus* of OT concepts in Greek garb." See Strathmann, "leitourgia" in *Theological Dictionary*, 4:215.

25. White, *Introduction to Christian Worship*, 23–24.

26. John Calvin exegetes this phrase as doing "public offices" or "public action." See Calvin, "Commentary upon the Acts of the Apostles," vol. 18 of *Calvin's Commentaries*, 1:498–99.

27. Nicholas Wolterstorff says, "In Philippians 2:30, for example, we hear of the liturgy of the Philippians to Paul; in Hebrews 8:6, of the liturgy of Christ; and in 2 Corinthians 9:12 the financial gift of the Corinthians to other churches is described as the ministry of this liturgy." See Wolterstorff, "Reformed Liturgy," 274.

28. White, *Introduction to Christian Worship*, 24.

29. *Constitution on the Sacred Liturgy*, 7.

30. White, *Introduction to Christian Worship*, 26.

31. De Jong, *Into His Presence*, 29, 52–53.

32. Saliers, *Worship and Spirituality*, 69.

A Reformed understanding of the priesthood of the baptized does not devalue the role of presider, but shows that, more than a mere onlooker, every participant is an active participant who has a liturgical role.[33] Through liturgy, baptized participants "rehearse God's actions in history"[34] and reveal the will of God. Participants in the worship are doing God's action for the world rather than doing it for their own benefit. Liturgy is not merely a human act, but a tool of communication between God and human beings. Liturgical theologian Bruce Morrill's definition is fitting: "[Liturgy] gives believers an explicit sense, a tangible presence, of the God hidden in their daily lives, as well as something of the specific content, through proclaiming and responding to sacred scripture."[35] The merit of this definition is that it designates liturgy as the response of the church to God's Word.[36] According to Simon Chan, liturgy and the church cannot be distinguished, because the church is comprised of the people who were called by God's Word and responded to it.[37] When we consider these definitions, we see that liturgy is the church's action and expression that responds to God's Word; it is a sort of dialogue between God and the human being. Its priority lies in God's Word, and it expresses the believer's faith with a specific form.[38]

Because liturgy is the church's confession and communication with God, it can include all persons, including children and the cognitively challenged. Through liturgical action, the church benefits, but this does not mean that church receives righteousness by its endeavor; rather, it creates an opportunity for learning that overcomes human understanding and reason. As Meeks insists, "What we say through body language is equally as important as what we say with our lips, in affecting both the conscious and unconscious levels of our being." This is because acting creates "a deeper spiritual relationship, incarnated."[39] "The Constitution on the Sacred Liturgy" says,

> The liturgy daily builds up those who are in the Church, making of them a holy temple of the Lord, a dwelling palace for God in the Spirit, to the mature measure of the fullness of Christ. At the same time it marvelously increases their power to preach Christ

---

33. Louis Weil's insistence on "baptismal ecclesiology" explains that performing liturgy does not mean "an act of the ordained clergy" in which people are mere onlookers, but "the work of the people"; each one has their own liturgical role in worship. Weil, *Theology of Worship*, 34.

34. Witvliet, *Worship Seeking Understanding*, 33.

35. Morrill, *Divine Worship*, 6.

36. Chan, *Liturgical Theology*, 41.

37. Ibid., 42.

38. Horton, *A Better Way*, 165–66.

39. Micks, *Joy of Worship*, 79.

and thus show forth the Church, a sign lifted up among the nations, to those who are outside, a sign under which the scattered children of God may be gathered together until there is one fold and one shepherd.[40]

Liturgy nurtures confession of faith and becomes a tool for communicating with God.

WHAT IS THE CHARACTER OF LITURGY?

What, then, is the specific character of liturgy? Liturgy, as work, is action itself.[41] Through action, participants experience oneness and gain power for transformation. Martimort says, "Liturgy brings into intense play all the activities of those who are present; that it has an objective and real result, independent of the edification that the participants feel; that it has a movement, a rhythm, a dynamic unity proper to it."[42] By acting together, the church "makes it possible for the liturgy to bring the entire Christian people together in oneness of mind and heart."[43] Liturgy is an act of the church as a faith community.[44] The Catholic understanding of liturgy as glorification of God and sanctification of humanity connects with the first question of the Reformed catechism, which suggests that our chief end is to worship and glorify God forever. The Westminster Shorter Catechism, asks, "What is the chief end of man?" with the answer: "Man's chief end is to glorify God and to enjoy Him forever."[45] This Reformed confession shows the human is in existence for worshipping God, *homo adorans*. Liturgy functions to glorify God and sanctify humanity at the same time, because Word and sacraments in the worship are the means of grace, and grace touches the whole person. Even John Calvin refused the concept of merit given by human act; however, he acknowledged the benefits that can be attained by performing the means of grace.[46]

---

40. "The Constitution on the Sacred Liturgy," in *Documents of Vatican II*, 1–2.

41. Chan, *Liturgical Theology*, 90.

42. Martimort, *Church at Prayer*, 13; Roy Rappaport says, "Unless there is a performance, there is no ritual." See Rappaport, *Ritual and Religion*, 37. According to him, "Liturgical orders are realized—made into res—only by being performed." "The act of performance is itself a part of the order performed." See Ibid., 37–38.

43. Martimort, *Church at Prayer*, 14.

44. Ibid., 240

45. Williamson, *Westminster Shorter Catechism*, 1.

46. I will discuss Calvin's thought on faith formation in more detail in the next chapter.

This raises the question, "If enjoying God is the end purpose of people, isn't it a sort of duty, not a voluntary love?" However, in the context of worship, people develop religious affection; affection is a great motivation for worshipping God, because it touches and transforms human acts and thoughts. The theology of liturgy does not belong solely to the Roman Catholic Church, but teaches us that liturgy is an important tool for worshiping God and forming Christian faith across denominations. Liturgy should be considered a two-way movement between God and human. As Moore-Keish says, "Liturgy is both anthropological rite and divine self-manifestation. Liturgy is a holy encounter, but it is also a profoundly human activity."[47]

Liturgy is not only a human rite, but also an encounter with the Triune God. It is acting in the context of worship that God presents. God promised to human beings, "For where two or three come together in my name, there am I with them" (Matt 18:20). By doing liturgy, people can encounter and have a fellowship with triune God.[48] Worship facilitates our relationship with God. Kimberly Belcher says, "Christian sacramental practice entails a participation in the Trinitarian mystery by which human persons are reconciled to God because of a mysterious connection between certain rituals in Christian life and the ministry of Christ, the incarnate word, whose existence is already Trinitarian."[49] Then, "for the Christian, the encounter with the triune God takes a communal, liturgical form."[50] Liturgy is "our gestures toward God, our metaphors for God."[51] In worship, people experience the presence of the Triune God, and they communicate with him in the liturgical act. The current liturgical form used in churches came not directly from God, but from the church as an act of faithfulness based on God's Word, by the illumination of the Holy Spirit. God gives a gift to people through worship; liturgy is not merely human action, but also God's action for the church.[52]

In liturgy, we taste heavenly worship; the form and contents of liturgy convey the meaning of the Bible and Christian faith.[53] Liturgy is the place of theology. In and through the liturgy, people learn how to worship God.[54]

---

47. Moore-Keish, *Do This in Remembrance of Me*, 62.
48. Pivarnik, *Toward a Trinitarian Theology*, xxi–xxii.
49. Belcher, *Efficacious Engagement*, 31.
50. Lathrop, *Holy Ground*, 44.
51. Ibid., 218.
52. Senn, *Introduction to Christian Liturgy*, 13.
53. Senn, *Christian Liturgy*, 41.
54. Ratzinger, *Der Geist der Liturgie*, 15. As von Allmen points out, "mais sans

The Role of Liturgy and Ritual in Public Worship

Liturgy is not merely repetitive action; in acting it, people gain "appropriate intention and construals."[55] Not only in preaching and teaching, but also in the action of liturgy, people learn the meaning of Christian faith. At this dimension, liturgy fortifies the believer's faith.[56]

Because liturgy delivers the meaning of Christian faith and fortifies that faith, liturgical form should sometimes be evaluated.[57] Liturgical theologian Frank Senn believes liturgical forms should be effective and relevant in delivering the content of the Gospel and expressing the culture of the liturgical assembly, and the Church has the freedom to re-evaluate and evolve the forms of worship to this end.[58] And according to Gordon Lathrop, a specific cosmology and worldview are melted in the liturgy of the local church.[59] However, liturgy itself must always reflect the Gospel. It should always be evaluated and reconstituted by central things: the Bible, Lord's Supper, and baptism.[60] Liturgy should reflect the contemporary culture and character of participants, but it should be firmly rooted in the Bible.[61]

Liturgy can be reoriented according to the local church's praxis. However, monumental liturgical tradition and form can exist in theological and anthropological fullness, even when used in the church for a long time.[62] According to Lathrop, worship has central elements. Even as there are various sorts of denominations, there is a common factor of worship around central things; for example, "meeting, gathering, book, washing, meal, song, speech, instead of divine service, evangelary, baptism, Holy Eucharist, offertory, sermon."[63] To honor this tradition is not merely to imitate the old, but to help transform it in a new manner.[64] Actually, the patterns in the worship service come from the Bible, and "what the communal acts and words of Christians mean to say about God in the course of the rite itself, is, at least

---

l'attitude, le geste et le movement, la liturgie de l'Eglise risqué aussi de se vider de son contenu, parce qu'elle n'a plus de contenant, ou parce que son contenant dement le contenu." von Allmen, *Celebrer le Salut*, 116.

55. Chan, *Liturgical Theology*, 87.

56. Martimort, *Church at Prayer*, 274.

57. Frank Senn says, "Liturgy expresses nothing less than a worldview." Senn, *New Creation*, xi.

58. Ibid., 44.

59. Lathrop, *Holy Ground*, 20, 37.

60. Ibid., 38.

61. Morrill, *Divine Worship*, 8.

62. von Allmen, *Celebrer le Salut*, 120.

63. Lathrop, *Holy Things*, 10–11.

64. Senn, *New Creation*, 121.

in its origin and intention, profoundly biblical."[65] However, "transformation occurs, when the reference of this human religious material is changed in Christian worship, the intention is to make clear that the new grace is for the very world that produced this religious language."[66] Liturgy can maintain its focus on the Bible throughout the centuries and even in the changes of cultural aspect.

WHAT IS THE POWER OF LITURGY?

Liturgy must re-orient "its participants in the world."[67] While doing liturgy, people contend with coded meaning. According to Lathrop, "worship, by repeatedly inserting the gathering into these directions, thus 'oriented' the community in both time and space and was intended to orient it, thereby, in a world of meaning and meaningful action."[68] Liturgy has power in that it inherits the church's faith and confession throughout the centuries and builds the faith community; it is a "constitutive and constructive act by which a community both produces its future and reconstructs its past."[69]

Liturgy benefits from tradition. It is a constitutive factor of the church community that also constructively forms the faith community. For example, consider the Reformed church's emphasis on the Ten Commandments in the worship.[70] John Calvin included singing the Decalogue in the public worship.[71] Today, there is resistance to including this element in the worship; however, reading the Decalogue formed a special spirituality for the Reformed Church throughout the centuries. By putting this act after the assurance of pardon or the absolution, people saw the Decalogue as the gratitude of a saved people, rather than a duty necessary for being saved.[72] Because biblical truth and confession of ancestral faith are merged in the liturgy, reading the Decalogue in public worship is a sort of public confession as a member of Christian Church. This liturgical act of reading the Decalogue, is constitutive and constructive at the same time.

Above all, the power of liturgy is in helping the personal and communal memory of Christian faith. Liturgy has been inherited by the church,

---

65. Lathrop, *Holy Things*, 24.
66. Ibid., 27.
67. Ibid., 51.
68. Ibid., 55.
69. Anderson, *Worship and Christian Identity*, 106.
70. De Jong, *Into His Presence*, 98.
71. See Maxwell, *History of Christian Worship*, 115.
72. Burgess, "Reformed Explication," in *The Ten Commandments*, 87.

such as the oral tradition impacted the process of the formation of the canon. Liturgy, in the memory of the people, handed down the memory of the faith community and helped to remember the truth of the Gospel. Participants who receive liturgical tradition develop it in the environment of worship. The constitutive factor has historically helped human memory and shaped faith formation. Peter Atkins says, "Without a memory there can be no liturgy. Without a liturgy there can be no memory of God for the people."[73] Liturgy and memory are inseparable. For example, through liturgy, people remember God's salvific act. The Word of God and the confession of ancestors are represented in the liturgical celebration, and deposited in the memory of worshipers. Engaging in liturgical action, singing and praying together, can revitalize participants' memory of God. According to Atkins, it is "by participation in the liturgy [that] each person is able to absorb naturally the corporate experience of the presence and power of God . . . It is the liturgy of the church which formulates and keeps alive the corporate memory of being church."[74] Since liturgy helps the communal memory of the church, which is essential in maintaining the church, it can be called formative.

HOW RITUAL AND LITURGY ARE RELATED

Before studying how liturgy is formative as a ritual practice, we must study the relationship between ritual and liturgy. These two terms have been used interchangeably, despite how distinctive they actually are. Senn says, "Liturgy is what Christians have performed in their public assemblies."[75] However, "ritual has to do not only with what a community does before God but also with what the members of a community do in interaction with one another. It is a pattern of behavior that expresses and forms a way of life consistent with the community's beliefs and values."[76] Liturgy is the act of "public assemblies" in the Christian worship; ritual also can be done in the worship; however, it is closer to "the pattern of behavior" which can express and form human feeling and faith. In general, anthropologists and ritual studies scholars have defined what ritual is.[77] The word is not often used in the Christian church, but "ritual" is a part of the worship practice; all worship is composed of various sorts of ritual. In the sense that ritual is a

---

73. Atkins, *Memory and Liturgy*, 24.
74. Ibid., 71.
75. See Senn, *Christian Liturgy*, 3.
76. See ibid., 3.
77. Bell, *Ritual*, 210.

way of behavior, ritual and liturgy are closely related. Since liturgy is a ritual action, forming the thoughts of the people and expressing human thinking and feeling, it can be formative in the process of developing people's faith.

What is ritual? In general, "ritual" can be defined as follows:

> Formal definitions of ritual work seek to differentiate ritual activity from other forms of behavior in terms of its distinctive features, usually identified as repetitive, prescribed, rigid, stereotyped, and so on. . . . Functionalist definitions approach ritual in terms of the purposes it serves in human life. Psychologists will focus on ritual behavior as it serves the needs of the individual. . . . Functionalist views of ritual often portray it as maintaining social cohesion and cultural coherence in the face of various kinds of threats. . . . Symbolic approaches to the definition of ritual look at it in terms of communication: it is an activity that conveys meaning.[78]

Because ritual is repetitive, prescribed, rigid, and stereotyped, it is not a private act, but a communal and public one. Ritual is sociological.[79] It impacts social and/or cultural cohesion. These formal and functionalist definitions imply that ritual is not a meaningless act, but delivers meaning to its participants. Its formality shows it has a certain special character that is different from that of ordinary acts. The symbolic approach shows that ritual helps people's communication. These three dimensions of ritual—formal, functionalist, and symbolic—are interrelated and cannot be separated. It's also significant that, as Catherine Bell says, that "ritual is not an intrinsic, universal category or feature of human behavior."[80] Ritual does not appear in the same form across centuries and regions. "It is a cultural and historical construction that has been heavily used to help differentiate various styles and degrees of religiosity, rationality, and cultural determinism."[81] The form of ritual will change over time as the social context changes.

Like ritual, liturgy is a public act and has formal, functionalist, and symbolic characteristics. Liturgy as an action is different from ordinary acts. Through participation in liturgy, people communicate with each other and God, opening up the possibility of transformation among worshippers and

---

78. Searle, "Ritual," in *Foundations in Ritual Studies*, 11–12.

79. Bradshaw, ed., *New Westminster Dictionary*, 407.

80. Bell, *Ritual*, ix.

81. Ibid. Bell shows "rituals enact the form of social relations and in giving these relations visible expression they enable people to know their own society." Douglas, *Purity and Danger*, 159.

contributing to the formation of faith. However, many reformed churches are reluctant to consider ritual's usefulness in worship.

HOW IS LITURGY FORMATIVE AS RITUAL PRACTICE?

In general, in reaction to medieval Catholicism, the Reformers and their successors tried to simplify and reform Catholic liturgy.[82] This is closely related to the notion that, as Charles Hodge says, liturgical worship has a tendency "to formality, and cannot be an adequate substitute for the warm outgoings of the heart moved by the Spirit of genuine devotion."[83] However, the Reformed Church was also creating new rituals in place of the Catholic ones; "liturgy was used by the reformers to promote the reform of doctrine, worship, and Christian life."[84] For example, the Reformers placed the factor of confession and preaching in the core of worship ordo.[85] Reformed theologians did not devalue the formative function of liturgy; rather, they worried about unnecessary ritual and liturgy moving people's focus from the Bible to merely human acts. According to Jonathan Smith, a Reformation "ritual could be perceived as a matter of surface rather than depth; of outward representation rather than inward transformation."[86] Reformers considered ritual as an unnecessary adjunct rather than an influence on the formation of faith. In addition, "ritual was to be classed with superstition (shallow, unreasoning action) or with habit (a customary, repetitive, thoughtless action)."[87] This sort of understanding made Reformed churches focus on the weak points of ritual rather than its merits. It was not commonly accepted that a ritual act could deliver meaning, or enhance people's understanding, and the possibility of an encounter with God, through repetition.[88] For example, even though Martin Bucer insisted on Christian freedom in using ritual and external ceremony, *he* argues in *Grund und Ursach* that the Word "in spirit and truth (John 4:23–24) served as warrant for the abolition of the gestures made by the priest during Mass (i.e., bowing, the sign of the

---

82. See Muir, *Ritual in Early Modern Europe*, 7–8. However, Moore-Keish says, "In Christian ritual, I will suggest later, rituals both mean and do." Moore-Keish, *Do This in Remembrance*, 90. Also see Winkler, *Praktisch Theologische Elementar*, 56.

83. Hodge, "Presbyterian Liturgies," 461. In Hart and Muether, *With Reverence and Awe*, 154.

84. Senn, *People's Work*, 231.

85. See Hart and Muether, *With Reverence and Awe*, 99.

86. Smith, *To Take Place*, 100.

87. Ibid.

88. Erickson, *Participating in Worship*, 18–19.

cross, kissing of the altar, striking of the breast, elevation of the hands)."[89] He believes in Christian freedom of choosing liturgy, but he doesn't seem to consider liturgy a neutral thing. In arguments against various sorts of liturgy, he grasped the power of liturgy for faith formation, even though these were negative images to him. However, Mary Douglas points out,

> It is a mistake to suppose that there can be religion which is all interior, with no rules, no liturgy, no external signs of inward states. As with society, so with religion, external form is the condition of its existence. As the heirs of the evangelical tradition, we have been brought up to suspect formality and to look for spontaneous expression. As a social animal, man is a ritual animal. If ritual is suppressed in one form it crops up in others, more strongly the more intense the social interaction. Without the letters of condolence, telegrams of congratulations and even occasional postcards, the friendship of a separated friend is not a social reality. It has no existence without the rites of friendship. Social ritual creates a reality that would be nothing without them. It is not too much to say that ritual is more to society than words are to thought."[90]

There is no religion without external signs and formality; in fact, the mind can be recognized as faithful by what is shown and expressed. Without expression, its authenticity cannot be checked, so the Reformers did emphasize the public confession of faith in worship. I believe the creed as spoken in the context of worship can be categorized as one of the important Reformed rituals in the worship.[91] While congregants confess the church's faith in unison, they are confirming the oneness of community in the presence of God; such public confessions encourage each other's faith, and vow fidelity to the Word of God. This liturgical act aroused the spirit of reformation, creating a bridge between Reformed leaders and church members. This ritual has been formative, not only for a person's faith, but also for the church as a faith community.

Ritual uses the human body. As Kimberly Belcher says, "rituals are effective because the physical formality of the body enables the social and cultural development of the whole human person."[92] This can help to "develop

---

89. Quoted in Thompson, *Eucharistic Sacrifice*, 110.

90. Douglas, *Purity and Danger*, 77; regarding social and cultural specifics of ritual form, see Rappaport, *Ritual and Religion*, 111.

91. Regarding the "dominant figure" of worship and its explanation in Strassburg, see Nichols, *Corporate Worship*, 55–56.

92. Belcher, *Efficacious Engagement*, 48.

certain desires and emotional capacities."[93] Ritual, through discipline of the body, inscribes a message in the body, and forms the human identity[94]—and it can be an important tool for faith formation. Even though we cannot explain "how practice forms us into graced beings" by "a mechanistic cause-effect relationship," it is certain that ritual as the action of the church forms the faith of people and community effectively.[95]

Currently, Reformed liturgical theologian Moore-Keish insists that "rituals both mean and do."[96] Ritual does not only show meaning, but *forms* meaning among the participants who perform it.[97] This meaning connects person to person, forming community in the presence of God: "Rituals relate and create . . . rituals are about doing in the sense of affecting the world as a whole: presenting models for a different world and even changing social structures. Rituals can transform."[98] Ritual is closely related to human nature, and it impacts human relationships and the inner mind of each participant.

In addition, gesture, posture, and symbol are good multimedia tools for memory. Paul Connerton says,

> To kneel in subordination is to display it through the visible, present substance of one's body. Kneelers identify the disposition of their body with their disposition of subordination. Such performative doings are particularly effective, because unequivocal and materially substantial, ways of saying; and the elementariness of the repertoire from which such sayings are drawn makes possible at once their performative power and their effectiveness as mnemonic system.[99]

John Calvin mentioned the propriety of kneeling in prayer as an example of proper church order.[100] He thought this act invokes piety and sincerity in the presence of God.[101] Even though he did not explain the

---

93. Ibid.
94. Ibid., 51.
95. Chan, *Liturgical Theology*, 93.
96. Moore-Keish, *Do This in Remembrance*, 90.
97. Ibid., 99.
98. Ibid., 90.
99. See Connerton, *How Societies Remember*, 59.
100. *Inst.* IV.x.29
101. John Witvliet, based on his reading of Calvin's commentaries and the *Institutes*, says, "Ceremony and symbols were, in Calvin's words, useful for encouraging and stimulating faith. He frequently referred to them as props, stimulants, and exercises." See Witvliet, *Worship Seeking Understanding*, 144.

effect of rituals and repetitive ceremony, it is probable that he recognized the relationship between kneeling and piety. However, in general, the Reformed Church has a tendency to reject ritual due to misunderstanding the difference between ritual and ritualism. According to Craig Erickson, the term comes from the Latin adjective *ritualis*, meaning "the form and manner of religious observances; a religious custom, usage, ceremony."[102] However, when people show "excessive devotion to ritual, it is better labeled as ritualism."[103] Erickson explains this phenomenon:

> When individual, church, and liturgy cease to function as co-workers, worship becomes ritualistic. In this situation, the individual has significant difficulty in appropriating the liturgy as an authentic expression of his or her own faith. Consequently, the individual is no longer able to participate knowingly, actively, and fruitfully . . . Devotion to God is eclipsed by an expressive devotion to ritual.[104]

If worship deviates from "devotion to God," or becomes confused with devotion to ritual, there is danger of falling into ritualism. According to Erickson, "Ritualism is a church-wide problem because it has to do with individual worshippers whose hearts and minds may or may not be able, for one reason or another, to pray through the liturgy regardless of its degree of development."[105]

Some people who reject ritual cite the Old Testament prophet's reproach against it in the context of abuse of the temple liturgy, worship of false gods, and disconnect between worship and ethics. Those who are suspicious of ritual also may insist that after the New Testament era, rituals and ceremonies that did not have biblical foundations were abolished by Jesus' crucifixion. But the Old Testament prophets did not repudiate rituals or ceremonies—only their abuse. As David Peterson points out, "It is interesting to note that certain psalms reflect prophetic perspectives. Four almost reach the level of condemning sacrifice (e.g., Pss 40, 50, 51, 69). Yet their intention seems to be to give expression to the true meaning implicit in the sacrificial rituals, insisting that prayer and praise, repentance, confession and obedience, are the essential requirements of God."[106]

---

102. Erickson, *Participating in Worship*, 14.
103. Ibid.
104. Erickson, "Liturgical Participation," 231–43.
105. Erickson, *Participating in Worship*, 16.
106. Peterson, *Engaging with God*, 45–46. In an essay "The Former Prophets and the Practice of Christian Worship," John Witvliet shows the significance of liturgical action. He argues that, according to the Old Testament, the former prophets did not negate

The Old Testament did not repudiate the use of ritual itself. Robert Webber discusses why people sometimes have negative responses to ritual:

> Some falsely assume that the worship of Israel was physical and the worship of the church should be spiritual. This is a false dichotomy that fails to recognize the overlap between the content of the Old Testament (the Exodus event) and the content of the New Testament (the Christ event). Worship in the Old and the New Testament has both spiritual and physical aspects. As we develop the physical side of Christian worship, we will see how Old Testament principles are still found in Christian worship. The radical difference is that they are informed by the event of Jesus Christ, the main content of the Christian faith.[107]

Ritual itself is not a bad thing for Christianity; it has been used to help participants proceed to God's presence; it also manifests, unwittingly, in churches that, for example, recite the Apostle's Creed or Decalogue all together, standing, and devoted in worship.

Rituals exist in other religions, of course, such as easily found rites of passage for transitions like births, initiations into adulthood, funerals, and healings.[108] Taking active roles in the community helps people form personal identities. Christian rituals are similar to other religions because human communication methods, like language, often share common factors. Therefore, ritual and its embodiment should not be repudiated. Of course, rituals may be corrupted.[109] Because of this, Reformed churches have been suspicious of rites and rituals, and have looked for safe ways to simplify or eradicate them in worship. Content is important. If people attempt to be faithful to the Bible and perform rites in the name of Jesus, those rites can be Christian.[110] Rituals have multiple contributions to offer. The function of ritual and ritualization can be explained as follows:

> 1) The first function that ritual and ritualization serve is to integrate into the human order those cosmic, biological, and social experiences that often are a source of anxiety if they remain exterior to the human person. 2) Ritual and ritualization speak

---

liturgical action itself: "When Israel is faithless, its worship is degenerate. When Israel is faithful, that faithfulness is expressed in corporate prayer and praise before God's face." See Witvliet, *Worship Seeking Understanding*, 26.

107. Webber, *Worship Old and New*, 38.

108. Cooke and Macy, *Christian Symbol and Ritual*, 25–33; van Gennep, *Rites of Passages*.

109. Senn, *Christian Liturgy*, 4, 8.

110. See Chan, *Liturgical Theology*, 88.

to the unconscious through the language of symbol, touching all aspects of human life. 3) Ritual and ritualization give life sense and value. Through ritual we make meaning about our lives and acquire a sense of orientation to why and where we are. 4) Fourth, ritual and ritualization facilitate the expression and catharsis of individuals and groups. 5) Ritual and ritualization help persons and communities address the unsettledness and unpredictability of life. 6) Even as ritual and ritualization mark, contain, and direct the flow of human life, they also reveal, convey, and enact the power and permanence of a group. 7) Finally, like integrating, structuring, meaning making, and identity-conferring functions described above, ritual and ritualization enable us to mark the cycles of human existence and to orchestrate or perform the grand passage of life.[111]

Ritual and ritualization help individuals and communities form their faith, using not merely cognition and understanding, but also a deeper dimension. In the context of worship, ritual that arouses human intellect, emotion, consciousness and sub-consciousness fosters communication, community, and the understanding of meaning by doing. Performing rituals makes meaning and forms identity. People can learn by acting and participating in ritual events with the community, even when they do not understand completely the process or logic of the work. The power of liturgy as ritual practice comes from repetition. By doing and repeating together, people share meaning and human reason is trained. Think of the relationship between mother and infant. They do not use language, but while interacting each other, they become attuned to each other's thinking and emotion. The mother can understand the baby's wants and response, and the baby learns to understand its mother's intentions. Likewise, by doing liturgy, God's meaning is shared more vividly and clearly among participants. Even when people cannot explain this practice logically, they experience the formative power of ritual tacitly in their body and mind through their participation in worship. This type of knowledge and learning is possible by and in the faith community. Liturgy and ritual enacted therein forms public memory and communal identity, and transforms minds and relationships.[112]

---

111. Anderson, *Worship and Christian Identity*, 61–69.
112. Ibid., 58.

LITURGY, RITUAL, AND FAITH FORMATION

Through the practice of liturgy and ritual, people receive the meaning encoded in the action, and by repetition, their minds respond to the Word of God. Eventually, it can impact the formation of faith. E. Byron Anderson argues:

> In the tension between *orthodoxia* and *orthopraxis* we come face to face with the fact that even as we perform liturgy, liturgy is also performing us. It is inscribing a form of the Christian faith in body, bone, and marrow as well as in mind and spirit ... liturgy not only expresses our thoughts and feelings but also impresses them, giving them shape and form by shaping and forming our attitudes so that they conform to those of Christ.[113]

This definition is an apt explanation of the relationship between liturgy and faith formation. Even as we perform the liturgy, liturgy forms our attitude of faith. For example, kneeling at prayer can be a Christian discipline. While the act of kneeling can make some contemporary Western Reformed Christians nervous, many US Lutherans and Korean Christians adopt this act in prayer meetings, regardless of denomination. While kneeling, people recognize praying as not just an expression of desire, but a humble acceptance of God's will. This act forms a Christian attitude, not only in the body, but also in the mind.

Liturgy itself cannot guarantee faith. However, it forms a belief system in the human mind. According to Roy Rappaport, "two broad classes of messages are transmitted in human ritual."[114] The first type of message is self-referential, the sort of information "concerning their own current physical, psychic, or social states to themselves and to other participants."[115] It is "confined to here and now."[116] The second is canonical, "the general, enduring, or even eternal aspects of universal orders."[117]

Let us consider the Korean practice of *Tongsung kido* in light of these two types of messages.[118] Everyone joins the worship service with their own prayer subject. This is a sort of self-referential message. However, while praying together and focusing on a common prayer subject, participants

---

113. See Ibid.
114. Rappaport, *Ritual and Religion*, 52.
115. Ibid.
116. Ibid., 53.
117. Ibid.
118. Korean "Tongson kido" is a "audible prayer" which prays "freely and fervently to God in a loud, outpouring unison." See Joo and Kim, "Reformed Tradition," 487.

come to consider the canonical message from the prayer. Within the prayer, people share a common feeling and mind. Praying together for others and the world, people realize that prayer is not merely a time to enumerate wishes to God, but is also a submission to God and an expression of love for neighbors.

Through participation, people come to make a "transforming decision on that state."[119] Participants in liturgy and ritual not only receive the message but also become "part of the order to which their own body and breath give life."[120] According to Rappaport, participation means a sort of acceptance, which does not necessarily signify belief; acceptance is not a private state, but a public act.[121] In other words, if a person joins the public liturgy and does not deny their faith in a public place, this can be called acceptance, and this acceptance becomes a structure in the mind of the individual. Of course, people can refuse to participate in a certain type of liturgy in public. However, if a person participates in public, such participation "constitutes an acceptance of a public order regardless of the private state of belief of the performer."[122] It is similar to the Reformed church's emphasis on confession in public. If a person refuses Christian confession, he or she can depart from the church; however, if he or she joins the confessional act, reciting the Decalogue or Apostolic Creed, the act signifies acceptance. While participation in a public act does not ensure the real status of the inner mind since no human can confidently know another's inner mind, such participation does contribute to the growth of the inner mind toward faith.

In order to receive information and meaning from ritual, Rappaport notes, "a participant must be trained, indoctrinated or otherwise prepared to receive the messages rituals transmit."[123] However, this does not negate the formative power of ritual. Consider eating and table manners. People do not need to learn how to eat; it is instinctive. But they must learn table manners to have a more profound table fellowship with other people. Liturgical participation is similar. Manners themselves are not the criteria for permitting participation. However, in order to gain a deeper relationship with God and others, participants need proper and continuing education. General acceptance itself cannot guarantee that ritual will instill belief. Information and understanding are key.[124] Above all, rather than having power in itself,

---

119. Rappaport, *Ritual and Religion*, 107.
120. Ibid., 118.
121. Ibid., 120.
122. Ibid., 121.
123. Ibid., 111.
124. Chan, *Liturgical Theology*, 87.

ritual provides public structure and prompts a decision of the inner mind. According to Rappaport, participation itself is necessary and important for the transformation of personality—a powerful idea, and helpful for the Reformed church. Participation itself cannot guarantee faith, but by engaging in liturgy and ritual, people receive a message coded in the ritual and liturgy. It informs the structure of faith and therefore, bodily participation itself is very important for faith formation.[125] As a person enacts liturgy, liturgy forms the person. Liturgy can enhance human understanding and memory; the act of the person requires a change in the mind of the person. As Simon Chan reminds us, "Grace can never be within our control," but grace "forms us not apart from practice."[126] Liturgy is not a tool for generating God's grace, but a tool for teaching and training the minds of God's people.

What, then, is the definition of faith formation? Generally, in the academic world, the terms "Christian formation," "spiritual formation," and "faith development" have been popularly used.[127] The term "faith formation" has even been used frequently in the ordinary church ministry. However, in books or articles, the term has rarely been defined. Currently, Sondra Matthaei defines it as signifying "our participation in God's work of inviting persons into relationship with God, self, others, and creation."[128] This definition has merit in showing that faith formation is very closely related to relationships, and that by participating in church and community, faith can be developed. However, the term "faith formation" does not mean people can produce faith by manipulating educational tools or systems.[129] Faith formation can be obtained by participating in the worship and life of the church in the work of the Holy Spirit. The beginning of faith is a gift from the Holy Spirit—but it is trained and grown by practicing liturgy. In this way, people receive the message and are continually educated in their faith, and form their Christian character. The term "faith formation" shows that the church and parents have an educational duty to create an effective environment for maturing faith. Christians are born by the work of Holy Spirit, but they are also made through worship and education.

Liturgy is a verb. The act of liturgy has formative power which human understanding and cognition do not, and harmonizes knowledge and affection. When people do liturgy, it widens understanding and brings them to

---

125. Senn, *People's Work*, 238. He says, "The act of participating in the performance of a liturgy opens one to the possibility of being exposed to the meanings encoded in that liturgy."

126. Chan, *Liturgical Theology*, 94.

127. Maddix, "Spiritual Formation," in *Christian Formation*, 240–41.

128. Matthaei, "Rethinking Faith Formation," 57.

129. Downs, *Teaching for Spiritual Growth*.

God's grace. The church has traditionally emphasized the cognitive dimension in forming faith; however, the term "faith formation" implies balance between liturgy and catechesis. Teaching and practice go hand in hand. From teaching, people understand the meaning of practice more clearly: practice inscribes teaching more vividly in the body and mind and gives the power of transformation.[130] Liturgy as a Christian practice is inseparable from faith formation.

---

130. Chan, *Liturgical Theology*, 89.

2

John Calvin's Thoughts on Liturgy and Faith Formation

CALVIN'S THEOLOGY OF WORSHIP has always influenced Reformed and Presbyterian churches.[1] To explore the formative aspect of liturgy among contemporary Reformed churches in the Calvinist tradition, we must review Calvin's thoughts concerning worship and ceremony. Reformed liturgical theologian John Witvliet believes the study of Calvin has focused too strongly on the *Institutes of the Christian Religion* at the expense of other significant imagery.[2] Calvin's commentaries, worship directory, letters, treatises, and catechism documents all further illuminate his thoughts on liturgy and ceremony.

A study of Calvin's thoughts on faith formation also clarifies his notions about the formative function of liturgy; he sought balance between intelligence and piety in both public worship and catechetical instruction. In later chapters, I'll revisit this in further discussion of liturgical theology and the formative power of liturgy in faith formation.

---

1. Lanning, "Foundations of Reformed Worship," 231–32.

2. See Witvliet, *Worship Seeking Understanding*, 129. Witvliet insists on the necessity of studying Calvin's commentary, church order, and catechetical documents.

CALVIN ON LITURGY

Generally, most Reformed churches think Calvin had a negative opinion regarding liturgy and ceremony.[3] According to Lanning, because of Calvin's work, "the Latin Mass was cast out along with all of its accessories," because he "proposed a return to the simpler form and manner of the ancient or pre-papal church."[4] That is why, as Geoffrey Wainwright points out, "it was Calvin who most strongly associated secondary (dare one simply say material) ceremony with devilry and idolatry."[5] Of course, when we see the outcome of Calvin's reform in the sixteenth century, especially his reformation in Geneva, this is quite clear. However, Witvliet insists, "The typical paragraph on Calvin in standard liturgical histories portrays Calvin as a stern and unrestrained iconoclast and an ardent opponent of popish forms ... Calvin's writings contain a surprising—and generally unacknowledged—amount about the value, purpose, and nature of Christian liturgy."[6]

Actually, Calvin did not repudiate liturgy itself. Witvliet says, "For Calvin, the abuse in public liturgy must be rooted out, but not liturgy itself."[7] Calvin emphasized "faithful" and "spiritual" worship which came from the heart.[8] Some theologians believe Calvin had few concerns about the practice of liturgy and was only interested in the "liturgy of the Word."[9] However, Calvin believed form should exist in worship; external form itself is not useless: "The inward worship of the heart is not sufficient, unless external profession before men be added. Religion has truly its appropriate

---

3. McKee, "Context, Contours, Contents," 187. McKee analyzes why Protestants were opposed to "the rites they inherited" as follows: "The first was ethical; like Christian humanists, Protestants thought that elaborate ceremonies were distracting and wasteful. More important, however, were the theological objections to sacramental liturgies as 'magical,' unbiblical 'good works.' All Protestants insisted that no rite is sacred or grace-giving in itself, but when rightly understood as a means of edification, a prepared and stable order of worship is useful and good. Thus, most of those who broke with Rome in fact prepared new or simplified liturgical forms in the languages of their peoples, giving particular emphasis to expository biblical preaching, communal participation in the sacraments, and congregational singing." See McKee, "Context, Contours, Contents," 187.

4. Lanning, "Foundations of Reformed Worship," 231.

5. Wainwright, *Doxology*, 266.

6. Witvliet, *Worship Seeking Understanding*, 127.

7. Ibid., 133.

8. Calvin, "Commentaries on Hosea," 233.

9. McKim, "Reflection on Liturgy," 306.

seat in the heart: but from this root, public confession afterwards arises, as its fruit."[10]

For example, regarding prayer, Calvin says, "The bodily gestures usually observed in prayer, such as kneeling and uncovering of the head (Calvin, *Com.* Acts 20:36), are exercises by which we attempt to rise to higher veneration of God."[11] That is to say, he did not repudiate the use of outward form in prayer; he *did* believe form should help enhance people's "veneration of God," because "prayer is not genuine unless the thoughts are turned upward."[12] Calvin goes on: "God, indeed, gave real tokens of his presence in that visible sanctuary, but not for the purpose of binding the senses and thoughts of his people to earthly elements; he wished rather that these external symbols should serve as ladders, by which the faithful might ascend even to heaven."[13] To him, external factors in worship are not efficacious in and of themselves, but rather tools to help people to encounter God and ascend the human mind as a ladder.[14]

Calvin likens the sacrament to a seal[15]—God's promise is sealed by the sacraments. Although the promise is certain by itself, the sacraments are necessary due to people's weakness.[16] Calvin thought that God helps people see the spiritual in the bodily[17], and "that the office of the sacraments differs not from the Word of God and this is to hold forth and offer Christ to us, and, in him, the treasures of heavenly grace."[18] However, it cannot be properly received without faith; it has no benefit in itself.[19] To receive and benefit from the Lord's Supper, one must testify to a confession

10. Calvin, "Commentaries on the Book of Genesis," 354.

11. Calvin, *Institutes,* III.xx.33.

12. Calvin, *Institutes,* III.xx.16.

13. Calvin, "Commentary on the Book of Psalms," 1:122.

14. Calvin says, "Visible sacraments were instituted for the sake of carnal men, that by the ladder of sacraments they may be conveyed from those things which are seen by the eye, to those which are perceived by the understanding," in Calvin, *Institutes,* IV.xix.15. For more mentions of the ladder imagery in discussions of the sacraments, see Calvin, "First Epistle to the Corinthians," 380, and *Sermons on 2 Samuel,* 229–43. Regarding Calvin's concept of ascension in spiritual theology, see Canlis, *Calvin's Ladder,* 3. Canlis believes that "human ascent is a matter of participating in Christ" in Calvin's thought. She also says, "For Calvin, the ladder is Christ—not in the facile explanation that 'Christ is the way,' but that our ascent is profoundly bound up in Christ's ascension, by our participation in his ascent." Ibid., 50.

15. Calvin, *Institutes,* IV.xiv.5.

16. Calvin, *Joannis Calvini,* 261.

17. Ibid., 118.

18. Calvin, *Institutes,* IV.xiv.17.

19. Ibid.

of faith.[20] Therefore, catechetical instruction is necessary in the scheme of Calvin's faith formation.

In addition, Calvin seems to recognize the effect of repetition in the process of faith formation. For example, Calvin's insistence on weekly communion was not merely because the Lord's Supper is an important factor in worship, but also because he anticipated a sort of formation or attitude of faith by centering the Word and the Eucharist weekly. Lee Wandel comments:

> One was not 'made completely one' with Christ in a single communion; one was 'made completely one' over time, through the interdependent activities of the Holy Spirit: preaching and the Supper. Frequent communion, therefore, for Calvin was essential to one's growth as a Christian—it transformed one in one's being and epistemology.[21]

This analysis is persuasive in that the Word and sacrament create a synergy; by weekly repetition, these elements transform and nurse the being and the understanding of the people. As Calvin himself says, "And hence it may be justly said, that such sacraments are ceremonies, by which God is pleased to train his people, first, to excite, cherish, and strengthen faith within; and, secondly, to testify our religion to men."[22] Calvin emphasizes that growth in, and discipline of, faith is established through sacraments as ceremonies; experience and participation nurture understanding.

There is also some formational imagery in Calvin's thoughts on prayer. He considers prayer not only a means of grace, but also a tool for discipline and spiritual growth. He believes that through prayer, God "may exercise us."[23] To this end, Calvin insists that people should allot time for daily prayers; "It is requisite for us to appoint special hours for this exercise, hours . . . when we rise in the morning, before we commence our daily work, when we sit down to food, when by the blessing of God we have taken it, and when we retire to rest."[24] Why did Calvin emphasize the regularity of prayer and of allotted times for prayer? Because this time "must not be a superstitious observance of hours, by which, as it were, performing a task to God, we think we are discharged as to other hours; it should rather be considered as a discipline by which our weakness is exercised, and ever and

---

20. Calvin, *Institutes*, IV.xiv.13.
21. Wandel, *Eucharist in the Reformation*, 171–72.
22. Calvin, *Institutes*, IV.xiv.19.
23. Calvin, *Institutes*, III.xx.3.
24. Calvin, *Institutes*, III.xx.50.

anon stimulated."[25] Calvin seems to intend some level of faith formation through the disciplines of worship and prayer.

From this, it can be noted that Calvin valued repetition in formation. But prayer as discipline is not merely private; it seeks also a public venue.[26] Calvin says,

> Since the glory of God ought in a manner to be displayed in each part of our body, the special service to which the tongue should be devoted is that of singing and speaking, inasmuch as it has been expressly created to declare and proclaim the praise of God. This employment of the tongue is chiefly in the public services which are performed in the meeting of the saints. In this way, the God whom we serve in one spirit and one faith, we glorify together as it were with one voice and one mouth and openly, so that each may in turn receive the confession of his brother's faith, and be invited and incited to imitate it.[27]

By praying together, imitating others' practices, people learn to confess faith by themselves.

Calvin believed that liturgy should be based on the Word of God. As Witvliet points out, inner worship from a faithful heart is more important than external liturgy, which can be enacted by a superstitious mind fixed on outward form and not focused on God.[28] Calvin considered primitive church worship, which he believed had a simple form, as an ideal, and tried to recover it based on what he believed it was like.[29] However, since it was and is still impossible to know much about primitive church worship, Calvin could not support this other than from a simplistic reading of scripture. As William Maxwell points out, "the structure of his Geneva rite is more meager; this was no doubt the result of the extreme opinions that prevailed there among the magistracy, who insisted that the rite be as 'simple' as possible."[30] In the eyes of the liturgical church, Calvin's liturgical stance can be seen as "non-liturgical," an artificial category which cannot shed much light on the meaning of liturgy. Calvin, based on his biblical interpretation

---

25. Ibid. Calvin insists that, through prayer, "our heart may always be inflamed with a serious and ardent desire of seeking, loving and serving him." Calvin, *Institutes*, III.xx. 3.

26. Calvin, *Institutes*, III.xx.47.

27. Calvin, *Institutes*, III.xx.31.

28. Witvliet, *Worship Seeking Understanding*, 129–33.

29. Hughes Oliphant Old says, "The reformers were willing to accept the tradition of the ancient Church in that it was a witness to the commandments of God and the practice of Christ and the Apostles." Old, *Patristic Roots*, 24.

30. Maxwell, *History of Christian Worship*, 115.

and knowledge of early church, tried to renew the worship rather than merely discard liturgy. To understand the core of Calvin's worship theology, three considerations are necessary: his sixteenth-century background, his exegetical principles, and his emphasis on *understanding* in doing worship theology.

First, the context surrounding the Reformation in the sixteenth century should be considered. As we see in debates with the Roman Catholics and Anabaptists, there were among the Reformers some differences of opinion as to how to deal with human factors in worship. Herman Selderhuis says, "Concerning liturgical matters . . . [Calvin] looks for the via media, seeking to neither underestimate nor overestimate the external aids."[31] Actually, Calvin did not take issue with the role of symbol or outward sign as an aid:

> The term sacrament, in the view we have hitherto taken of it, includes, generally, all the signs which God ever commanded men to use, that he might make them sure and confident of the truth of his promises . . . If he had impressed memorials of this description on the sun, the stars, the earth, and stones, they would all have been to us as sacraments. For why is the shapeless and the coined silver not of the same value, seeing they are the same metal? Just because the former has nothing but its own nature, whereas the latter, impressed with the public stamp, becomes money, and receives a new value. And shall the Lord not be able to stamp his creatures with his word, that things which were formerly bare elements may become sacraments?[32]

Calvin has an open mind about the concept of sacrament. To him, anything can be sacramental if God wants to use it: even though the object itself does not have power, its use can have value through public acceptance of it. Regarding this, Baillie comments,

> There is a very interesting passage in Calvin's *Institutes* in which he bases the Christian sacraments on this broader basis of nature, recognizing that God can take any one of His created elements and use it sacramentally, apart from the sacraments in the narrow and proper sense.[33]

While overcoming both the limitation of Zwingli's thought and Roman Catholicism's sacramental theology, Calvin chooses a middle or third way. He has a balanced view of the relationship between the Word and

---

31. Selderhuis, *Calvin's Theology*, 205.
32. Calvin, *Institutes*, IV.xiv.18.
33. Baillie, *Theology of the Sacraments*, 45.

sacrament. In his liturgy, "heaven and earth are connected in the church service through God's presence with his gathered people."[34]

The second consideration is how Calvin's exegetical principles, *brevitas et facilitas*, were traits of Calvin's hermeneutics and impacted his worship theology.[35] While discussing Calvin's commentary and the opinions of theologians such as Parker and Battles, Richard Gamble observes that "Calvin keeps his teaching style simple" and "makes his commentaries understandable to the dullest student."[36] This could have influenced Calvin's worship theology. John Leith says, "Simplicity is a recurring theme in all of Calvin's writings, and it was a characteristic of his practice . . . he applied it to liturgy, polity, and style of life."[37] Simplicity for Calvin is closely related to faithfulness and the power of the Gospel.[38]

The third consideration is the term that best describes Calvin's effort in worship renewal: "worship seeking understanding."[39] Calvin says, "In all prayer, public and private, the tongue without the mind must be displeasing to God. Moreover, the mind must be so incited, as in ardor of thought far to surpass what the tongue is able to express."[40] Mind is more important than gesture; however, "the bodily gestures usually observed in prayer, such as kneeling and covering of the head (Calvin, Com. Acts 20:36), are exercises by which we attempt to rise to higher veneration of God."[41] Calvin

---

34. Selderhuis, *Calvin's Theology of the Psalms*, 204. Martha Moore-Keish says, "Unlike Zwingli, however, Calvin is clearly seeking a balance: of Word and sacrament, and of objective gift and subjective responses." See Moore-Keish, *Do This in Remembrance*, 35.

35. "Brevity" and "facility" (usefulness or appropriateness) are traits of John Calvin's biblical hermeneutics. Regarding this topic, see Gamble, "Brevitas et facilitas," 3. David C. Steinmetz says Calvin's methodology contributed to the Reformed scholarship. See Steinmetz, "John Calvin on Isaiah 6," 158.

36. Gamble, "Brevitas et facilitas," 3.

37. Leith, *Introduction*, 83, 84. Regarding the simplicity of liturgy in Calvin's thought, see Brienen, *De liturgie bij Johannes Calvijn*, 163–65. He says, "De 'simplicitas' van de liturgie staat dan ook in verband met het bijbels gegeven, dat het nu de tijd is om God te aanbidden in geest en waarheid." Ibid., 165.

38. Calvin, "First Epistle to the Corinthians," 76–78.

39. McKim, "Reflections on Liturgy and Worship," 308; Leith, *Introduction*, 210. Boulton says, "Reformed worship was in the first place a matter of verbal, catechetical, intellectual engagement with God's word revealed in Scripture and expounded from the pulpit." See Boulton, *Life in God*, 33.

40. Calvin, *Institutes*, III.xx.33.

41. Ibid. Also, Calvin believed that "the ceremony of lifting up our hands in prayer is designed to remind us that we are far removed from God, unless our thoughts rise upward: as it is said in the psalm, 'Unto thee, O Lord, do I lift up my soul' (Ps 25:1)." Calvin, *Institutes*, III.xx.5.

insisted the act and symbol of worship should be clearly understood.[42] He also insisted on the necessity of knowledge of God to escape from idolatry or "contaminating the right worship of God"[43]; people without knowledge cannot worship God rightly, and are susceptible to idolizing external aids rather than concentrating on God. Right worship requires teaching from God's Word.[44] Without knowledge of God, a human cannot please God, but through knowledge, one can acquire a "confidence in him and fear of him."[45] This is more than the accumulation of knowledge about God; it is combined with piety.[46] Calvin emphasizes the importance of this knowledge as follows:

> The knowledge of God which we are invited to cultivate is not that which, resting satisfied with empty speculation, only flutters in the brain, but a knowledge which will prove substantial and fruitful wherever it is duly perceived, and rooted in the heart. The Lord is manifested by his perfections. When we feel their power within us, and are conscious of their benefits, the knowledge must impress us much more vividly than if we merely imagined a God whose presence we never felt.[47]

This does not refer merely to the cognitive, but also to human piety and the response of the heart; to Calvin, knowledge is not the outcome of speculation, but is experiential. The key is the right understanding of God, rooted in personal encounters with God. For Calvin, knowledge of God integrates the contents of faith and the assurances of the mind.

With these three considerations of Calvin's worship theology in mind, we must analyze Calvin's writings and then look at his definition of worship to know his attitude on the use of liturgy and thought on faith formation.

In Calvin's writings, the term "liturgy" does not appear in either French or Latin.[48] However, he frequently used the "etymological mean-

42. Calvin, *Institutes*, IV.xiv.3–4.

43. Dowey, Jr., *Knowledge of God*, 3.

44. Calvin, *Institutes*, II.viii.1.

45. Calvin, "First Epistle to the Corinthians," 95. In his commentary on Hosea 6:6, Calvin says, "The knowledge of God is required as necessary to faith . . . for where there is no knowledge of God, there is no religion." Calvin, "Commentaries on Hosea," 233.

46. Beeke, *Puritan Reformed Spirituality*, 1.

47. Calvin, *Institutes*, I.v.9.

48. Peter, "Calvin and Liturgy," 239–40. According to Peter, the term first appeared sixteen years after the death of Calvin. McKee says, "'liturgy' and 'devotional acts' are not Calvin's terms. He prefers to speak of the obligations of devotion generally, with 'public' or 'common prayers' for what is here named liturgy is called *Form of Prayers*." See McKee, "Context, Contours, Contents," 183.

ing of the word, which signifies public service (laos + ergon)."⁴⁹ To Calvin, liturgy means public worship. Even though Calvin did not include a chapter dealing with liturgy in his *Institutes*, his first edition of the *Institutes* (1536) contains an order for public worship. He says,

> First, then, it should begin with public prayers. After this a sermon should be given. Then, when bread and wine have been placed on the Table, the minister should repeat the words of institution of the Supper. Next, he should recite the promises which were left to us in it; at the same time, he should excommunicate all who are debarred from it by the Lord's prohibition. Afterward, he should pray that the Lord, with the kindness wherewith he has bestowed this sacred food upon us also teach and form us to receive it with faith and thankfulness of heart, and, inasmuch as we are not so of ourselves, by his mercy make us worthy of such a feast. But here either psalms should be sung, or something be read, and in becoming order the believers should partake of the most holy banquet, the ministers breaking the bread and giving the cup. When the supper is finished, there should be an exhortation to sincere faith and confession of faith, to love and behavior worthy of Christians. At the last, thanks should be given, and praises sung to God. When these things are ended, the church should be dismissed in peace.⁵⁰

The term frequently used in Calvin's writing to refer to what we now call "liturgy" is the "ceremony (caerimonia)."⁵¹ In his "Reply to Sadolet" (1539), he describes ceremony as an "exercise for the people in offices of

---

49. Peter, "Calvin and Liturgy," 240. Also see Calvin, "Commentary upon The Acts of the Apostles," 1:499; Calvin, "Commentary on the Second Epistle," 314.

50. Calvin, *Institutes of the Christian Religion*, 122–23. Also, Calvin's service book of 1545 contains some information about Calvin's worship. See Text 35, vol. xxxiv, 194–6 in Maxwell, *History of Christian Worship*, 116.

51. However, according to Old, "The one word that Calvin uses more than any other to speak of worship is the word cultus." He says, "It seems to be the closest word he uses for our word *liturgy* . . . The Latin word *cultus*, however, was a good choice for Calvin because it referred to both the inner religious affections and the outward religious observances . . . In other words, it has a broader meaning than the word *liturgy*, which more properly designates the public service of worship," Old, "Calvin's Theology of Worship," 414. I think *cultus* has a broader meaning than liturgy, because *cultus* includes the "subject aspect of worship" and "private devotion," as Old points out. Therefore, regarding the aspect of public act, I think liturgy has a close relationship with the term "ceremony." Also, it should be noticed that regarding the matter of public worship, Calvin frequently used the term "ceremony." Cf. Calvin, *Institutes*, II.vii.1; IV.x.29; IV.xix.3.

piety,"[52] a public tool for helping the discipline of faith. This can help ensure the "safety of the Church" with "doctrine, discipline, and the sacraments."[53] However, Calvin insists that the Roman Catholic Church had "more than enough of ceremony," and that most of its ceremonies were "vitiated by innumerable forms of superstition."[54] Therefore, he insists on the propriety of abolishing those ceremonies, such as venerating Mary in worship, which he believed had "degenerated into a kind of Judaism" and "filled the minds of the people with superstition and could not possibly remain without greatly obstructing the piety they should be promoted."[55]

Calvin considered ceremony a tool of faith discipline; however, he wanted to retain only "those [ceremonies] which seemed sufficient for the circumstances of the time."[56] Regarding church discipline and ceremony, he says,

> Lastly, as he [God] has not delivered any express command, because things of this nature are not necessary to salvation, and,

---

52. Calvin, "Reply to Sadolet," 232. Also, he says that through ceremony, people are "trained to godliness, and might make greater and greater progress in faith and in the pure worship of God." See Calvin, "Commentary on the Prophet Isaiah," 56.

53. Calvin, "Reply to Sadolet," 232.

54. Ibid.

55. Ibid. Calvin says, "It should be established that God is to be worshiped in accordance with his decision, not ours . . . God rejects anything that does not correspond to his will." See Calvin, *Calvin's Ecclesiastical Advice*, 52. Bard Thompson points out Calvin sought true worship and warned against the "admixture of human invention." See Thompson, *Liturgies of the Western Church*, 194. Old says, "The most important criticism which the Strasbourg Reformers had of the old forms of worship was that they were of merely human origin. The reformers knew that many of the liturgical traditions which they had inherited were not of truly ancient tradition." See Old, *Patristic Roots*, 24. Calvin says, "We must always remember that ceremonies are on different levels. On the one hand there are those which were pure at the beginning but which later, when the sun of truth came upon them, either became clouded and were finally abolished (as Christianity succeeded Judaism), or deteriorated into sinfulness by usage (as Judaism was used by the Jews in a superstitious and literal manner). On the other hand are the sheer superstitions that the devil devised to falsify the worship of God." See Calvin, *Calvin's Ecclesiastical Advice*, 67.

56. Calvin, "Reply to Sadolet," 232. While explaining the act of kneeling in prayer, Calvin insists that human and divine factors exist at the same time. Calvin's opinion has a close relationship with liturgical theology. Martin Bucer, who influenced Calvin's worship theology, emphasized public worship space and the Christian year in *De Regno Christi* and the *Censura*. It is somewhat interesting, considering the Reformed church's objection against ritual. However, Bucer thought that if ritual could contribute to our increase of faith, we can use ritual. Also, Christians have freedom to make ritual not only in contents, but also in methods. However, at the same time, he warns that rituals made for worshipping God should not be distorted. See Bucer, "De Regno Christi," 248–56; Bucer, "Censura," 136–42.

for the edification of the Church, should be accommodated to the varying circumstances of each age and nation. It will be proper, as the interest of the Church may require, to change and abrogate the old, as well as to introduce new forms. I confess, indeed, that we are not to innovate rashly or incessantly, or for trivial causes.[57]

He recognized the necessity of ceremony for helping the faith of the Church, but he did not consider ceremony essential for attaining salvation itself. His point comes from the idea that ceremony should be proper for the edification of the Church, and should accommodate to the cultural background and character of the congregation. Rather than abrupt change, Calvin cautiously purified the ceremony based on Bible and context.

Eventually, he insisted that ceremony must have "facility in observance, and significance of meaning which consists in clearness."[58] He states,

> God neither cares for nor values ceremonies considered only in themselves; that he looks to the faith and truth of the heart; and that the only end for which he commanded and for which he approves ceremonies is that they may be pure exercises of faith, and prayer, and praise.[59]

To Calvin, ceremony is an outward tool for helping and disciplining human faith. While ceremony does not create faith by itself, it does help nurture the process of faith formation by disciplining the minds of believers. Ceremony is a tool given to people for training and enhancing their piety through prayer, song, and preaching, and has value only when connected to God's Word.[60] Regarding the use and role of liturgy, Calvin insists there is crucial difference between the New Testament era and the Old Testament era, and therefore some liturgical materials that were helpful under law are no longer necessary.[61] The essence of worship does not change, but the people who live after Christ do not need to be subjected to an outdated "ceremonial yoke."[62] This would be true because "these outward rites are,

---

57. See Calvin, *Institutes*, IV.x.30; also see *Institutes*, IV.v.5; IV.x.12–13; IV.x.15; IV.x.25–30; IV.x32. Calvin insists, "We ought to give attention to bodily exercise in such a manner as not to hinder or retard the practice of godliness." See Calvin, "Commentaries on the First Epistle to Timothy," 110.

58. Calvin, *Institutes*, IV.x.14.

59. Calvin, "Necessity of Reforming the Church," 191. Calvin considers faith as the core of worship. Calvin, *Institutes*, II.viii.11.

60. Calvin, "Commentary on the Book of Psalms," 1:410.

61. Selderhuis, *Calvin's Theology*, 207.

62. Calvin, "Commentary on the Book of Psalms," 2:271.

therefore, themselves of no importance, and acquired only insofar as they are useful in confirming our faith."[63]

Therefore, he says, "let not church despise church because of a difference in external discipline."[64] This may seem to undermine his challenge to the Roman Catholic Church, but for him, the problem in Roman Catholic worship was not merely a difference of ritual and ceremony. He took issue with what he saw as excessive dependence on ceremony rather than a primary focus on God's Word.[65] External differences in discipline did not justify the separation of the Church; however, every church's ceremony should follow the teaching of the Bible.

Calvin had much concern about the form of worship, because outward rites and aids are necessary for believers who live in this world.[66] According to Robert Kingdon, the Geneva Church of Calvin naturally used many rituals, noted here:

> Genevan services were often accompanied by other rituals. Baptism had to be celebrated in church, before a congregation with an ordained minister presiding, not in private as before the Reformation. They usually took place after the sermon toward the end of a service, most commonly one of the very early or late Sunday services, not the main one. Marriages also were celebrated during a service, usually before the main service began. Another ritual sometimes accompanying a service was a ceremony of reparation, in which people apologized in public, most commonly for having participated in a Catholic service elsewhere. A number of times there was a ceremony of reconciliation, in which people who had been involved in public quarrels formally forgave each other and were welcomed back into the general community.[67]

We cannot consider worship at Geneva as "non-liturgical"; rather, it was an attempt to revise and purify the liturgy and rituals according to the Reformed church's biblical interpretation and theological opinion. Calvin says,

63. Ibid.
64. Calvin, *Institutes*, IV.x.32.
65. Calvin sees Roman Catholic worship as depraved by paganism. See Brienen, *De liturgie*, 146. Brienen says, "Het is met recht, date r gesproken wordt over het beginsel van de continuiteit in de liturgie van de Reformatie." Ibid., 171. He believes Calvin's liturgy has a common factor with the Roman Missal. That is to say, according to Brienen, Calvin did not invent a new liturgy, but purified it. See Ibid., 172.
66. Calvin, "Commentary on the Book of Psalms," 4:52–53.
67. Kingdon, "Worship in Geneva," 55.

> Let us know and be fully persuaded, that wherever the faithful, who worship him purely and in due form, according to the appointment of his word, are assembled together to engage in the solemn acts of religious worship, he is graciously present, and presides in the midst of them.[68]

He wanted to worship God with "due form" based on God's Word; the aim is "to praise God, to confess faith and grow in it, to advance in one's knowledge of the word, to confess and experience the unity of faith, and to commemorate God's blessings."[69]

What, then, is "pure and due form" for Calvin? It means having a biblical foundation that helps us concentrate on God.[70] At the same time, he warns that "all fictitious worship is condemned in the Church, and is the more suspected by believers, the more pleasing it is to the human mind."[71] For Calvin, "pure and due form" means that which helps people's minds concentrate on God, not a worship form that pleases the human mind. The biblical foundation of worship form and content are important to him, but it is uncertain whether he intended to use only the outward form of worship designated in the Bible, or merely to be faithful to biblical patterns of worship.

The posterity of Calvinism, especially the Puritan Reformed Church, insisted on the importance of the "regulative principle" of worship.[72] This is "quite simply the doctrine that only what God has instituted or commands (or that which is a necessary logical consequence of what God has instituted or commanded) may be an acceptable element of worship."[73] However, the Puritans deviated from Calvin. The difference, as Gore points out, is that "for Calvin, then, the requirement could be described quite simply as

---

68. Calvin, "Commentary on the Book of Psalms," 1:122.

69. Selderhuis, *Calvin's Theology*, 202.

70. Calvin, "Necessity of Reforming the Church," 191–93.

71. Calvin, *Institutes*, IV.x.11. Also, in the context of baptism, Calvin said, "First, whatever is not commanded we are not free to choose. Secondly, nothing which does not tend to edification ought to be received into the Church." Calvin, "Form of Administering the Sacrament," 118.

72. Reymond, *New Systematic Theology*, 869.

73. See Gore Jr. *Covenantal Worship*, 38; John Calvin insists on the importance of simplicity of worship to maintain the message of the Gospel. See Calvin, "Commentaries on the Four Last Books," 1:263. He says, "when the right and proper method of worshipping him is in question, he whom we ought to obey, and on whose will we ought to depend, alone has authority over our souls." Calvin, *Institutes*, IV.x.8.

whatever is consistent with the Scripture. That is not the same as the Puritan whatever is commanded by Scripture."[74] Calvin says,

> I know how difficult it is to persuade the world that God disapproves of all modes of worship not expressly sanctioned by His Word. The opposite persuasion that cleaves to them, being seated, as it were, in their very bones and marrow, is that whatever they do has in itself a sufficient sanction, provided it exhibits some kind of zeal for the honor of God. But since God not only regards as fruitless, but also plainly abominates, whatever we undertake from zeal to His worship, if at variance with His command, what do we gain by a contrary course? The words of God are clear and distinct, "Obedience is better than sacrifice." ... Every addition to His word, especially in this matter, is a lie. Mere "will worship" is vanity.[75]

This tract was an appeal to Emperor Charles for the necessity of Church and worship reform. In this paragraph, Calvin does not insist on strict Biblicism, but emphasizes that worship should be proper to the principle and spirit of the Bible; "ceremonies, in order to be exercises of piety, must lead us directly to Christ."[76] The reason why Calvin emphasized this is centered in his recognition of human nature. According to him, people tend to do as they see fit rather than obeying the Word of God.[77]

> The human mind, in its wantonness, is ever and anon inventing different modes of worship as a means of gaining his favour. This irreligious affectation of religion being innate in the human mind, has betrayed itself in every age, and is still doing so, men always longing to devise some method of procuring righteousness without any sanction from the Word of God.[78]

People's minds harbor the vestiges of superstition; "we perceive in the human mind an intemperate longing for perverse worship, a longing which no curbs are able to restrain."[79] These considerations of the human nature produced a negative view of any additions made by humans into

---

74. See Gore, *Covenantal Worship*, 89.

75. See Calvin, "Necessity of Reforming the Church," 128–29. Jordan says, "The Reformers had realized that God's commands are found in Scripture in precept, principle, and example. Their heirs tended to exchange this holistic openness to the Word of God for a quest for explicit commands." Jordan, *Sociology of the Church*, 28.

76. Calvin, *Institutes*, IV.x.29.

77. Calvin, "Necessity of Reforming the Church," 192.

78. Calvin, *Institutes*, II.viii.5.

79. Calvin, "Commentaries on the Book of Joshua," 268.

the worship. Actually, his point is right in that people's religious minds are not always connected to worshipping God; people invent some forms of ritual or worship to satisfy their own religiosity. Calvin's distrust of human nature resulted in the belief that human sin can spoil worship; to preserve the purity of God's Word, Calvin was inclined to minimize human additions to the worship practice.[80]

However, Calvin was more inclusive than his successors in the Reformed Church, especially the Puritans in England.[81] In the letters to the Brethren of Wezel, he says,

> We do not hold lighted candles in the celebration of the Eucharist nor figured bread to be such indifferent things, that we would willingly consent to their introduction, or approve of them, though we object not to accommodate ourselves to the use of them, where they have been already established, when we have no authority to oppose them . . . But should our lot be cast in some place where a different form prevails, there is not one of us who from spite against a candle or a chasuble would consent to separate himself from the body of the church, and so deprive himself of the use of the sacrament. We must be on our guard not to scandalize those who are already subject to such infirmities, which we should certainly do by rejecting them from too frivolous motives . . . For as we have said, it is perfectly lawful for the children of God to submit to many things of which they do not approve. Now the main point of consideration is how far such liberty should extend. Upon this head let us lay it down as a settled point, that we ought to make mutual concessions in all ceremonies that do not involve any prejudice to the confession of our faith, and for this end that the unity of the church be not destroyed by our excessive rigor or moroseness.[82]

As we see, Calvin understands liturgy to be a tool for helping human weakness. His priority is to preserve church unity. In this respect, he tries to admit the use of ritual practices that have already been used in other

---

80. Todd Billings says, "Calvin is not being negative about humanity, but negative about sin." Billings, *Calvin, Participation*, 45. In *The Necessity of Reforming the Church*, Calvin says, "In short, as God requires us to worship him in a spiritual manner, so we with all zeal urge men to all the spiritual sacrifices which he commends . . . This, I say, is the sure and unerring form of divine worship, which we know that he approves, because it is the form which his Word prescribes." See Calvin, "Necessity of Reforming the Church," 187–88.

81. Calvin, *Institutes*, IV.x.27; 30; Leith, *Introduction to the Reformed Tradition*, 173.

82. "Letters of John Calvin, 3: 30–31," 174.

churches. However, such freedom is possible only within the boundaries of confession and conscience. To Calvin, the matter of selecting the liturgy was related to the edification of believers and the church community.[83] John Leith notes, "He did not needlessly attempt to ascribe to theological significance every act or accessory of worship."[84] Also, according to Brennen, Calvin's vision of liturgy has freedom in it, even though it should be based on God's Word.[85]

Therefore, Calvin is not only tolerant of some ritual, he is open to revising the ritual practice. In 1561, he voiced discontent about worship practices in the Geneva Church: "I have taken care to record publicly that our custom is defective, so that those who come after me may be able to correct it the more freely and easily."[86] He did not deny the use of liturgy; he considered it necessary to remind the people of "God's present goodness."[87] He recognized the necessity of external symbols if people "come with pure hearts to seek him in a spiritual manner."[88] Liturgy was a supportive ladder to heaven through worship. However, he worried about human complacency, and believed God would not be satisfied if people kept rituals and ceremonies without holiness of heart.[89] If people do not worship God spiritually, but focus on outward ceremony without the affection of the heart, it is merely meaningless play.[90]

CALVIN ON FAITH FORMATION

Did Calvin have a plan for faith formation? Of course, the modern term "faith formation" is not mentioned in his writing. However, it is evident that Calvin has a notion of faith formation.[91] Joel Beeke reminds us that "Calvin

---

83. Calvin, "Form of Administering Sacraments," 118.

84. Leith, *Introduction*, 210; Calvin, *Institutes*, IV.x.30.

85. Brienen, *De liturgie*, 154. Also, see Jansen, "Calvin on a Fixed Form," 282–87.

86. Text 35, vol. xxxviii, i. p 213 in Maxwell, *History of Christian Worship*, 118.

87. Calvin, "Commentary on the Book of Psalms," 1:446. While seeing Calvin's commentaries on Gen 8.20; 33:20; 35: 7; Jer 7:21; Dan 9:1–3 and the *Institutes* IV.i.1. and IV.x.31, John Witvliet says, "Ceremonies and symbols were, in Calvin's words, useful for encouraging and stimulating faith. He frequently referred to them as 'props,' 'stimulants,' and 'exercises.'" See Witvliet, *Worship Seeking Understanding*, 144.

88. Calvin, "Commentary on the Book of Psalms," 2:130.

89. Ibid., 260.

90. Calvin, "Commentary on the Book of Psalms," 5:168; Calvin, "Commentary on the Book of Psalms," 2:101.

91. Boulton, *Life in God*, 24. Joel Beeke says, "In expounding faith's maturation process, Calvin asserts that assurance is proportional to faith's development. More

does allow for varying degrees of faith. Though secondary sources often downplay them, Calvin uses such concepts as 'infancy of faith,' 'beginnings of faith,' and 'weak faith' even more frequently than does Luther."[92] What did Calvin say about "faith" and "practicing" the liturgy?

In order to understand this, we must first understand what "faith" meant to Calvin. Among the many places he mentions faith, "The True Method of Giving Peace to Christendom and Reforming the Church" gives an integrative and core definition of faith:

> First, that it is an undoubting persuasion, by which we receive the word brought by Prophets and Apostles as truth sent from God. Secondly, that what it properly looks to in the Word of God is the free promises, and especially Christ, their pledge and foundation, so that, resting on the paternal favour of God, we can venture to entertain a confident hope of eternal salvation. Thirdly, that it is not a bare knowledge which flutters in the mind, but that it carries along with it a lively affection, which has its seat in the heart. Fourthly, that this faith does not spring from the perspicacity of the human mind, or the proper movement of the heart, but is the special work of the Holy Spirit, whose it is both to enlighten the mind and impress the heart. Lastly, that this efficacy of the Spirit is not felt by all promiscuously, but by those who are ordained to life.[93]

While ideas about faith can, of course, be found throughout his commentaries, articles, and books,[94] it is not an exaggeration to say that this statement encompasses the core of Calvin's thoughts on faith. First, Calvin points out that faith comes from the work of the Holy Spirit.[95] He thinks faith can be given by the Holy Spirit to arouse human intelligence and emotion.[96] This is closely related to predestination and providence. This sort of

---

specifically, he presents the Holy Spirit not only as the initiator of faith, but also as the cause and agent of its growth (3.2.33–36). Faith, repentance, sanctification, and assurance are all progressive (3.2.14; 3.3.9)." See Beeke, "Appropriating Salvation," 282; regarding the growth of faith, see Calvin, "Commentary on the Gospel," 1:88–90; Regarding the relationship between sacrament and growth of faith, see Calvin, *Institutes*, IV.xiv.7.

92. Beeke, "Appropriating Salvation," 282.

93. Calvin, "True Method," 250.

94. Regarding Calvin's mention of faith throughout his works, see Beeke, "Appropriating Salvation," 270–300.

95. Also, Calvin emphasizes the role of the Holy Spirit in faith formation. See Calvin, "Catechism of the Church," 102–07.

96. Calvin says, "The secret efficacy of the Spirit, to which it is owing that we enjoy Christ and all his blessings. Calvin, *Institutes*, III.i.1. Calvin added "an epiclesis

faith is not mere accumulation of knowledge, but very close to the character of "affection."[97] Faith is certainty, which is focused on Christ, who is the promise of God.

Among all his characterizations of faith, the most interesting is that of faith as "knowledge." He says, "[Faith] is a firm and sure knowledge of the divine favor toward us, founded on the truth of a free promise in Christ, and revealed to our minds, and sealed on our hearts, by the Holy Spirit."[98] Dowey considers knowledge a central category of Calvin's theological structure.[99] However, knowledge, to Calvin, does not merely mean cognition, but includes piety. Calvin says that "an empty and confused knowledge about God must not be mistaken for faith, but that knowledge which is directed to Christ, in order to seek God in Christ; and this can only be done when the power and offices of Christ are understood."[100] Faith is closer to the heart than it is to intelligence.[101] He emphasizes confession of faith and catechetical instruction, but was not seeking Scholasticism; rather, he sought affection, which was combined with knowledge of God and piety. Therefore, he says, "We cannot say that God is known where there is no religion or piety."[102]

Faith includes both *cognito* and *fiducia*. For Calvin, two kinds of knowledge are given to people: one is "knowledge by faith (*scientia fidei*)

(invocation) of the Holy Spirit, the Collect for Illumination (prayer invoking the Holy Spirit) before the reading of scripture" in his liturgy. See White, *Protestant Worship*, 68. Old says, "There is a baptismal epiclesis and a Communion epiclesis. The point of an epiclesis is that we realize that our liturgical doing must be Spirit-filled. It is 'valid' not because of what we have done, but because of what God's Spirit does with it and through it." See Old, "Calvin's Theology of Worship," 421. This shows Calvin's emphasis on the role of the Holy Spirit in worship.

97. Doumergue, *Le Caractere*, 74.

98. Calvin, *Institutes*, III.ii.7.

99. Dowey, *Knowledge of God*, 247.

100. Calvin, "Commentaries on the Epistles of Paul," 257.

101. Beeke, *Puritan Reformed Spirituality*, 1–2. Beeke says, "For Calvin, *pietas* designates the right attitude of man towards God. This attitude includes true knowledge, heartfelt worship, saving faith, filial fear, prayerful submission, and reverential love." See Ibid., 2. Elsie McKee gives a brief but important explanation of *pietas*: "*Pietas* represents generally a very positive concept of the human attitude of adoration and service of God. True piety implies knowledge, but its primary emphasis is commitment, devotion, attitude. *Pietas* can cover worship generally, but it is also commonly used to designate the first table of the law, especially when worship is distinguished from service of neighbor. Calvin can distinguish *pietas* from outward ecclesiastical ceremonies, but he often speaks approvingly of the exercises or duties of piety as outward manifestations of the first table of the law." McKee, "Context, Contours, Contents," 175.

102. Calvin, *Institutes*, I.ii.1. Calvin says, "I call 'piety' that reverence joined with love of God which the knowledge of his benefits includes."

and the knowledge of experience (*scientia experentiae*),"[103] or knowledge of God is gained by faith and experience. According to Beeke, "bare experience (*nuda experiential*) is not Calvin's goal, but experience grounded in the Word, flowing out of the fulfillment of the Word. Experimental knowledge of the Word is essential."[104] To this point, Calvin said, "Hence we conclude that the knowledge of faith consists more of certainty than discernment."[105] To attain certainty or trust in faith formation, people apply God's Word to their existence in the experience of worship and sacrament.

This experience comes from the Gospel. Gerrish says, "The phrase *facti eius participes*, is perhaps an echo of Hebrews 3:14. In his commentary on this verse, Calvin states that we are admitted to this participation by faith."[106] For Calvin, knowledge of God is a sort of experiential knowledge, gained by experiencing God.[107]

Faith, participation, and union with Christ

According to Calvin, the concept of participation has a close relationship with faith, sacrament, union with Christ, justification, and sanctification.[108] What does participation mean to Calvin, and how can people accomplish it? Todd Billings says, "This participation takes place in the communal context of the church and its sacramental life, which is connected to an interrelated set of outwardly moving mutual love in the church, love of neighbor, love

---

103. Beeke, *Puritan Reformed Spirituality*, 40. Gerrish says, "The cognitive strand in Calvin's concept of faith never excludes mystery, nor does the mystical strand leave him speechless. Calvin's notion is that faith, even as cognition, is somehow enabled to go beyond the normal limits of human knowing, but that the result is nonetheless knowledge even if it is not comprehension (Inst. 1559, 3.2.14)." Gerrish, *Grace and Gratitude*, 76.

104. Beeke, "Appropriating Salvation," 285.

105. Calvin, *Institutes*, III.ii.14.

106. Gerrish, *Grace and Gratitude*, 83.

107. Regarding this, we need to know the meaning of the Hebrew word *yada*. In the Hebrew, real faith came from God. People come to know faith while having fellowship with God. Therefore, worship experience is very important. In the Old Testament, the meaning of knowing firstly can be known in the book of Hosea. See Wolff, "Wissen um Gott," 182–205. Boulton says, "Hence the term 'knowledge' in the definition of *pietas* does not refer to a speculative, abstract, or merely mental affair, but rather to a concrete, relational, affective, and experiential one, what we might call a knowledge of as opposed to merely a knowledge about." Boulton, *Life in God*, 47.

108. Billings says, "A theology of participation is seen as the essential reintegrating factor, integrating the connections between divine love and human love and a Trinitarian soteriology of reciprocity." Billings, *Calvin, Participation, and the Gift*, 12.

of the needy, and love manifested through justice and equity in society."[109] For Calvin, participation happens through a life of worship and sacrament, and the place in which the love of God is connected to a love of neighbor.[110]

Joel Beeke argues that "the heartbeat of Calvin's practical theology and piety is communion (*communio*) with Christ. This involves participation (*participatio*) in his benefits, which are inseparable from union with Christ."[111] Through union with God, people participate in the "benefit" of Christ.[112] Calvin believes that as Father and Son are one, humans are united to Jesus Christ.[113] This union and communion "entail the giving of new identity such as that in Christ."[114] By participating, people are united to God and enjoy the trinitarian communion.

At this point, it should be considered that the most important thing is the priority of God's grace. Before the resolution of people, God's calling exists; Calvin says, "Christ is given to us by the kindness of God."[115] What benefit then does God give to us? Calvin says, "We obtain in particular a twofold benefit; first, being reconciled by the righteousness of Christ, God becomes, instead of a judge, an indulgent Father; and, secondly, being sanctified by his Spirit, we aspire to integrity and purity of life."[116] That is to say, by participating in Christ, people receive double grace, justification and sanctification.[117] According to Calvin, not only justification, but also sanctification is given as grace. Also, by participation, "Christ . . . becomes ours making us partners with him in the gifts with which he was endued."[118]

According to Calvin, the believer is "partaker of all his benefits, but also of himself" because "Christ is not external to us, but dwells in us; and not only unites us to himself by an undivided bond of fellowship, but by

---

109. Billings, *Calvin, Participation, and the Gift*, 15.

110. Billings says, "In prayer, the sacraments, and obedience to the law, believers are incorporated into the Triune Life." Ibid., 17. "In the first edition of the *Institutes*, Calvin develops the theme of participation in Christ in relation to three major topics: The Lord's Supper, baptism, and justification." See Ibid., 70.

111. Beeke, "Appropriating Salvation," 273.

112. Julie Canlis points out that "participation in Christ" is one of the important subjects in Calvin's *Institutes*. See Canlis, *Calvin's Ladder*, 55.

113. John Calvin, "Sermon on 1 Samuel 2: 27–36," cited in Billings, *Calvin, Participation*, 52.

114. Billings, *Union with Christ*, 11.

115. Calvin, *Institutes*, III.xi.1.

116. Ibid.

117. Calvin says, "As Christ cannot be divided into parts, so the two things, justification and sanctification, which we perceive to be united together in him, are inseparable." Calvin, *Institutes*, III.xi.6.

118. Calvin, *Institutes*, III.xi.10.

a wondrous communion brings us daily into closer connection, until he becomes altogether one with us."[119] Through the Holy Spirit, believers "become partakers of the divine nature."[120] Through God and the Holy Spirit, people come "into participation in the Father."[121] By participation, people can have communion with the Trinity.[122] During the administering of the Word and sacraments, believers experience the Trinity.[123] As Billings notes, "the creature is not identical to the Creator, and this participation is always in Christ, through the Spirit."[124]

It is important to note the importance of participation itself. Though many people emphasize the presence of God in the Lord's Supper, this is not the reward of human faith, but the self-giving faith that comes from God's promise.[125] Thus, God's self-giving faith has priority.[126] At the same time, this promise requires faithful reaction from his people.[127] Participation is not merely an automatic tool for receiving grace, but rather a dynamic opportunity to strengthen relationships with God.[128] Participation permits believers to approach the means of grace and enhance their understanding and faith. Calvin says, "The blessings in which his happiness consisted were not his own, but derived by divine communication."[129] Therefore, participa-

119. Calvin, *Institutes*, III.ii.24.

120. Calvin, *Institutes*, I.xiii.14; also see Calvin, *Institutes*, III.i.2; Calvin says, "Hence, too, we infer that we are one with the son of God; not because he conveys his substance to us, but because, by the power of his Spirit, he imparts to us his life and all the blessings which he has received from the Father." Calvin, "Commentary on the Gospel," 2:184.

121. Calvin, *Institutes*, I.viii.26.

122. Calvin, *Institutes*, III.xi.5. Julie Canlis says, "We remember that, in Calvin's definition of the Trinity, the names Father, Son, and the Spirit refer to an immanent relationship (and thus personal communion) rather than segregated economic function." See Canlis: *Calvin's Ladder*, 133. Cf. Calvin, *Institutes*, IV.xv.6. Julie Canlis says, "While Aquinas used the inner perichoretic life of the Trinity as the model, Calvin stuck to the biblical economy and limited participation to our inclusion into Jesus and his vicarious humanity, full stop." Canlis, *Calvin's Ladder*, 137.

123. Billings, *Calvin, Participation*, 114.

124. Ibid., 60.

125. Calvin says, "I conclude, that Christ's body is really, that is, truly given to us in the Supper, to be wholesome food for our souls. I use the common form of expression, but my meaning is, that our souls are nourished by the substance of the body, that we may truly be made one with him." Calvin, "First Epistle to the Corinthians," 379.

126. Canlis, *Calvin's Ladder*, 71.

127. Calvin, *Institutes*, IV.xi.16.

128. Julie Canlis says, "In Calvin, participation is not a principle. It is a way of living such that everything forces us to be in relationship." Canlis, *Calvin's Ladder*, 76.

129. Calvin, *Institutes*, II.ii.1.

tion in worship and sacrament, which is the place of union and communion with God, is important.[130]

Faith formation starts from infant baptism

For Calvin, faith is a gift from God, given by the work of Holy Spirit.[131] To accommodate human weakness, God assists faith using the means of grace. Even though God "might perfect his people in a moment, chooses not to bring them to manhood in any other way than by the education of the church."[132] Calvin insists, "In particular, [God] has instituted sacraments, which we feel by experience to be most useful helps in fostering and confirming our faith."[133] To Calvin, the sacraments are an important factor in the process of faith formation: "[The sacraments] are aids and means to our incorporation in Jesus Christ, or, if we are already of his body, to confirm us therein more and more until he unites us wholly with himself in the life of heaven."[134] So, what is Calvin's thought on infant baptism as the starting point in the process of faith formation?

In Calvin's scheme of faith formation, infant baptism, the parents' confession and duty of teaching, and the educational mission of the church community are delicately interrelated. Calvin thinks the believers in the Old and New Testament era were born holy, because of the covenant with Abraham.[135] In the womb, they belong to the everlasting covenant.[136] Peter Lillback says, "The implication for the practice of baptism is that the offspring of Abraham are heirs of the promise, even those who became his offspring by faith. Thus the children of Abraham's offspring by faith are also made full partakers of the promises, since they are now part of his family."[137] Calvin insisted on the inclusiveness of covenant in the context of infant baptism. This is the starting point of faith formation of Calvin's scheme;

---

130. Julie Canlis says, "We will now proceed into Calvin's Christology, to the man Jesus Christ, who will redeem humanity through his death and persuade them once again of God's love for them. However, this will not be mere cognitive persuasion. Jesus will be noticeably 'set apart' by a sinless relationship of trust and communion with God the Father, which he reopens to all humanity through participation in his person." Canlis, *Calvin's Ladder*, 88.

131. Calvin, *Institutes*, III.ii.30.

132. Calvin, *Institutes*, IV.i.5.

133. Calvin, *Institutes*, IV.i.1.

134. Wendel, *Calvin*, 318.

135. Calvin, *Institutes*, IV.xvi.12; Lillback, *Binding of God*, 251.

136. Calvin, "True Method," 275.

137. Lillback, *Binding of God*, 252.

next, it is connected to the family and church's continuing education in the Christian faith, because infants cannot confess their own faith. The practice of infant communion requires the parents' oath to educate the child in the catechism.[138]

According to Robert Kingdon, this is one of the most fundamental differences between the Catholic Church, which relied heavily on home instruction, and the Reformed Church, which insisted "that catechism by professional clergymen supplement home instruction. Calvin and his fellow clergymen did not abandon home instruction."[139] This is one of the reasons why Calvin emphasized the importance of Christian mood *and* the role of church education. Although he valued cognition and the ability to understand regarding worship and the sacraments, on the matter of infant baptism, he says, "Though these [repentance and faith] are not yet formed in them, yet the seed of both lies hid in them by the secret operation of the Holy Spirit."[140] Of course, Calvin did not consider a child's faith the same as an adult's.[141] He notes, "I would not rashly affirm that they are endued with the same faith which we experience in ourselves, or have any knowledge at all resembling faith (this I would rather leave undecided)."[142] However, as Gerrish points out, Calvin believed that "the influence of a mother church on a child is never wholly a matter of instruction; it operates at subconscious levels that leave ample room for Calvin's profound sense of the mystery of the Sacrament and the secret working of the Spirit."[143] Calvin recognized the importance of the environment and adult guidance for young children; these statements suggest that he intended faith formation to be fostered among children by allowing them to experience public worship, by nurturing them in a Christian family, and by teaching them through the Catechism. Through these channels, children become accustomed to the Christian mood and tacitly learn about Christian faith.[144] Even so, Calvin

---

138. Calvin, *Joannis Calvini*, 35–36.

139. Kingdon, "Catechesis," 295.

140. Calvin, *Institutes*, IV.xvi.20. However, Calvin denies the possibility of infant faith. See Pitkin, "Heritage of the Lord," 186.

141. Ibid.

142. Calvin, *Institutes*, IV.xvi.19. Calvin says, "But it is perfectly clear that infants must be placed in a different class." Calvin, *Institutes*, IV.xvi. 23.

143. Gerrish, *Grace and Gratitude*, 119.

144. Boulton insists, "The pedagogical program Calvin had in mind is more comprehensively immersive and formational than what the terms 'instruction' or 'education' often connote in modern English." See Boulton, *Life in God*, 57.

did not devalue the importance of confession of faith, and his emphasis on infant baptism was supported by catechetical instruction for children.[145]

Infant baptism requires catechetical instruction

John Calvin endorsed the propriety of infant baptism based on the continuity of God's covenant, and especially the practice of circumcision in the Old Testament. He believed the sign of baptism is prior to its understanding.[146] At the same time, he often emphasizes catechetical instruction from an early age in his writings.[147] He insists that "infants of tender age be so instructed that they are able to give reason for the faith"[148]:

> There be a brief and simple summary of the Christian faith, to be taught to all children, and that at certain seasons for the year they come before the ministers to be interrogated and examined, and to receive more ample explanation, according as there is need to the capacity of each one of them, until they have been proved sufficiently instructed.[149]

The church could enhance a child's understanding by checking their memory, correcting errors, and clearing up any misunderstandings or uncertainties. At age ten, children could confess their faith in front of the church community in a question-and-answer format.

---

145. Karen Spierling says, "According to Calvin's defense of infant baptism, the full significance of the sacrament was realized through the diligent instruction of the baptized children and the teachings of Reformed faith." See Spierling, *Infant Baptism*, 193; Zachman, *John Calvin as Teacher*, 135.

146. Calvin, *Institutes*, IV.xvi.21.

147. Calvin, *Institutes*, IV.xix.13; Calvin, *Letters of John Calvin*, 177. Calvin wrote two catechisms in 1537 and 1545. For a more detail explanation, see Watanabe, "Calvin's Second Catechism," 224–32. In particular, we should note the changes of form in the second document into a question-and-answer structure. Watanabe says, "It seems that Calvin considered this form to be more effective for the instruction of children because 1) short sentences are more conducive to a clear expression of the faith, and 2) they lend themselves more readily to confession of faith by word of mouth. The form by which the minister asks and the child answers is a sort of oral confession of faith in the young believer elicited by the minister. In Calvin, this is not a method of explanation of faith or a method of developing theological theory but rather an exemplary form of confession by young believers." See Ibid., 227. At this point, I propose that Calvin was not a stern judge who intended to prohibit young children's access to worship and sacrament, but rather that he wanted to help them gain understanding and the appropriate knowledge for oral confession.

148. See Calvin, "Articles Concerning the Organization," 48.

149. Ibid., 54.

Robert Kingdon says, "The obvious intention of this catechism was to make sure that every child in the community could ultimately repeat from memory a set of basic summaries of the faith: the Apostle's Creed, the Ten Commandments with their New Testament supplement, the Lord's Prayer."[150] Eventually, this public practice might expose lazy parents who did not participate in their child's faith education.[151] It was clear in the "Draft Ecclesiastical Ordinances (1541)" that the religious upbringing of children was the responsibility of their parents, and in 1549 the council went so far as to impose a fine of three *solz* on parents who did not send their children to catechism; furthermore, "parents were expected to keep their children under control at all church services, but children who disrupted the service even under the watch of their parents could expect to be disciplined by the Consistory."[152]

Calvin comments, "It has always been a practice and diligent care of the church, that children be rightly brought up in Christian doctrine."[153] He emphasized that the right foundation of biblical understanding leads to right piety and right worship.[154] Children who could not yet express their testimony of faith at the time of baptism should get an opportunity to testify in the presence of the church community.[155]

To best help children in their faith formation, Calvin insisted on the necessity of cooperation between church and family for education.[156] The Sunday midday service at the Geneva Church was for teaching the catechism to little children,[157] and the Registers of the Consistory of Geneva City, under the guidance of John Calvin, emphasized the participation for all citizens and inhabitants and outlined clear guidelines for how catechism should be taught to children.

> All citizens and inhabitants are to bring or convey their children on Sundays at midday to Catechism . . . A definite formulary is to be composed by which they will be instructed, and on this, with the teaching given them, they are to be interrogated about what has been said, to see if they have listened and remembered well. When a child has been well enough instructed to pass the

---

150. See Kingdon, "Catechesis," 304.
151. Calvin, *Institutes*, IV.xix.13.
152. Spierling, *Infant Baptism*, 199–201.
153. Calvin, "Catechism," 88.
154. Calvin, *Institutes*, I.ii.2; Calvin, "Commentary upon The Acts," 2:154–61.
155. Calvin, "Articles Concerning the Organization," 54.
156. Kingdon, "Catechesis," 300.
157. Zachman, *John Calvin as Teacher*, 139.

> Catechism, he is to recite solemnly the sum of what it contains and also to make profession of his Christianity in the presence of the Church. Before this is done, no child is to be admitted to receive the Supper; and parents are to be informed not to bring them before this time. For it is a very perilous thing, for children as for parents, to introduce them without good and adequate instruction, for which purpose this order is to be used.[158]

Calvin's aim for catechetical instruction, unlike the Consistory's directive, goes beyond mere mastery of the content of Christian doctrine, calling instead for full, informed participation in the public worship.[159] Of course, children had to memorize the Lord's Prayer, the creed, and the Ten Commandments. Therefore, Robert Kingdon points out,

> It raises the possibility that the people of Calvin's Geneva . . . did not need to understand what these texts really meant, that these texts had no real influence on their behavior. In short, these texts could have become mantras, held to have magical value simply in their repetition.[160]

However, weekly catechism class itself, along with public worship, reinforced the process of faith formation for baptized children due to repetition and participation.

This catechetical instruction proceeded with cooperation between parents and the church.[161] To Calvin, the family is responsible for nurturing and educating children in matters of faith. He believed God gave parents the educational duty of nurturing their children.[162] He insisted that parents properly use gentleness and austerity harmoniously, believing that the best way for parents to teach children was to be good examples.[163]

---

158. Calvin, "Draft Ecclesiastical Ordinance," 69. In the catechism service, "those adults who were deemed to have an insufficient grasp of the evangelical faith" should participate. See Zachman, *John Calvin as Teacher*, 140; Also, Kingdon says, "Adults who were not able to recite from memory these basic texts were not permitted to receive communion." Kingdon, "Catechesis," 305. For more information about the Geneva Church's Sunday worship practice, see Calvin, *John Calvin*, 98–134.

159. Calvin, "Catechism," 88.

160. Kingdon, "Catechesis," 307.

161. James Smith says, "The rituals of Reformed worship very tangibly remind us that the mundane and monumental task of raising children is not something we can do on our own. It takes the village of God's peculiar people." See Smith, *Letters to a Young Calvinist*, 82.

162. Calvin, *Ioannis Calvini*, 51:783.

163. Calvin, *Ioannis Calvini*, 33:43.

After confessing the faith, children and adults alike are developed and nurtured by joining in the sacrament and public worship. Robert Kingdon, says, "The basic instruction provided in catechism classes was reinforced by church service."[164] According to Boulton,

> An ideal picture emerges of Genevan life as a life lived in and through liturgical, disciplinary, paideutic forms and formation: twice-weekly mandatory worship in church among the gathered assembly (Sundays and Wednesday), as well as optional pubic worship on all other days; daily morning and evening devotions at home among the household (parents, children, and servants); and over the course of each day, a regular cycle of dedicated times for individual or small-group prayer.[165]

Through all these activities, Calvin's intent that faith formation be nurtured and fostered through practicing the worship is evident.

When discussing Calvin's idea of faith formation through practice, it is helpful to note his emphasis on the weekly celebration of the Lord's Supper. According to Boulton, "Christian paideia, the formative education toward genuine and full humanity" is "oriented toward union with God in Christ, and for Calvin, the sacred supper is the sacrament . . . of that mystical union." Boulton concludes that "Calvin placed the supper at the heart of his theological work, and called for its weekly celebration in Christian churches."[166] Why did Calvin insist on the Lord's Supper at every Sunday worship? We can surmise that Calvin anticipated the effect of worship by repeating and reminding, because Calvin considered the sacrament as an "exercise of faith."[167] Calvin did not merely emphasize the necessity of adding frequency, but seems to keep in mind the formation of sincere faith by repeating the worship practice. Wandel says,

> Those who received the earthly elements in faith were not alone somatically or spiritually. For Calvin, the Supper, like preaching,

---

164. Kingdon, "Catechesis," 306.

165. Boulton, *Life in God*, 40. According to Boulton, Calvin insisted that "Psalm singing should be pervasive, in church, at home, and in the fields," that "moral and spiritual life should be accountable," and that "regular Bible study for clergy and laypeople was held on Friday." Ibid., 43–44. Boulton believes that the "disciplines of prayer and the sacred supper" were important practices for Christian discipline in the thought of John Calvin. See Ibid., 166.

166. Ibid., 42.

167. Calvin, "Genevan Confession," 29. John Calvin says, "We believe that the sacraments which our Lord has ordained in his Church are to be regarded as exercises of faith for us, both for fortifying and confirming it in the promises of God and for witnessing before men."

was to be a praxis-repeated over years, and with that repetition, deepening both understanding and faith. The two, following Calvin's definition of the sign, exist in interdependence with one another. Together and in dynamic with one another, they educate the faithful, how to read God's representations, verbal and visual.[168]

Wandel considers the Lord's Supper, for Calvin, as a sort of tool for helping faith formation, like the Word of God, and these two have interrelated functions. Also, Wandel notes the interaction between understanding and faith in Calvin's thought: understanding fortifies faith, and through faith, people gain deeper understanding. Faith is not a once-and-for-all event; rather, faith is possible through repetitive practice and participation.

Without participation, people cannot fully understand. Participation in worship can be the starting point of understanding and union with God. Wandel believes Calvin anticipated that "faith would be nourished, knowledge of God's episteme deepened, and therefore, the ability to discern God in his signs, increased."[169] The core of Calvin's intent was nourishing of faith and increasing knowledge of God by participating in public worship—the Word and sacraments, which efficiently deliver God's Word to the human mind through hearing and seeing. Participation in worship, by enhancing human understanding, gives the generative power for development. Boulton supports this:

> It [the sacramental supper] helps us learn by doing. It helps us gain the kind of knowledge that comes only through experience, sensation, and practice. It helps us "feel in ourselves the working of that unique sacrifice," that is, Christ's sacrifice by which "he gave his body to be made bread" (4.17.1, 5). It helps us say of the supper, with Calvin, "I rather experience than understand it," and thereby be, in faith, "persuaded of what we do not grasp" (4.17.32; 3.2.14).[170]

Understanding is strengthened by the cooperation between the visible Word and invisible Word. Participation is a necessary part of the process of faith formation. Calvin insists that even though the sacraments are an appendage of doctrine, sacraments are at the same time the essence of doctrine.[171] He makes a balance between learning the doctrine and participation in the sacrament as a way of knowing God.

---

168. Wandel, *Eucharist in the Reformation*, 164.
169. Ibid., 166.
170. Boulton, *Life in God*, 185.
171. John Calvin says, "Since the sacraments of both testaments have the same

God, through the sacraments, assures us of salvation and grace.[172] And through the sacraments, people are combined into a mystic body of Christ. This is a mystery which human cognition cannot grasp—not a matter of cognition, but of experience and feeling.[173] Doumergue points out that Calvin believed it is not enough to know through the Bible, but that we need to feel and experience.[174] As Calvin says,

> Faith is more about the heart than the mind, more about tenderness than intelligence. The root of the faith must be the heart, faith is not merely about reason and conjectures; it requires true expression. Faith is truly the eye of understanding/knowing; faith is not providing lip service about spiritual things; faith stems not from what is said but from the depth of the soul.[175]

Faith is a matter of heart, closely related to experience and essential for spiritual growth. Even though Calvin has generally been understood as prioritizing reason and intelligence, he did try to find balance between knowledge and assurance of faith in the process of faith formation. Therefore, he did not devalue the role of experiencing and practicing sacrament and public worship as a formative experience of Christian.

CALVIN'S THOUGHTS ON LITURGY AND FAITH FORMATION AS FOUND IN THE WORSHIP DOCUMENTS

Calvin recognized the relationship between worship and faith formation. He did not use the term, "formation," but his emphasis on the practice of

---

Author, the same promises, the same truth, and the same fulfillment in Christ, we justly say that they differ from each other in external signs, but agree in those things which I have mentioned, or, in one word, in the reality. For as they are appendages of doctrine, but the substance of the doctrine is the same, so the same rule holds in regard to the Sacraments." See Calvin, "Acts of the Council of Trent," 172.

172. Calvin, *Corpus Reformatorum*, 737.
173. Calvin, *Institutes*, II.xvi.3, III.vi.2, III.xxv.2.
174. Doumergue, *Le Caractere*, 71. Calvin says, "Now, should any one ask me as to the mode, I will not be ashamed to confess that it is too high a mystery either for my mind to comprehend or my words to express; and to speak more plainly I rather feel than understand it." Calvin, *Institutes*, IV.xvii.32.
175. "Le consentment de la foi est plutot du coeur que du cerveau, de l'affection que de l'intelligence." "Il faut que la racine soit au coeur" "la foi ne se contente point de raisons probables et de conjetures vraisemblables; elle requiert la verite expresse" "La foi est vraiment l'oeil de l'entendement; -il nous faut apporter la bouche spiritueele de la foi; -la foi seule est la bouche par maniere de dire et l'estomac de l'ame." Commentaires, Saint Jean VI, 69, 63, 56. In Doumergue, *Le Caractere*, 74.

and participation in public worship, prayer meetings, the weekly Lord's Supper, and catechesis was aimed at forming sincere believers. To him, liturgy and faith formation are closely related.

In Calvin's documents on worship, there can be found many considerations on the formative function of liturgy.[176] In the "Articles Concerning the Organization of the Church and of Worship at Geneva 1537," Calvin considered church order and regulation closely related to the frequent celebration of the Lord's Supper. In other words, Calvin seems to believe that the practice of Lord's Supper can be a tool for helping faith formation and maintaining spiritual order in the community. According to Calvin, "to maintain the Church in its integrity, the discipline of excommunication is necessary."[177] This is not just a tool for maintaining authority, but for leading to right spirituality. Robert Kingdon says, "This was a punishment far more severe than most of us in the twentieth century can appreciate. Communion was still regarded as possessing an almost magical value, being essential for the mental and physical well-being of every adult."[178] For Calvin, frequent communion and the practice of excommunication were interdependent tools for spiritual formation: the Lord's Supper is a means of grace; therefore, it nurtured and nourished faith. Excommunication, although seemingly negative in the process of faith formation, is positive in its aim, because it makes people examine the status of their faith and return to the place of grace. The person who is excommunicated from joining the Lord's Supper comes to discern the status of faith, and then can be retrained according to the guidance of the church. According to Calvin, excommunication is "to cleanse [the church], to restrain evil desires, to remove shameful behavior, and to correct wrong ways of acting."[179] It can be a tool for fostering and preserving faith not only for the church, but also for private individuals.[180]

---

176. Calvin believed that people could be disciplined in the worship. See Calvin, "Commentary on the Book of Psalms," 3:353–54. Even though Calvin did not consider worship as a tool, it is certain that Calvin's thought on worship is formative.

177. Calvin, "Articles concerning the Organization," 48.

178. Kingdon, "Calvin and the Family," 96. However, excommunication itself was not a perpetual penalty. Kingdon says, "Monter demonstrates that almost every excommunicant purged himself or herself and was permitted to take communion again within the quarter, within three months. It was unusual for an excommunication to be extended for a second or third quarter." Ibid., 97.

179. Calvin, *Calvin's Ecclesiastical Advice*, 112.

180. While studying Calvin's commentary on Ps 22:22–24, Old says, "Commenting on the text 'in the midst of the congregation I will praise thee,' Calvin says that the purpose of public thanksgiving is that the faithful might encourage each other. This is called an exercise because the act of thanksgiving on the part of one member of the congregation encourages others to give thanks. It is an exercise because the expression

Through the Lord's Supper, believers experience the oneness of body, and excommunication itself becomes not merely a system of penalty, but the method of discipline to introduce the right way. The Lord's Supper is a sort of discipline that sustains the church and people.[181]

Secondly, Calvin insists on singing the Psalms "in the form of public devotions by which one may pray to God, or to sing his praise so that the hearts of all be roused and incited to make like prayers and render like praises and thanks to God with one accord."[182] This was his contribution to Reformed worship, and through it, he intended to raise faith and edification.[183] According to McKee, "The Psalms were not simply the texts of the most important biblical prayer book for Calvin personally; they were also the core of the worship and devotional life of the whole people of God, gathered as a body or living out their vocations from day to day."[184] While singing communally, people could more actively participate in the public worship, which contributed to communal piety, because the Psalm was the "communal prayer book."[185]

Thirdly, we can find Calvin's liturgical ideas and his thought on the relationship between liturgy and faith formation by looking at the arrangement of the Decalogue and confession of faith in his liturgy. During the period from 1538 to 1541, after Calvin was expelled from Geneva, he worked at Strassburg with Martin Bucer and was influenced by Bucer's worship theology.[186] However, there are some differences between Calvin and Bucer. Poll says, "Calvin separated the Words of the institution from the Fraction and Distribution by a long exhortation, with Fencing of the Tables. It was

---

of thanksgiving builds up and increases thanksgiving." Old, "Calvin's Theology of Worship," 483.

181. Peter says, "He wanted an organic integration of the sermon and communion and saw the Lord's Supper and the thanksgiving as the climax of divine worship." Peter, "Calvin and Liturgy," 246.

182. Calvin, "Articles Concerning the Organization," 48.

183. Regarding the use and performance practice of psalmody in worship, and its spirituality in Calvin's Geneva, see Witvliet, *Worship Seeking Understanding*, 203–29. John Witvliet insists that "Psalm singing was a discipline, a discipline of sung prayer." See Witvliet, "Spirituality of the Psalter," 210. Regarding Calvin's use of psalm in Geneva, see, Jenny, *Luther, Zwingli, Calvin*, 225–30.

184. Calvin, *John Calvin*, 85.

185. Ibid., 86.

186. White, *Protestant Worship*, 64. Bard Thompson evaluates the relationship as follows: "Impressed by the Strassburg rite, Calvin appropriated it as his model. . . . His service-book came from the press in 1540." Thompson, *Liturgies of the Western Church*, 189.

entirely Calvin's own work."[187] Also, Calvin "did not ask [children] to make a personal confession of their faith, but merely demanded that they should be informed of the fundamental parts of the Christian Catechesis and in this manner should render an account of their faith."[188]

There was no "definite form" of worship in the French church in Strasburg until Calvin arrived in 1538.[189] When we see the sequence and contents of worship, his scheme for faith formation through liturgy becomes clearer. Van de Poll says,

> Calvin sometimes connected the confession of sin with the Decalogue. After each commandment there follows the Kyrie eleison. But in his Strasburg liturgy, he allowed the first table of the law to be sung after the Absolution, and the second after the prayer for instruction in God's law. But then the function of the law was not accusatory, but laudatory and glorifying. The minister moved to the pulpit while the congregation sang the second table.[190]

Calvin was concerned about the piety aroused by the sequence of confession-absolution-Decalogue. The Decalogue occurs after confession of sin and absolution because "Calvin understood our obedience to be a response of thanksgiving for grace, not a means to gain it."[191] Next, after the prayer by the pastor, the latter part of the Decalogue is narrated.

What did Calvin wish to accomplish with this sequence? It seems he intended that through worship, the worshipper would be reminded of the law and of God's grace and hence be brought to a right confession. Calvin's liturgy reflects a deep consideration of formation, although at this time, there was no concept of faith formation like that of the current Christian education field. However, Calvin's liturgical ideas and practices regarding public worship, as well as his catechesis, have common ground with modern liturgical catechesis. It is certain that he considered that the sequence and arrangement of factors of worship could impact the formation of the believer's faith.

Regarding his worship theology and practice, there has been some critical reflection. Liturgical historian James White points out, "The tone of the service is prolix and verbose, never lacking a chance to instruct, whether

---

187. See van de Poll, *Martin Bucer's Liturgical Idea*, 113–14.
188. See Ibid., 101.
189. Ibid., 112.
190. Ibid., 113–14.
191. Chapell, *Christ-Centered Worship*, 49, cf. Calvin, *Institutes*, II.vii.12.

in the form of prayer, spoken rubric, or exhortation."[192] According to him, the Reformers were mindful of the duty to teach the lay people impacted by Roman Catholicism; they appealed to human reason and cognition, which is the character of Reformed worship. White says,

> Such an introspective piety came to be characteristic of Reformed churches. If God's decrees were inscrutable, human beings at least could examine themselves to see if there was hope they might be among the elect . . . Thus Reformed piety tended to be highly penitential, with a strong inward focus on human unworthiness.[193]

White makes a good point, but for Calvin, the Geneva Church liturgy made people inspect their own minds as worshippers, which also formed the particular piety of the Reformed Church. This was the outcome of formation that came from repetition of liturgy.

---

192. White, *Protestant Worship*, 65.
193. Ibid., 66.

3

Liturgy as a Tool for Christian Faith Formation and Learning

STUDIES ON THE FORMATIVE FUNCTION OF LITURGY

To what degree can liturgy help the process of faith formation? To find a proper answer, a study of the clear meaning of faith will be necessary. What is faith and what dimensions does it include? What does it mean to form faith?

To begin, a theological study of the human body is needed, because faith does not merely happen in the brain, but develops in the embodied action of liturgy—sitting down and standing up, raising hands, kneeling, and so on—affirming the body as a tool for discipleship and faith formation.[1] People perform liturgy, but liturgy forms people. So, we must also discuss the relationship between embodiment and faith formation.

Some may ask if embodiment is necessary to the process of faith formation. In general, due to the dualistic concept that the spirit is good and the body is wicked, people tend toward a negative view of the role of the body in the process of faith formation. However, people receive and practice God's Word with their whole person through embodiment, not merely through hearing and abstract thought.

---

1. Shepherd, *Worship of the Church*, 61.

What does the Bible say about the relationship between body and soul? Does spiritual worship in the Bible mean the exclusion of the body? If so, is there any relationship between the body and soul, or is the body merely a tool for imprisoning human reason? If not, can we consider the human body a tool for spiritual growth? Do contemporary education and ritual studies reveal bodily participation and experience as efficient learning media and facilitators for mature faith?

Faith does not depend only on cognition, but also affection and volition, and therefore, the process of faith formation engages not only the intellect, but the whole person, including the body. Liturgical practice in worship touches the human intelligence as one part of a whole being. Through participation in worship, the human body becomes a tool for learning and disciplining the soul. While engaging in liturgical action, people learn more vividly, which facilitates thinking and understanding.

To study the impact of liturgy on faith formation, it is essential to explore the meaning of faith. Despite the attempts of many theologians and philosophers throughout the centuries to define faith, a clear definition is still difficult. However, in this thesis, I will adopt Yust's definition of faith as "not a set of beliefs; or . . . a well-developed cognitive understanding of all things spiritual. It is an act of grace, in which God chooses to be in relationship with humanity."[2] This experience of fellowship is not just a matter of cognition, but of the whole person. Based on this definition, I will study the relationship between the performance of ritual and the formation of faith.

AFFIRMING THE HUMAN BODY

What is the benefit of embodiment in the process of faith formation and Christian spirituality? Traditionally, the church has not been deeply concerned with the body. In general, the body has been considered fragile and easily exposed to sin. Throughout the centuries, many Christians have tended to focus on the life of the soul while underestimating the role of the body in the process of faith formation.

This dualistic separation has made it difficult for Christians to perceive the wholeness of the human being, and has led to an inward, subjective faith and worship. Think about a worship style focused only on preaching, without significant incorporation of bodily movement. This kind of church would practice the Lord's Supper infrequently, and would tend to characterize Christian discipline as hearing the Word and internalizing it in the mind. Without the regular practice of the Lord's Supper in worship,

2. Yust, *Real Kids, Real Faith*, 4.

such a church would favor a focus on personal sanctification and receiving the blessing; the ideas of oneness of community and loving one's neighbor would be largely absent. If the soul is considered the only part of the human being that can communicate with God, and the body to be inferior and vulnerable to temptation, it will be much less common for bodily movement or liturgy to be included in worship ceremonies.

Liturgical practice throughout much of church history attests to the fact that the body is not merely a tool that leads people to sin, or an organ inferior to the soul. In fact, the Bible affirms the body—especially in the context of the incarnation and resurrection of Jesus Christ. As Herman Bavinck points out, "creation culminates in humanity where the spiritual and material worlds are joined together."[3] According to Scripture and Reformed confessions, the human being does not merely "bear or have" the image of God—the human being is the image of God; "we, having been conformed to the image of Christ, are now again becoming like God (Rom 8:29; 1 Cor 15:49; 2 Cor 3:18; Phil 3:21; Eph. 4:24; Col. 3:10; 1 John 3:2)."[4] Embodiment is appropriate and does not negate the importance of the soul. Moltmann says,

> Embodiment is [God's] goal. All the paths of his spirit and all the words of his speech end in the lived form and configuration of his body. According to the biblical traditions, embodiment is also the end of God's work of reconciliation: "The Word became flesh...." By becoming flesh, the reconciling God assumes the sinful, sick and mortal flesh of human beings and heals it in community with himself. God's eternal Logos becomes a human body, a child in the manger, a savior of the sick, a tortured human body on Golgotha.[5]

If it were not for the incarnation, people could not know and understand God. The metaphor Calvin uses is that in order to make it possible for humans to understand, God used "baby talk"—embodiment—as a method of communication.[6] Rodney Clapp says, "The insistence on the resurrection and the spiritual body underscores just how much orthodox Christian spirituality esteems the body. From creation to and beyond the final judgment, Christian spirituality values the body."[7] Therefore, conservative reformed churches should consider the necessity and propriety of using

---

3. Bavinck, *Reformed Dogmatics*, 511.
4. Ibid., 554–55.
5. Moltmann, *God in Creation*, 245–46.
6. Calvin, *Institutes*, I.xiii.1, III.xi.20.
7. Clapp, *Tortured Wonders*, 47.

liturgy as an embodied act, and the possibility of spiritual discipline while using bodily movement in the worship.

This should not be interpreted to mean that the body is more important than the soul. Rather, it shows how mind and body are closely related; "Christian spirituality is not a freedom from the body, but a freedom within the body."[8] Christian spirituality uses the body as a tool for greater understanding of God while recognizing the body's limitations. In faith formation, the body and spirit, conscious and the unconscious, are all harmoniously balanced; not separate, but united in mystical method.[9] Of course, just as people cannot easily articulate the doctrine of the Trinity in words, it can also be challenging to explain the relationship between the soul and body; however, it can be said that the body itself is not inherently evil.[10] Lecerf's metaphor can be useful in this discussion: "The union between soul and body, whatever ontological realities are implied in this expression, is much closer than that which unites a pilot and his craft."[11] Body and soul exist not as two separate elements in parallel or proximity, but as two elements made one through chemical cohesion.

Affirming the body can be connected to the necessity of liturgy for faith formation, because the human being has the quality of being embodied.[12] As James Smith points out, recognizing the "incarnational affirmation of liturgy" can help people affirm the necessity of liturgical practice. God does not devalue human need; rather, God lovingly recognizes our weakness and limited understanding. The incarnation shows that the body does not hamper faith formation, but is rather a necessary tool for growth. The practice of the body can be a tool of piety. James Smith says, "Our bodies are students even when we don't realize it, and because we are fundamentally oriented by this habitus, this incarnate education ends up being the more powerful."[13] It can be said that God teaches human beings through embodiment. As Smith insists, "Just as God communicates to humanity through the incarnation

---

8. Hollinger, *Head, Heart, Hands*, 108–09.

9. Moltmann, *God in Creation*, 259.

10. Regarding current studies on the relationship between mind and body, see Green, ed., *In Search of the Soul*; Van Peursen, *Body, Soul, Spirit*; Hollinger, *Head, Heart, Hands*, 109.

11. Lecerf, *Introduction*, 92.

12. James Smith says, "In other words, an incarnational affirmation of liturgy and the aesthetics of worship are the fruit of an incarnational ontology (an account of the nature of reality) and a holistic anthropology (an account of the nature of reality) and a holistic anthropology (an account of what it means to be human)." Smith, *Who's Afraid of Postmodernism?* 136.

13. Smith, *Imagining the Kingdom*, 97.

of the Word of flesh—the image of the invisible God (Col 1:15)—so God continues to speak to the Church through the material symbols of bread and wine but also through images and dance."[14] The material world itself does not belong to sinfulness. Everything belongs to a sovereign God: "God himself affirms materiality as a good thing."[15]

Christian faith is not only inward, but also should be the embodiment of an outward faith.[16] Public worship has many liturgical practices through which faith can be embodied, formed, and reformed. For example, through "adorning ourselves for worship, kneeling in prayer, drawing our breath in song," faith can be formed.[17] Smith says,

> The sacramental imagination begins from the assumption that our discipleship depends not only—not even primarily—on the conveyance of ideas into our minds, but on our immersion in embodied practices and rituals that form us into the kind of people God calls us to be. It is only Cartesian thinking things that can do without liturgy; for we embodied creatures, whether ancient or postmodern, the rhythms of ritual and liturgy are gracious practices that enable discipleship and formation.[18]

Western theology's emphasis on reason has underestimated the role of bodily practice and discipline. Liturgy itself has a deep relationship with human nature and discipline.

Smith's ideas can be a starting point for dialogue with liturgical theology. Christian discipleship cannot be formed using only cognitive methods. Without embodied practice, efforts that only concentrate on cognitive learning in faith formation can easily fail. Because a human being is a whole person, the soul as well as the body must be trained. How, then, can the church use this principle to make faithful disciples of Christ? We can find solutions in the practices of liturgical worship. If the bodily aspect in faith formation is affirmed, then liturgy as a formative practice of the church can be affirmed. Smith comments, "We are not conscious minds or souls housed in meaty containers; we are selves who are our bodies; thus, the training of desire requires bodily practices in which a particular telos is embedded."[19] Enacting the liturgy starts from the discipline of the body, and, by repetition, impacts the spirit; in the process, telos and affection are

14. Smith, *Who's Afraid of Post Modernism?* 77.
15. Chan, *Spiritual Theology*, 138.
16. Paulsell, "Honoring the Body," 16.
17. Ibid., 26.
18. Smith, *Who's Afraid of Postmodernism?* 140.
19. Smith, *Desiring the Kingdom*, 62.

aroused. Embodiment has a close relationship with practice. Practice forms a web of meaning and delivers it into the mind and body. Related to this, Dorothy Bass and Craig Dykstra say, "Practices are filled with meaning, and the meaning goes far beyond our own spiritual life to touch all the suffering of humanity. Taking part in Christian practices can cultivate qualities we did not have before and open our eyes and hearts to the activity of God's Spirit in the wider world."[20] Understanding grows through practice itself.[21] As Taylor says, "If the understanding makes the practice possible, it is also true that it is the practice that largely carries the understanding."[22]

Practice and understanding are not two things, but one. People learn the Christian faith while participating in the liturgy. A stance that permits participation in the sacraments and public worship only for those exhibiting a certain level of understanding misses the connection between learning and prayer. Bass and Dykstra also comment, "A Christian community at worship is a community gathered for rehearsal. It is 'practicing' the practices in the same way a child practices catching a ball or playing scales."[23] In the repetitive factors of worship, human affection can be formed.[24] Above all, practice is necessary for the senses, to accumulate ritual knowledge through embodiment and the dimension of sense.[25] Because humans are embodied beings, the practice of liturgy is necessary; through practicing and repeating it in worship, faith is formed and nurtured.

Furthermore, bodily practice has a close relationship with spiritual worship. According to Rodney Clapp,

> Paul's statement [Rom 12:1–2] links and intertwines the disposition and comportment of the physical body with the "renewing of your minds" and "spiritual worship." The "living sacrifice" of bodies is not contrasted to "spiritual worship"—that sacrifice simply is "spiritual worship." Paul clearly speaks in the context of the formational social body that is the church, as the immediately following sentences indicate (12:3–5). From that context he refers to the tangible, material bodies of the members of the church, citing a number of practices that include visible, physical aspects—contributing to the needs of the saints, showing

---

20. Bass and Dykstra, "Growing in the Practices of Faith," 200–01.
21. Smith, *Desiring the Kingdom*, 65.
22. Taylor, *Modern Social Imaginaries*, 25.
23. Dykstra and Bass, "Times of Yearning," 9.
24. Ronald Grimes says, "Ritualizing the event is the best way to ensure that the meanings absorbed are those that represent our most profound aspiration." Grimes, *Deeply into the Bone*, 71.
25. Ibid., 344.

hospitality to strangers, rejoicing and weeping, associating with the lowly, feeding enemies (12:13–20). It does not occur to Paul to separate the body from the mind, the physical from the spiritual, let alone pit them against each other. Showing hospitality and feeding enemies, actions that must be done with and through bodies, are instances of "spiritual worship." The transformational "renewing of your minds" can flow or follow from these palpable, earthy exercises of Christian spirituality.[26]

While remaining faithful to the meaning of the original text in Romans, Clapp has also created a working meaning of spiritual worship. God does not merely implant the concept of faith in the brain; rather, God renews the human mind using the whole person through practice and participation. Spiritual worship does not rule out the body, but renews the mind while "training" or disciplining the body. In the same vein, Ronald Grimes says, "We need interlocking, rather than polarized, conceptions of religion, spirituality, and ritual."[27] We need to affirm the formative power of liturgy while affirming the body and embodiment using integrative thinking, not dualistic positions.

THE IMPORTANCE OF THE BODY IN THE LEARNING PROCESS

Humans grow through learning. Learning can be defined as "a long-term change in mental representations or association as a result of experience."[28] It is also "the means through which we acquire not only skills and knowledge, but values, attitudes, and emotional reactions as well."[29] Based on this, it is clear that learning can occur through the body; the body stabilizes the memory through habituation and fortifies it with the help of emotion.[30] We do not learn only by the work of the mind, but by interaction between body and mind.[31] Merleau-Ponty insists on the centrality of the body in perception and meaning, describing the body as "a nexus of living meanings."[32] Because the body is important in these ways, bodily experience is also important. Merleau-Ponty notes that:

26. Clapp, *Tortured Wonders*, 229–30.
27. Grimes, *Deeply into the Bone*, 70.
28. Ormrod, *Human Learning*, 4.
29. Ibid., 7.
30. Assmann, *Erinnerungsraume*, 20.
31. Merleau-Ponty, *Phenomenology of Perception*, 111.
32. See Ibid., 175.

> Our bodily experience of movement is not a particular case of knowledge; it provides us with a way of access to the world and the object, with a "praktognosia" which has to be recognized as original and perhaps as primary. My body has its world, or understands its world, without having to make use of my "symbolic" or "objectifying function."[33]

This understanding of the human body as the foundation of perception and learning leads us to several points.

Experience is very important in the learning process. Through experience, a person accepts new information and makes room for understanding. Mead argues that "intelligence and knowledge are inside the process of conduct."[34] Mind and self develop while interacting, imitating, and communicating with other people or objects. Through experience, we learn how to decide and lay the foundation for the next act.[35] We can say that perception is a sort of "integration of experience."[36] Past experience becomes fodder for reflection and development through its continued presence in the action of the body.

What is the relationship between the memory of the past and one's current perception? According to Mark Solms' studies, human memory proceeds via a sequence of encryption, storage, and reminiscence.[37] Generally, experience of the past impacts present perception, and mingled perception and experience form a specific image. Knowledge gained through a learning experience and encoded in the brain controls the process of perception.[38] This can be supported by brain research; experience promotes the growth of individual brain cells.[39] In the process of learning and exercise, the brain is reconstructed to maximize the process of reaction.[40] Experience helps us not only form memory but also understand new information; it prepares us to systematize events in the future, helping to inform action the next time this event is encountered.[41]

---

33. Ibid., 162.
34. Mead, *Mind, Self, and Society*, 93.
35. Ibid., 98.
36. Polanyi and Prosch, *Meaning*, 108.
37. Solms and Turnbull, *Brain and the Inner World*, 141.
38. Ibid, 154.
39. Kalat, *Biological Psychology*, 116.
40. Ibid., 118.
41. Gluck, et al., *Learning and Memory*, 89.

Thus it is that the human body and senses join together through experience.[42] Pierre Bourdieu says,

> The world is comprehensible, immediately endowed with meaning, because the body, which, thanks to its senses and its brain, has the capacity to be present to what is outside itself, in the world, and to be impressed and durably modified by it, has been protractedly (from the beginning) exposed to its regularities.[43]

Through experience, sense and cognition are integrated. Perception can be developed by the interrelation between experience and repetitive messaging. In fact, cognitive ability and perception originate and develop through the process of experience. While interacting with others and experiencing the world around them, humans form cognitive systems. Discussing Helen Keller's story, Horst Ruthrof comments,

> We learn from her written documents that only once the relationship was established between her sense interpretations of her surroundings and language in the form of tactile spelling into her hand was she able to deal with language in a semantic sense. Once that was achieved, learning to speak proved a relatively simple affair.[44]

Until she learned how to connect verbal and nonverbal facts, Keller could not acquire the meaning of language.[45] Until she understood the relationship between sense and interpretation, she was considered severely handicapped. By the growth of understanding through experience, she was able to communicate with others and understand their communication. The anecdote that Sullivan, Keller's teacher, was able to teach the difference between the terms "mug," "milk," and "drinking" only after Helen experienced the tactile sensation of water on her hand shows how bodily senses and learning are closely related. Horst says, "No sooner has this semantic event occurred than Helen understands the principle of word meanings as

---

42. Paul Connerton shows how act and ceremony impact memory. See Connerton, *How Societies Remember*, 10.

43. Bourdieu, *Pascalian Meditations*, 135. Also, he says, "To deny the existence of acquired dispositions, in the case of living beings, is to deny the existence of learning in the sense of a selective, durable transformation of the body through the reinforcement or weakening of synaptic connections." Ibid., 136. In addition, he insists that "we learn bodily." Ibid., 141.

44. Ruthrof, *Body in Language*, 23.

45. Ibid., 30; Helen Keller says, "There is nothing, however, mystic or uncertain about what we can touch . . . I derive much knowledge of everyday matter from the jars and jolts which are to be felt everywhere in the house." See Keller, *World I Live In*, 17.

a generalized consequence."[46] For all of us, bodily participation and experience are necessary to connect learning and memory. They make learning possible. In the same vein, Paul Connerton says, "Our bodies, which in commemorations stylistically re-enact an image of the past, keep the past also in an entirely effective form in their continuing ability to perform certain skilled actions."[47] The body remembers previous events; through ceremony and act, the body learns meaning tacitly, which impacts the next act. However, this does not devalue cognitive memory; as Connerton says, "bodily practices of a culturally specific kind entails a combination of cognitive and habit-memory."[48] Through practicing ritual, people reflect on a visceral level, and can gain ritual knowledge. Acting accumulates knowledge and perception in the human body. It can be so powerful that "effective ritual knowledge lodges in the bone, in its very marrow."[49]

To see how this is possible, we can turn to neuroscience, the case of split-brain people in particular.[50] James Kalat says,

> When a split-brain person views a display briefly in the right visual field, thus seeing it with the left hemisphere, the viewer can name the object easily. But the same person viewing a display in the left visual field (right hemisphere) usually can neither name nor describe it. I say "usually" because a small amount of information travels between the hemisphere through several smaller commissures.... Nevertheless, even a patient who cannot name an object correctly points to it with the left hand. The person sometimes even says, "I don't know," while pointing to the correct choice. (Of course, a split-brain person who watches the left hand point out an object can then name it.)[51]

This experiment shows that even a person with brain damage who cannot articulate a process can have other kinds of cognition and perception. In other words, even people who cannot articulate a certain piece of knowledge or process can have a dimension of learning and thinking. Ritual knowledge is similar. It arouses the conscious and subconscious at the same time. D'Aquili and Newberg say, "The subconscious is not completely separated from consciousness; however, these underlying feelings

46. Ruthrof, *Body in Language*, 65.
47. Connerton, *How Societies Remember*, 72.
48. Ibid., 88.
49. Grimes, *Deeply into the Bone*, 7.
50. A "split-brain person" is one who has had physical surgery to separate the two hemispheres of the brain as a remedy for severe epilepsy.
51. Kalat, *Biological Psychology*, 424.

and experiences often affect how we behave."[52] Bodily practice combines cognition and senses, consciousness and subconsciousness, and enables them to impact each other, giving meaning and wisdom to the learner. For Helen Keller, it is certain that nonverbal factors gleaned through experience greatly impacted the formation of perception. As she herself reported, the sense and perception she experienced through her hand was the starting point for connecting the senses and cognitive power. She says, "With the dropping of a little word from another's hand into mine, a slight flutter of the fingers, began the intelligence, the joy, the fullness of my life. Like Job, I feel as if a hand had made me, fashioned me together round about and molded my very soul."[53] Keller makes clear that bodily experience and perception are closely related; intelligence and formation of meaning develop through real experience.

Rudolf Arnheim makes a similar point, arguing that sensory thoughts are composed of perception from the sense organs.[54] And D'Aquili and Newberg say, "All of [the] sensory areas in the brain are connected to the outside world and allow the mind/brain and consciousness to create a loop between the internal and external worlds."[55] This is intuitive recognition organized in interactive networks.[56] It is clear that experience can be the starting point of thinking and cognition; it is also clear that experiences should be repeated to arouse more effective learning and understanding.

THE EFFECT OF REPETITION IN THE HUMAN LEARNING PROCESS

For an experience to be an effective method of learning, the experience needs to be repeated. Ritual knowing is powerful and formative because it is repeated weekly in Christian worship. So, how exactly does repetition help nurture knowing and learning?

Repetition triggers a heightened neural state. Then, it vitalizes comprehension in the human learning system and. D'Aquili and Newberg argue that:

> There is something about repetitive rhythmic stimuli that may, under the proper conditions, bring about the unusual neural

---

52. d'Aquili and Newberg, *Mystical Mind*, 65.
53. Keller, *The World I Live In*, 2.
54. Joly, *L'Image et les signes*, 21.
55. d'Aquili and Newberg, *Mystical Mind*, 68.
56. Joly, *L'Image et les signes*, 21.

state consisting of simultaneous high discharge of both the arousal and the quiescent system . . . Such driving of the autonomic nervous system by rhythmic stimuli powerfully activates the holistic operator, allowing various degrees of gestalt perception.[57]

The power of repeated ritual comes from "rapid rhythmicity, marked ritual actions, and olfactory drive," which can lead to "powerfully reinforced arousal stimulation, which can ultimately lead to quiescent breakthrough."[58] Rather than becoming a tedious experience, repetition supports cognition through the senses; in repeating liturgical actions, participants comprehensively learn Christian worship. Repeating the events of listening to God's Word and participating in the Lord's Supper every week is an experience of the rhythm of liturgical worship. This rhythm forms the participant's responses in both the conscious mind and the subconscious, arousing the senses and providing a comprehensive educational environment that helps people gain understanding through cognitive and intuitive recognition. As Don Saliers points out, "'tasting' can be the opening to 'seeing,' as in the psalm refrain, 'O taste and see that the Lord is good' (Ps 34:8)."[59] The Bible contains many additional references to sensory experiences as well, which have been repeated in worship throughout the centuries.

Repetition delivers meaning to participants. According to Bourdieu, with the help of repetition, people become acclimated to "the structure and tendencies of the world," adapting "endlessly to partially modified contexts" and learning "to construct the situation as a complex whole endowed with meaning."[60] When a ritual is repeated regularly, no two instances will be exactly alike, and as participants observe and adapt to these small changes, the whole of these repeated experiences becomes more complex, more personal, and more practiced. Brett Webb-Mitchell says, "Repetition is like repainting a wall in a house; each coat overlaps the last and results in a smooth finish. Repetition of gestures is similar: the more we repeat them, the more polished they are."[61] As participants gain better and better command of the actions, their attention can shift from performance to mindfulness and reflection on the meaning of the action. Rather than a continuity of meaningless action, repetition forms and polishes the web of meaning. Repetitive acts deliver meaning more profoundly than single, unrelated stimuli; repetition forms

57. d'Aquili and Newberg, *Mystical Mind*, 90.
58. Ibid., 101.
59. Saliers, *Music and Theology*, 2.
60. Bourdieu, *Pascalian Meditations*, 139.
61. Webb-Mitchell, *Christly Gestures*, 132.

habits—not merely mechanic repetition or automatic process, but a sort of experiential knowledge based on familiarity.[62] In this way, repetition helps a person learn to act voluntarily. Bergson says,

> The true effect of repetition is to decompose, and then to recompose, and thus appeal to the intelligence of the body. At each new attempt it separates movements which were interpenetrating; each time it calls the attention of the body to a new detail which had passed unperceived; it bids the body discriminate and classify; it teaches what is the essential; it points out, one after another, within the total movement, the lines that mark off its internal structure.[63]

Repetition fosters more comprehensive understanding. Although repetitive action is sometimes characterized as "mindless," it actually frees the participant to think about the content and significance of the action, and therefore it is effective for the church to use "the same forms and the same responses over and over again."[64]

Furthermore, repetition gives reflective power not only to the mind but also the body. Blaise Pascal poetically writes, "The heart has its reasons which reason itself does not know."[65] While participating as members of their specific congregations and repeating the familiar rituals, people learn "practical comprehension."[66] This is not a form of consciousness, but rather is connected to habitus, "which constructs the world and gives it meaning."[67] Experience and action can inscribe social meaning onto the body. When people participate in community ritual, social symbols impact their memories and reinforce patterns of behavior and conduct established by the group.[68] Bourdieu says, "The inherited and therefore immediately attuned habitus, and the corporeal constraint exercised through it, are the surest guarantee of direct and total adherence to the often implicit demands of these institutions."[69] Repetitive action conveys a continual

---

62. Merleau-Ponty, *Phenomenologie de la perception*, 168.
63. Bergson, *Matter and Memory*, 137–38.
64. Senn, *Introduction to Christian Liturgy*, 207.
65. Pascal, *Pensees and Other Writings*, 158.
66. Bourdieu, *Pascalian Meditations*, 142.
67. Ibid.
68. Ibid., 145; Collins, *Interaction Ritual Chains*, 37. Reformed theologian Louis Berkhof affirms the habitus in the process of faith formation. See Berkhof, *Systematic Theology*, 503.
69. Bourdieu, *Pascalian Meditations*, 152.

message to the mind and facilitates reaction, producing generative power for transformation.

Knowing through habitus is hard to explain logically, because it does not always work at the level of consciousness. For example, people have similar difficulty explaining logically how to stay afloat when swimming. One can explain the principles of buoyancy, respiration, and lung function to someone else, but the learner cannot swim well without experiencing the act of swimming. And by practicing swimming repetitively, he can learn to be afloat—not through scientific explanation, but through using the body itself.[70] Similarly, repetition during participation in ritual conveys meaning and teaches a responsive pattern efficiently while arousing the senses and mind, cognition and subconsciousness.

RITUAL PRACTICE AND TACIT KNOWING

Worship is composed of several rituals. Standing together, singing, raising hands, kneeling, reading; all of these are rituals. These ritual practices accompany the possibility of faith and impact human consciousness and subconsciousness at the same time. In ritual, there is an implied story and meaning; when we act, our actions impact body and mind.[71] Volf sees that "in most cases, Christian practices come first and Christian beliefs follow—or rather, beliefs are already entailed in practices, so that their explicit espousing becomes a matter of bringing to consciousness what is implicit in the engagement of the practices themselves."[72] Ritual itself does not confer faith automatically, but the meaning included in faithful practice can impact consciousness and subconsciousness.

In Verda and Eli Carmeli's study of "holiday awareness," a group of mentally challenged youngsters made significant advances in "symbol recognition" over the course of twelve weeks.[73] Similarly, worship practice can enhance recognition of religious symbols among children and the cognitively challenged, and repetitive participation can help foster understanding. Those who are cognitively challenged are sometimes unable to use verbal language, but "they have highly creative ways of using their eyes, head, limbs, and body."[74] It is certain that thinking progresses when people act, even when they cannot articulate it. Remembering our swimming ex-

---

70. Polanyi, *Personal Knowledge*, 49.
71. Webb-Mitchell, *Christly Gestures*, 128.
72. Volf, "Theology for a Way of Life," 256.
73. Carmeli and Carmeli, "Holiday Awareness," 123.
74. Harrington, *A Place for All*, 15.

ample, it is not an exaggeration to say that experience and participation is an important part of learning and understanding.

Liturgy is a method for helping young children and cognitively challenged individuals understand faith. Faith begins in the practice of ritual behaviors. Don Richter says, "For almost everyone, faith begins in practice rather than belief . . . in words and songs and gestures and things we do with and for our bodies, with and for one another. We learn to pray by praying."[75] People first experience the practice of worship before they gain knowledge and understanding of doctrine. Through practice, they become accustomed to the Christian mood and the contents of Christian faith. While praying, people learn the method of prayer; while singing hymns, people develop their piety in image, word, and emotions. Practice locates people in the narrative of God and nurtures growth through the messages encoded in the worship practice. Participation itself in worship is formative and makes knowing possible, even when people cannot articulate how they know a specific piece of knowledge.

Michael Polanyi states, "We can know more than we can tell."[76] Generally, we feel that to explain something to another person is proof of our knowing. However, even when we cannot explain something expressively, we can still understand. As Polanyi explains, "The premises underlying a major intellectual process are never formulated and transmitted in the form of definite precepts. When children learn to think naturalistically, they do not acquire any explicit knowledge of the principles of causation."[77] As noted earlier, Polanyi claims that epistemology is neither objective nor subjective; it should be personal.[78] According to him, recognition and knowing happen naturally in the process of participation and relationships with others—not just through conceptual recognition. Polanyi and Prosch say, "Generally, all comprehensive entities are known by our indwelling in them, and to this extent we participate in them as if their subsidiaries were parts of our body."[79] If a person cannot articulate logically about a certain thing, it does not signify an absence of knowledge. People come to know by indwelling in reality, by "immersing oneself in the particulars of subsidiary

---

75. Richter, "Embodied Wisdom," 24.
76. Polanyi, *Tacit Dimension*, 4.
77. Polanyi, *Science, Faith and Society*, 42.
78. Polanyi, *Personal Knowledge*, 18.
79. Polanyi and Prosch, *Meaning*, 138.

awareness by means of embodied activity" while synthesizing and internalizing.[80] Tacit knowledge is a sort of epistemology without insight.[81]

To explain the tacit mode, Polanyi uses the concept of "subsidiary and focal awareness." He gives this example: "When we use a hammer to drive in a nail, we attend to both nail and hammer, but in a different way."[82] The process involves two sorts of awareness. The intention to drive the nail is "focal awareness," the sense of the hand that holds the nail is "subsidiary awareness," and the two types of awareness are "mutually exclusive."[83] If one concentrates on the sense of the hand holding the nail, instead of driving the hammer, the action will not be successful. To successfully drive the hammer without hitting the hand, focal awareness and subsidiary awareness should be balanced. This can be acquired by indwelling and acting. In studying indwelling, we must see the body as a tool for understanding.[84] According to Polanyi, "we know other minds by dwelling in their acts."[85] While participating and interacting with others, we come to know and learn things naturally. The idea that all thoughts have a bodily foundation is the most important concept of the tacit mode.[86] Let us think of an intercessory prayer in public worship. This prayer makes church members aware of other people in the worship place and the world and reminds them that we are all brothers and sisters in Christ. Praying repeatedly together in the Holy Spirit and indwelling in the worship place, people are reminded of and feel the connection between self and others.

The possibility of tacit knowing is as strong for cognitively challenged persons and young children as it is for adults who are not cognitively challenged. Although the expressions of children and the cognitively challenged may be seen to lack logic or clarity, knowledge is possible in their minds and bodies. Mary Harrington argues,

> It is often wrongly presumed that religion requires abstract knowledge, or formal operational functioning. Actually, the

---

80. Gill, *Tacit Mode*, 52. I have discussed this in Moon, "When is it Appropriate for Children to Participate in the Lord's Supper?" 30–47.

81. See Torrance, ed., *Belief in Science*, 145.

82. Polanyi, *Personal Knowledge*, 55.

83. Ibid., 56.

84. See Polanyi, *Knowing and Being*, 183.

85. Polanyi and Prosch, *Meaning*, 48.

86. According to Bourdieu, "Practice has a logic which is not that of the logician." Bourdieu, *Logic of Practice*, 86. Also, "practical belief is not a 'state of mind,' still less a kind of arbitrary adherence to a set of instituted dogmas and doctrines ('beliefs'), but rather a state of the body." Ibid., 68. Bourdieu's thought is very similar to Michael Polanyi's.

practice of religion is very concrete. If one is open to the witness of those with mental retardation who have faith according to their capacity, it is easy to see how concrete faith is.[87]

The "patterns of unconsciously learned behavior" are so powerful that they are difficult to change.[88] Ideas and habits, once formed, are not easy to modify.[89] Ongoing participation in ritual and liturgy can affect personal faith formation permanently, as a tattoo engraved in the skin.

Brett Webb-Mitchell considers ritual as wisdom inscribed in the body, connecting it with Aristotle's concept of *phronesis* [practical wisdom]. He says, "*Phronesis* does not ascend to a level of abstraction or generality that leaves experience behind. Rather, like any other virtue, there is openness in the experience of *phronesis*, in which one is continually involved in a learning process."[90] The purpose of ritual repetition is not to form an abstract concept, but rather to provide an opportunity for learning and awareness. For example, by the action of kneeling to pray repetitively, rather than formal instruction in the theological concept of prayer, we learn submission and humility in the presence of God. The effect of ritual can be considered a sort of *phronesis*.

When cognitively challenged persons and young children observe liturgy as Francis observes, they have an opportunity to experience the knowledge of faith in the symbolic dimension, even though they may be unable to explain their experience logically.[91] A single droplet falling does not have power, but the repetition of many droplets falling over a long time can make a beautiful lime cave; likewise, weekly religious participation and communion with others can create beautiful religious imagery and tacit knowledge in the minds of children and mentally handicapped participants.

At this point, I insist that practical theology is more important than any other theological method. The power of religion does not come merely from an accumulation of knowledge, but from reflection and experience; it is more than mere human experience—it is an encounter between God and human. All people should be included in religious meetings to experience those moments of relationship with God.

As participants in religious rituals and as members of religious groups, we react to various types of spiritual stimulation. Each person has a unique

---

87. Harrington, *Place for All*, 34.
88. Castleman, "Liturgy for a Lifetime, 72.
89. Ibid.
90. Webb-Mitchell, *Christly Gestures*, 181.
91. Francis, "Celebrating the Sacraments," 88.

liturgical role in worship, and develops religious affection and virtue while performing this role. Kant says,

> By playing this role, people are gradually aroused to a full exercise of the virtues whose externals they have cultivated for a space, and they acquire the disposition itself. No. It is more: it is a question of affirming a role given to us in a religious context and of schooling ourselves to become existentially identified with it.[92]

In the worship, individuals gain knowledge of faith. In the *Institutes*, Calvin explains that the sacrament "represents the promises of God as in a picture, and places them in our view in a graphic bodily form."[93] Our understanding requires a "visible word"; Liturgy as a symbolic work of God's grace can be a vivid experience and learning tool.

The practice of ritual is not meant to create a conditioned reflex, such as in the experiments of Pavlov.[94] Liturgical ritual does not train people like animals to produce an automatic response; it is not a magical phenomenon. It touches the tacit dimension of human knowledge and helps widen understanding and memory.

IS FAITH MERELY A MATTER OF KNOWLEDGE?

Although I am using Yust's definition of faith, it is still important to discuss Marcus Borg. He argues directly against the Reformed Church's excessive emphasis on human reason in faith formation, pointing out that people sometimes understand faith as "a certain set of beliefs . . . 'believing' a set of statements to be true, whether cast as biblical teachings or doctrines or dogma."[95] This preoccupation with "beliefs" in the modern period has made Christian faith an intellectual concern, a "head matter," whereas previously, "the most common Christian meanings of the word 'faith' were . . . matters of heart."[96] But faith cannot be considered only a matter of knowledge; faith has a deeper and more complex dimension. Borg points out that until the sixteenth century, the word "orthodoxy" was taken to mean "right worship" or "correct worship."[97] If you performed the liturgy and practice correctly,

---

92. Kant, *Anthropologie*, 6:442, quoted in von Balthassar, *Theo-Drama*, 54.
93. Calvin, *Institutes*, IV.xiv.6.
94. Gluck, et al., *Learning and Memory*, 18–19.
95. Borg, *Heart of Christianity*, 25.
96. Ibid., 26.
97. Ibid., 29.

you were orthodox.[98] Borg does not criticize the importance of orthodox faith itself; however, he cautions that the idea of faith as belief is "relatively powerless," and reminds us that people can subscribe to the church's set of beliefs without experiencing any actual spiritual transformation.[99] Faith as belief can be nothing more than conceptual faith, an abstract form that does not foster an individual's personal and social transformation. According to Borg, "what we believe is what we belove. Faith is about beloving God."[100] Not merely a matter of reason, faith involves the whole person in a relationship with a beloved and loving God.

It cannot be denied that right knowledge is essential to orthodox faith.[101] As systematic theologian Horst Pöhlmann points out, faith is closely related to its concrete historical contents.[102] Even though Paul espouses the importance of personal trust in God, he also emphasizes right belief in the sense of orthodoxy.[103] Anyone can have a religious attitude, what Calvin calls "the seed of religion."[104] But it is not automatically connected to the worship of God; it can be expressed with other religions, which is why "right knowing" or orthodox knowledge is necessary. However, "right knowing" is not merely dogmatic agreement. Cognitive agreement with a dogmatic statement itself is not the same as having faith. Faith is not knowledge about God, but knowledge of God that leads to loving and enjoying God; and it depends on God's revelation and will.[105] A person's knowledge of God cannot be evaluated by to the eloquence of their faith statement, but by their attitude and affection for God; even though a person has knowledge of God, expression or logical explanation differ according to learning and verbal ability. We must escape from the limitation of thinking of faith as only a cognitive phenomenon. Religious experience has dimensions far deeper than that of human cognition, and traditions that prioritize doctrinal knowing tend to overlook the non-rational factor in religious life, and the potential of religious experience. Rudolf Otto addresses this stance as follows:

98. Ibid.
99. Ibid., 30–31.
100. Ibid., 40.
101. Berkhof, *Systematic Theology*, 503.
102. Pohlmann, *Abriss der Dogmatik*, 61.
103. Ibid., 98. Lecerf says, "Scripture is the unique source of religious knowledge. Faith does not derive this knowledge from itself but is merely the receptive organ which takes cognizance of it." Lecerf, *Introduction to Reformed Dogmatics*, 20.
104. John Calvin insists everyone has "the seed of religion." This means every person has the potential for religious attitude. However, he points out that this tendency is not directly connected to seeking God. See Calvin, *Institutes*, I.iv.1.
105. Lecerf, *Introduction*, 108.

> The common dictum that orthodoxy itself has been the mother of rationalism is in some measure well founded. It is not simply that orthodoxy was preoccupied with doctrine and the framing of dogma, for these have been no less a concern of the wildest mystics. It is rather that orthodoxy found in the construction of dogma and doctrine in no way does justice to the non-rational aspect of its subject. So far from keeping the non-rational element in religion alive in the heart of the religious experience, orthodox Christianity manifestly failed to recognize its value, and by this failure gave to the idea of God a one-sidedly intellectualistic and rationalistic interpretation.[106]

Reformed Orthodoxy has understood God in a cognitive dimension, an attitude at one time essential to protect the church from heresy or the impact of other religions, but which underestimates the multi-dimensional aspects of Christian faith and church life. In fact, recently, churches have come to study how to make sincere believers because they recognize a knowledge-centered approach to faith formation fails to connect with the transformation of a life. An alternative proposal is offered by Louis-Marie Chauvet:

> One becomes a Christian only by entering an institution, and the modes of Christian behavior which may appear the most "personal" (meditative prayer, for example) or the most "authentic" (concern for others) are always the expression of an apprenticeship interiorized for a long time and of habits inculcated by institutional and highly ritualized processes.[107]

Chauvet's concept depends on the interrelationship between scripture, ethical practice, and sacraments.[108] According to him, these three factors form Christian identity. In particular, "the sacraments, which inscribe faith in the body of participants, symbolically give a role to play to all these modalities of the human being as 'speaking body.'"[109] Worship "trains us in lamenting, confessing, adoring, and lifting our cries for the whole world."[110] A Christian is made through worship. Faith is given by God, but it is nurtured through the act of worship, not just by learning and memorizing. Worship has a formative dimension; even though human effort alone is not enough to somehow "obtain" faith, God utilizes worship as a tool for faith formation.

106. Otto, *Idea of the Holy*, 3.
107. Chauvet, *Sacraments*, 112.
108. Ibid., 28.
109. Ibid., 114.
110. Saliers, *Worship and Spirituality*, 2.

In worship, God reveals himself and works in our minds, encompassing both cognitive and mystical dimensions.

Dennis Hollinger insists, "Head faith tends to focus on rationality, logic and ideas; it has great difficulty dealing with any sense of mystery, ambiguity, the unknown wonder, awe or transcendence insofar as it touches one personality."[111] Faith has a deeper dimension which reason cannot explain. Take, for example, the doctrine of the Trinity. Is it possible to articulate the traits of the Trinity? The Trinity itself is a mystery. Of course, people can know its doctrine through reading or hearing scripture, but there is a realm in the doctrine of the Trinity which human reason cannot explain. Faith is something above human reason. Daniel Migliore says, "Faith is faith in the living God, and God is and remains a mystery beyond human comprehension."[112]

I do not dismiss the necessity of reason and cognition in faith. As Migliore points out, "How could we obey the will of God if we had no knowledge of what that will is? How could we rightly worship or pray or serve a God who is totally unknown and unknowable?"[113] Balance is important in the process of faith formation:

> Taken alone . . . passion and action render a fragmented faith that only further engenders a fragmented self and a fragmented church. Isolated from the other dimensions, our mind can never truly be the mind God intended; our affections can never truly be the affections God intended; and our actions can never truly be the actions God intended. What we need today, in a fragmented world, is a whole faith of the head, heart and hands, with each dimension feeding and sustaining the others.[114]

Traditions that emphasize experience, and those which emphasize knowledge, both have strong and weak points.[115] However, historically, a stance that adheres strictly to only one aspect of faith—cognition—has hampered the growth of faith. Yet, the very goal of liturgical worship, as Louis Weil argues, "is to enable those who participate in it to live more deeply the mystery of salvation which the rites evoke in signs."[116] The Word and liturgical action create synergy in faith formation. By combining Word

---

111. Hollinger, *Head, Heart, Hands*, 94.
112. Migliore, *Faith Seeking Understanding*, 3.
113. Ibid., 23.
114. Hollinger, *Head, Heart Hands*, 16.
115. Ibid., 32–33.
116. Weil, "Growth in Faith," 206.

Liturgy as a Tool for Christian Faith Formation and Learning

and liturgical action, we learn Christian faith with head and body at the same time:

> We do not really know until we do, and we learn as we do. As Paul stated in Colossians 1:9–10, "We have not ceased praying for you and asking that you may be filled with the knowledge of God's will in all spiritual wisdom and understanding, so that you may lead lives worthy of the Lord, fully pleasing to him, as you bear fruit in every good work and as you grow in the knowledge of God." The pattern here is knowledge ... action ... knowledge.[117]

Knowing and doing are not two divided categories, but are intermingled and simultaneous in the process of forming knowledge—and faith. We may believe we know and understand something, but this knowledge is not perfect until put into practice. A person can memorize the Bible's teachings, but if they are not practiced in everyday life, this person cannot be said to have true knowledge. As Dykstra and Bass write, "Beliefs and practices," that is, knowing and doing, "can and should be understood in relation to one another."[118] According to them, "Christian practices thus involve a profound awareness, a deep knowing: they are activities imbued with the knowledge of God and creation," and participation in these practices increases our knowledge and understanding of the Trinity.[119] This is very similar to Don Browning's idea of "practice to theory and back to practice."[120] According to Browning, "theology can be practical if we bring practical concerns to it from the beginning."[121] Therefore, according to him, "practices are meaningful or theory-laden," and theory (knowing) and practice (doing) are not independent, but accompany each other, because "theory is always embedded in practice."[122] This assertion can be supported by the thought of Miroslav Volf, who says, "Practices are essentially belief-shaped, and beliefs are essentially practice-shaping." According to Volf, "right practices well practiced are likely to open persons for insights into beliefs to which they would otherwise be closed."[123] Practice and belief are not separate, but compose a sort of simultaneous bundle—a Mobius strip. Practice should not be undermined; it is a fundamental factor in the formation of faith.

---

117. Hollinger, *Head, Heart, Hands*, 131.
118. Dykstra and Bass, "Theological Understanding," 21.
119. Ibid., 24–25.
120. Browning, *Fundamental Practical Theology*, 7.
121. Ibid., 5.
122. Ibid., 6, 9.
123. Volf, "Theology for a Way of Life," 254, 257.

The power of doing comes from repetition and from reflection that is gained from repetition. There is wisdom in the act of practice. Repetitive acts deepen reflection, and reflection fosters belief and faith. As Edward Farley comments,

> Theory meant that aspect of the habitus, or wisdom, in which the divine object evokes acknowledgement, belief. Practice meant that aspect of the habitus, or wisdom, in which the divine object sets requirements of obedience and life. Both reside in the single existential habitus called theology. Theory/practice is based on what could be called a phenomenology of theology as a habitus.[124]

Theology is not merely theoretical, but is practical at the same time.

Some Christians abhor the idea of habitus from fear of designating a meaningless, repetitive act absent of cognitive engagement as "holy." However, habitus impacts not only practice, but theory. From repetition, people gain deeper, more profound knowledge of the meaning of the act because the wisdom of the act is included in the act itself.

Knowing and doing are closely related. Like the chicken-and-egg question, knowing and doing are not a matter of sequence; they are coincidental. As Myers notes, "it is that we are likely not only to think ourselves into a way of acting but also to act ourselves into a way of thinking."[125] Repetition and practice are also necessary in faith formation; they fortify human faith. In fact, as Bernard Cooke says,

> For many of us the first experience of this kind of [experiential] Christian witness came when we were children. There, at home, gathered around mother as she read to us from books about faith and from scripture itself, we instinctively and without question accept what she read as fact.[126]

The contents of what this mother reads are implanted in the mind of the listener in the form of tacit knowledge. As time goes on, it becomes part of the listener's consciousness and understanding.[127] Faith is naturally formed through experience and repetition. This upholds the propriety and merit of liturgical practice. James De Jong asserts,

---

124. Farley, "Theology and Practice," 27.
125. Myers, *Social Psychology*, 136.
126. Cooke, *Formation of Faith*, 31.
127. Ibid., 36.

> The liturgy, then, is not ritual magic which works a protective spell over our existence. It is the sum and substance of our lives. It is the presentation of ourselves to the Lord for his benediction. It is also the pattern by which we cut the cloth of our experiences. Another way of putting it, turning things just around, is to say that life is the incarnation of the liturgy.[128]

Liturgy is the responsive pattern of believers who received God's grace. It is not magic, but is powerful in its impact on humans' response to God and the Christian way of life. Through repetition, liturgy fortifies human resolution and facilitates a transformation.

RITUAL PRACTICE AND MEMORY

The idea of ritual and liturgy as a way to enhance faith formation not only through the mind, but also through the body can be supported by Bourdieu's concept of "habitus," a "system of durable, transposable dispositions, structured structures predisposed to function as structuring structures, that is, as principles which generate and organize practices and representations that can be objectively adapted to their outcomes without presupposing a conscious aiming at ends or an express mastery of the operations necessary in order to attain them."[129] By repetition, habitus structures thinking and reaction efficiently, which is then accumulated in the body and mind. Habitus is "internalized as a second nature," not mindless, mechanistic action, but rather something that imparts "reflexive freedom of subjects."[130] While performing an action repetitively over time, "spontaneity without consciousness or will" becomes possible. Through habitus, "past experiences" are "inscribed in human bodies."[131] Habitus not only helps establish memory and automatic response, but can also lead to more profound understanding as new knowledge is accumulated in the body and mind, forming the basis for transformation.[132] Although an individual habit may seem like a small detail, habits as repetitive acts are not neutral, but have

---

128. De Jong, *Into His Presence*, 120.
129. See Bourdieu, *Logic of Practice*, 53.
130. Ibid., 56
131. Bourdieu, *Pascalian Meditations*, 138.
132. James Smith says, "Habits are inscribed in our heart through bodily practices and rituals that train the heart, as it were, to desire certain ends. This is a noncognitive sort of training, a kind of education that is shaping us often without our realization. Different kinds of material practices infuse noncognitive dispositions and skills in us through ritual and repetition precisely because our hearts are so closely tethered to our bodies." Smith, *Desiring the Kingdom*, 58.

formative power in a person's life. James Smith calls them "meaning-laden, identity-forming practices that subtly shape us precisely because they grab hold of our love—they are automating our desire and action without our conscious recognition."[133] The power of habitus cannot be understated. Above all, because liturgy uses not merely cognition but all the senses, it can help to form human affection and enhance understanding. Louis Weil insists, "The way in which liturgy forms Christians in faith is primarily around such elemental factors as touch and taste and smell, and through the repetitious, yet not monotonous, character of ritual acts."[134]

So, considering the effects of habitus, we should study the relationship between ritual practice and memory. One of the important benefits of liturgy and ritual is in helping to form human memory. As Paul Connerton insists, "commemorative ceremonies" and "bodily practices" help form memory, and memory is "sedimented in the body."[135] In doing liturgy together, people both vividly receive communal memory and renew it at the same time. Traditionally, the church has endeavored to remember God's commandments. This effort has been expressed in several rites in worship. Atkins says, "At the heart of all worship is the act of remembrance."[136] Remembrance is not merely a reminder of the past, but a way "to link past, present, and future in a single fold."[137] Through remembrance of the salvific act of Jesus Christ, and the anticipation of his coming, people can experience anamnesis at the place of worship.[138]

Liturgy promotes memory

Recent studies show how act and experience impact the brain and memory.[139] When people act, "the brain can transmit information as a result of eternal stimuli, or creative thought patterns, or from the recall of a memory."[140] The act vitalizes the brain; the brain then receives information and forms a

---

133. Ibid., 83.
134. Weil, "Growth in Faith," 215.
135. Connerton, *How Societies Remember*, 102.
136. Atkins, *Memory and Liturgy*, 25.
137. Ibid., xi.
138. Robert Webber says, "Biblical remembering is much more than an intellectual recalling. Biblical remembering brings God's saving events to mind, body, and soul. Biblical remembering makes the power and the saving effect of the event present to the worshiping community." Webber, *Ancient-Future Worship*, 43.
139. See Solms and Turnbull, *Brain and the Inner World*, 139–56.
140. Atkins, *Memory and Liturgy*, 5.

Liturgy as a Tool for Christian Faith Formation and Learning

pattern of response.[141] This pattern, or memory, can be activated by various practices and methods. This is related to Edgar Dale's studies, which show that people learn most effectively when they are involved in direct, active, and purposeful learning experiences.[142] According to Connerton, memory of the past can be structured and maintained by ritual performance.[143] Don Saliers also shows the intimate relationship between liturgy and memory: by "participation in the living memory and symbols of the community," people can remember the salvific history of God and connect their faith with the past.[144] Let us think about reciting or singing the Ten Commandments in worship. While speaking or singing it weekly, people are repeatedly reminded of the contents of the Decalogue which God gave to Moses, and these contents are structured in the memory of the people; people not only come to remember it, but also experience it as fully present and in the presence of God. Similarly, in the Lord's Supper, the bread and wine bring to our minds the body and blood of Jesus Christ. While participating in the Lord's Supper—listening, eating, drinking, singing, and communicating—people are continually reminded of the story of Jesus Christ.

These examples show that ritual helps us remember the Christian story more efficiently and vividly. Performing a task (reading, hearing, seeing, writing, and doing) is the most efficient method in the learning process; we "retain items of information which engages significantly one or more of our senses and evoke strong feelings."[145] In this way, liturgical worship is a tool for memory, because liturgy incorporates the senses and establishes a pattern of memory and response. Robert Webber notes that we remember God's saving deeds in worship through "historical recitation" and "dramatic reenactment."[146] Preaching, creeds, and songs "[draw] the worshiper into the action, not as an observer, but as a participant."[147] The sacraments also work to enhance memory, because they "not only speak God's Word but also re-enact it in our midst."[148]

Public liturgy leads to commemorative memory, and this communal remembrance develops the worship community.[149] Christian worship can

141. Ibid., 7–8.
142. See Dale, *Audio-Visual Methods*, 108.
143. Connerton, *How Societies Remember*, 4.
144. Saliers, *Worship and Spirituality*, 13–14.
145. Atkins, *Memory and Liturgy*, 17.
146. Webber, *Ancient-Future Worship*, 48
147. Ibid., 48–51.
148. Birch, "Memory in Congregational Life," in *Congregations*, 33.
149. Ibid., 23.

be considered a ritual act of congregational remembering. Although its central purpose is celebration, it is based on the remembrance of what God has done in Jesus Christ, and of who we are called to be as God's people, Christ's Church.[150]

According to Connerton, social memory is formed through commemorative ceremonies and bodily practices, and is maintained and delivered by performance.[151] Connerton shows how rituals can powerfully impact communal remembrance and consciousness. He says, "our experiences of the present largely depend upon our knowledge of the past, and that our images of the past commonly serve to legitimate a present social order."[152] This denotes the importance of memory and experience in the present. He also emphasizes that social memory can be sustained by commemorative ceremonies "only insofar as they are performative," because performativity has a deep relationship with habit, and habit is also related to bodily automatisms.[153] While explaining various sorts of memory, Connerton emphasizes the importance of habit memory, explaining that "habits of affection and behavior are not to be learned by precept, but only by living with people who habitually behave in a certain manner."[154] Habit memory is not identical with the cognitive memory of rules and codes. Rather, it is related to community ritual; by participating in community rituals, people gain vivid memories and impressions. Liturgical action helps this communal memory.

Formation of social memory involves not just habit formation, but also imitation:

> If we are wired to imitate then this will have major implications both for behavior and for liturgy. When in liturgy we receive information in word and action that we are valued, cared for and loved, and that the appropriate response is thanksgiving, acceptance, and return of value to God, then we are establishing a memory pattern for helpful behavior.[155]

By imitating religious acts, people receive information encoded in the ritual itself; we receive others' sentiments and produce our own attitudes and responses. Imitation is a starting point for individual faith formation. The liturgical act does not aim at automatic response, but at sustaining communal action and thought. As Gadamer describes it, imitation and

---

150. Ibid., 32–33.
151. Connerton, *How Societies Remember*, 7, 40.
152. Ibid., 3.
153. Ibid., 4–5.
154. Ibid., 30, 36.
155. Atkins, *Memory and Liturgy*, 12.

representation are not merely repetitive acts, but formative acts that can impact the minds of those who engage with them.[156] Through liturgical practices, people come to think about the meaning of the acts and widen their horizons of understanding.

It is through repetition that a person's short-term memory becomes long-term memory.[157] However, repetition itself does not convey meaning automatically. As Atkins points out, "Retention requires both repetition and a weighing of significance."[158] According to Atkins, to gain meaning, "a sense of application and a sense of belonging to the group" are necessary.[159] For more efficient memory, worshippers must know why an act is important and reinterpret its meaning in their faith community. Therefore, for gaining meaning, liturgy and teaching should occur at the same time.

As a means of habit formation through imitation and instruction, worship also provides a means of covenantal renewal.[160] Why and how did God, throughout the Bible, renew the covenants with his people? God understood humans' weakness of volition and limits of memory and revitalized memory of the Word through various forms of symbolic action, which are repeated as liturgical action. In worship, people remember and anticipate God through the Word and sacrament. Memory connects the past and present, makes people confront the presence of God, and requires resolution in front of God's Word.[161] As Brevard Childs says, "The act of remembering serves to actualize the past for a generation removed in time from those former events in order that they themselves can have an intimate encounter with the great acts of redemption. Remembrance equals participation."[162] Through remembrance, we stand in the presence of God in the same way as those who lived in the Biblical era. Memory brings the contents of the Bible to life here and now. Liturgy not only helps form memory, but also brings people to an encounter with God, and helps them make a resolution in the presence of God.

---

156. Gadamer, *Truth and Method*, 114.

157. Ormrod, *Human Learning*, 168.

158. Atkins, *Memory and Liturgy*, 72.

159. Ibid.

160. John Witvliet says, "Christian worship is like a covenant-renewal service in which the gathered reaffirm the vows made with God in Christ. Guided by liturgy, in a worship service, we renew the promises we made to God, and we hear again the promises God has made in Christ." Witvliet, *Worship Seeking Understanding*, 30.

161. Childs, *Memory and Tradition*, 56.

162. Ibid.

Body, matter, and symbol can be tools for remembrance

The interaction of body, matter, and symbol aids the formation of memory and contributes to the overall formative power of worship. According to Bergson, "memory is just the intersection of mind and matter."[163] Memory is real, just as matter is real. Its medium is the human body. Certain knowledge is acquired by a special image, which is given through and by the human body.[164] At the same time, the human body responds to a certain object. To Bergson, body, matter, and spirit are closely related. The growth of understanding happens in centering the body amid the interrelationship of other images.[165] Body and matter are necessary for perception and memory. Clifford Geertz insists man understands culture "in webs of significance he himself has spun," and that humans receive information and expand understanding through a web of meaning that expands while centering the human body.[166] Just as a spider repeats a single action again and again to create a web, people form a web of meaning while doing acts repetitively. The body is an important organ that receives information and forms responses through perception. This process requires education.[167] Through learning, while using the senses and collecting information, people expand their net of thought. Experience deepens thought, as well as impacts current perceptions and thought.

In order to remember, it is necessary to use various channels that help our memory. Traditionally, the Reformed Church has not been hospitable to the use of symbols in worship. Bruce Birch points out that "many congregations suffer from a poverty of visual image and symbol. We should not think that enhancement of congregational memory is solely accomplished by words."[168] Even though God's word is the most important factor in the Christian worship, it is also important to remember that God gave not only the audible Word, but also the visual Word in the sacraments. The sacraments do not signify that the Word is insufficient for enhancing faith; rather,

---

163. Ibid., xii.

164. Ibid., 3.

165. Ibid., 43.

166. Geertz, *Interpretation of Cultures*, 5. William James says, "The world experienced (otherwise called the 'field of consciousness') comes at all times with our body as centre, centre of vision, centre of action, centre of interest. Where the body is is 'here'; when the body acts is 'now'; what the body touches is 'this'; all other things are 'there' and 'then' and 'that.'" James, "Experience of Activity," 70. Merleau-Ponty's opinion is also similar; see Merleau-Ponty, "Eye and Mind," 295.

167. Bergson, *Matter and Memory*, 45.

168. Birch, "Memory in Congregational Life," 40–41.

Liturgy as a Tool for Christian Faith Formation and Learning

they help facilitate understanding. Throughout the centuries, the church has used "holy space, holy symbols and holy time . . . which assist us to recall memories of the presence of God and our relationship with God."[169] Symbols are necessary for helping human memory and understanding religious concepts, just as they are necessary for understanding the world clearly.[170] Through symbols, the deeper, inward dimensions of the world—that which transcends verbal communication—can be manifested. Religious knowledge, because it is mystical, cannot always be clearly manifested, because human cognition cannot understand the deeper dimensions of God. Religious symbols help understanding and memory, and denote the presence of God. As Gadamer insists, "The representational function of a symbol is not merely to point to something that is not present. Instead, a symbol manifests the presence of something that really is present."[171] This is not idolatry, but a function of religious symbols that remind participants of the presence of God. When worshippers see the cross in the sanctuary, they do not worship the cross, but are continually reminded of God's sacrifice and love. This symbol of God's love and presence helps people's religious mind and memory. Rather, by revealing a mystery, a symbol can help foster understanding and memory: "It is especially true of religious symbols that they not only function as distinguishing marks, but that the meaning of these symbols is understood by everyone, unites everyone, and can therefore assume a sign function."[172] Symbols are not only representational, but also formative.

The symbolic dimension included in a ritual can help memory and understanding by forming and delivering meaning.[173] Gadamer claims, "A symbol . . . is not limited to the sphere of the logos, for a symbol is not related by its meaning to another meaning, but its own sensory existence has meaning. As something shown, it enables one to recognize something else."[174] Symbol "has a metaphysical background" and can lead people "beyond the sensible to the divine."[175] Symbols transcend human cognition;

---

169. Atkins, *Memory and Liturgy*, 98.

170. Theißen, *Die Religion*, 35.

171. Gadamer, *Truth and Method*, 146–47.

172. Ibid., 147.

173. Theißen, *Die Religion*, 172. Gadamer defines symbol as such: "A symbol is the coincidence of sensible appearance and suprasensible meaning." Gadamer, *Truth and Method*, 67. Ann and Barry Ulanov say, "Often, even with the large possibilities of figurative speech at our disposal, a gesture or a bodily movement will, as we all know, say what we mean better than any word." See Ulanov, *Religion and the Unconscious*, 243.

174. Gadamer, *Truth and Method*, 63.

175. Ibid., 64.

while engaging the human senses, they help religious sensitivity. Saliers says, "Each of the human senses plays a constituent role in the formation and expression of a theologically determined spirituality. In most historic theistic traditions, seeing and hearing have a primacy of place in awakening, sustaining, and deepening awareness of the divine-human relationship."[176] Matter and symbol, while touching the "sense" dimension, can be tools for spiritual formation and expression. However, matter or symbols themselves do not contain meaning. Take, for example, the wedding ring: the ring itself cannot include the essence of the marriage, but whenever the ring is seen, people are reminded of the meaning of the wedding and the necessity of a faithful relationship.[177] The material symbol reminds us of a previous event and makes the memory more vivid.

Jesus incarnate is the divine descending and becoming human; through this event, people can meet and understand God. Incarnation can be a starting point for use of liturgy, matter, and symbol in the Christian worship. This does not amount to idolatry, but shows the usefulness of symbols in the church—the table, cross, and font. Matter and symbol should be understood as they relate to God's incarnation and accommodation. They are tools God uses; however, vigilance about their misuse or misinterpretation is important. Their use in worship should be guided by the Word and Holy Spirit.

Liturgy as action is also symbolic. Gordon Lathrop says, "When we come to church . . . we see before us or near us bread, wine, and water. Even before their use, these things are already symbols—that is, they gather together many meanings in one focused place, giving us a means actually to participate in those meanings."[178] There are many symbols in the worship—but how do they form meaning? Lathrop goes on to say:

> The words are symbols, gathering places of multilayered meaning and means to participate in that meaning. They are also sacred, even before we hear their content, suggesting transcendence simply in the way they are used, evoking our longing for speech that does not lie but works, a kind of speech we do not much know in our time, either in public or in private.[179]

Rituals and ceremonies in worship, centering on the Word and Eucharist, arouse participants' hearts, minds, and bodies are aroused. This juxtaposition and layering of symbols create opportunities for faith formation.

176. Saliers, *Music and Theology*, 1.
177. Atkins, *Memory and Liturgy*, 28.
178. Lathrop, *Holy Things*, 95.
179. Ibid., 99.

Liturgy as a Tool for Christian Faith Formation and Learning

Piaget's understanding of assimilation and accommodation can be a framework for understanding such formation.[180] By assimilation and accommodation, human intelligence is developed; likewise, participants in the worship get their forms of faith from the interrelationship between assimilation and accommodation. In worship, a child imitates others and plays the role of participant. The child then accommodates these actions within his or her existing mental schemas and assimilates these new schemas through repetition. Eventually, this forms the child's religious character and attitude. The presence of symbols actively juxtaposed and layered in worship rituals and ceremonies informs participants, and they respond. These rituals and ceremonies create opportunities for transformation. Liturgy with symbolic dimensions both forms and delivers meaning:

> Only as they are put together do they bring their symbolic resonance to the faith of the community . . . But when this cross is set next to the content of the ordo, when the book tells the story of the cross, the bath washes into its meaning, the cup gives to drink from it, the resonance of the symbol is transformed . . . the symbol comes into its own when it is properly subordinated to the primary interactions of the ordo. We need such symbols—evoking our hope for the union of the four directions . . . but we need them to be subjoined to the central juxtapositions of the ordo.[181]

Symbol not only arouses conscious and subconscious to aid memory, but also gives power for transformation.

Liturgy forms identity

Liturgy that incorporates the body and symbolic action facilitates remembrance. Hence, liturgy helps form both individual and communal identity. Peter Atkins says, "Memory is a vital part of our discovery of a sense of self."[182] Through liturgy, people are reminded of past events, and this memory forms their identity. Furthermore, the nature of remembrance affects the current state of the inner mind. Happy, warm memories can produce a contented, peaceful state of mind; unhappy, tortured memories have the power to create an unstable mind in turmoil. Communal remembrance is similar. The contents of communal remembrance affect the identity of the

---

180. Regarding the Piagetian concept of accommodation and assimilation, see Phillips, *Piaget's Theory*, 13–16.

181. Lathrop, *Holy Things*, 103.

182. Atkins, *Memory and Liturgy*, 3.

community, and, as Aleida Assmann notes, if the community's foundation of common knowledge is lost, communication between the generations is lost.[183] Without remembrance, individuals and communities risk losing identities that have been handed down. Remembering can be considered the essential factor in forming identity.[184] To help form memory, communal content and use of common symbols should be periodically repeated.[185] Through this repetition, memory, via the action of the body, is inscribed in the body and soul.[186]

According to James Smith, habitually practiced action can train not only the emotions, but also the "formation of our unconscious."[187] Liturgy is composed of "rituals and practices that constitute the embodied stories of a body politic," and hence liturgical action shapes our identity and faith.[188] Repetition forms human thinking and attitudes toward faith; it fosters continuity with the past and conveys the meaning of the past to the people who perform the rites.[189] Atkins explains how a person "borrows" from the memory of a community: through "natural sharing, observation and modeling," communal memory impacts each individual's mind. Sharing in ritual, "hearing and repeating the corporate songs and sayings," plays a role in faith formation.[190]

When participating in worship, a person learns and remembers Christian faith. He or she learns communal remembrance, and other community members' confessions and attitudes of faith become a part of his or her own. As Jerome Bruner says,

> Self-making, anomalously, is from both the inside and the outside. The inside of it, we like to say in our Cartesian way, is memory, feelings, ideas, beliefs, subjectivity. Part of this insidedness is almost certainly innate and species-specific, like our irresistible sense of continuity over time and place and our postural sense of ourselves. But much of self-making is from outside in—based on the apparent esteem of others and on the

---

183. Assmann, *Erinnerungsraume*, 13.
184. Antze and Lambek, eds., *Tense Past*, vii.
185. Assmann, *Erinnerungsraume*, 132.
186. Ibid., 155.
187. Smith, *Imagining the Kingdom*, 38.
188. Ibid., 109.
189. Ibid., 45.
190. Atkins, *Memory and Liturgy*, 69–70.

myriad expectations that we early, even mindlessly, pick up from the culture in which we are immersed.[191]

Formation of identity proceeds by the interconnection between inner development of self and outward influences, such as environment and culture. In the same way, the repetition of liturgy forms the identity of the community as it impacts its participants' individual identities. Liturgy activates memory, and memory appeals to individuals to live according to God's Word.[192] Ritual and liturgy can touch the mind in ways that mere reading and studying cannot. Discussing Plato's *Phaedrus*, Assmann insists that although the written word is efficient in depositing memory, it is no substitute for dynamic, productive memory such as anamnesis.[193] For Plato, the written word gives superficial wisdom, not real wisdom that comes from experience and memory:

> So not you, as the father of letters, have been led by your affection for them to describe them as having the opposite of their real effect. For your invention will produce forgetfulness in the souls of those who have learned it, through lack of practice at using their memory, as through reliance on writing they are reminded from outside by alien marks, not from within, themselves by themselves. So you have discovered an elixir not of memory but of reminding.[194]

Plato, not merely seeking to amass new memories, seeks anamnesis. He believes that the letter does not lead to a change in the actions of people; rather, the human internalizes memory by action that leads to transformation.[195] Plato thought that for many, the letter, which is outside the body, takes the place of memory. The letter diminishes the vividness of memory. The most important thing is embodiment; to respond with the whole person, inscription and embodiment are necessary. Therefore, habit itself is very important; the letter of the body forms through habitus, which controls

---

191. Bruner, *Making Stories*, 65.

192. Robert Webber says, "When we remember God's mighty, saving deeds, we are inspired to worship him, to contemplate his mighty deeds, and to obey him. Remembering is that powerful." Webber, *Ancient-Future Worship*, 45. He presents very important texts for proving the importance of memory in Christian worship. See Ibid., 46–47.

193. Assmann, *Erinnerungsraume*, 185.

194. Plato, *Phaedrus*, 62.

195. However, Plato's thought is fragmentary. Based on Humboldt's thought, Agamben says, "It is through language, then, that the individual as known to us is constituted as an individual, and linguistics, however far back it goes in time, never arrives at a chronological beginning of language, an 'anterior' of language." Agamben, *Infancy and History*, 56.

consciousness and subconscious. Doing liturgical action, people can learn and experience the Word of God more vividly.

Hence, the goal and merit of liturgy and ritual is not merely to enhance memory:

> The goal of the liturgy is to enable those who participate in it to live more deeply the mystery of salvation which the rites evoke in signs. Its purpose then reaches further than merely the articulation of correct doctrine. The purpose of the liturgy is to incorporate those who share in its action into a faith which is not only professed but lived.[196]

Liturgical action is essential for faith formation. By transforming cognition and character, liturgy helps connect faith and practice in participants' lives. Liturgy is transformative.

Throughout church history, there has been a tendency to emphasize preaching, or the Word, as the sole method for fostering faith formation. Right knowledge and professing the faith are both essential to faith formation, but this approach leads to a type of abstract faith that does not effectively help a person live faithfully. Through repetition and interaction, liturgy helps people to live more faithfully to God's Word and will.

The person and the Triune God are both present at the place and time of worship. Bodily participation, through horizontal communication with others and vertical communion with God, can change people's thought. People no longer consider God as an object of perception but instead, experience God in personal encounters.

LITURGY AND TRANSFORMATION

Through liturgy, people encounter and have fellowship with God. Through participation in the worship, people gain the opportunity to be transformed. Therefore, liturgy as action is important. As Wilfred Smith says, "Much religious faith has sought and found for itself an expression in ritual practice."[197] This shows the potential of ritual practice in the process of faith formation. However, at the same time, by doing liturgy repeatedly, and through the experience of worship, people have the possibility of being transformed. Atkinson says, "The aim of structured liturgical worship is to allow the worshipper to enter into a communal flow of adoration and praise of God, and in turn absorb the presence of God and attend to the instructions from God

---

196. Weil, "Growth in Faith," 206.
197. Smith, *Meaning and End of Religion*, 178.

as to how life should be lived."[198] Liturgical worship introduces people to the presence of God, giving them opportunities for encounters with God, and then the visible and invisible Word penetrates the mind and requests resolution.[199] Participants then must answer this call; liturgy disciplines the human mind through the human body.[200] In this way, liturgy can be an important tool for Christian discipline.

Of course, liturgical participation itself does not guarantee human transformation. Worship and ritual do not automatically result in a person's or a community's transformation.[201] As Louis Weil says, "The liturgy does not create a disposition of trust in God, nor does the liturgy teach correct doctrine."[202] This does not signify the ineffectiveness of liturgy, but discounts the school of thought that considers liturgy to be a kind of magic. That is to say, mere repetition of action itself cannot guarantee an automatic change of inner mind; rather, liturgy and ritual are necessary as a helping hand for the discipline of the human mind—but need a deeper dimension to effect transformation.[203]

The starting point of liturgy's transformative power lies in God's initiative. Through Word and sacrament, God reveals his will and teaches the right way of life. Look at the covenantal renewal in the Old Testament. Prior to the rites, God gave the covenant. By the words of institution, people received God's promise, and responded to it. Then, ritual taught participants discipline to be able to adhere to God's Word. Through ritual, participants "rehearse that narrative through our bodies," and receive meaning in the structure of narrative and symbol.[204] Saliers says, "The ethos of God as the transformative power of liturgy relocates our tendency to look for immediacies of feeling. Over time, authentic liturgy deepens our disposition to perceive the world as God's creation."[205] Through liturgical acts, people learn how to follow God's way, which can be the great motive for human transformation. This is why participating in and doing liturgy is so important, since, as Chan insists, "with participation there is already some spiritual progress."[206] Participation itself is a formative factor that helps bring about

198. Atkins, *Memory and Liturgy*, 111.
199. Anderson and Foley, *Mighty Stories*, 42.
200. Smith, *Desiring the Kingdom*, 25.
201. Chan, *Liturgical Theology*, 89.
202. Weil, "Growth in Faith," 211.
203. Driver, *Liberating Rites*, 169.
204. Ibid., 27; Collins, *Interaction Ritual Chains*, 44.
205. Saliers, *Worship as Theology*, 37.
206. Chan, *Spiritual Theology*, 108.

human transformation. Through participation, people encounter God, and live in the grace of God.[207]

Through an encounter with God—in worship—people gain a sense of love, and this impacts human beings and their direction. James Smith says, "Our ultimate love/desire is shaped by practices."[208] Practice creates love and affection. Baron von Hugel said, "I kiss my child not only because I love it; I kiss it also in order to love it."[209] While doing liturgy, people can gain wisdom and learn how to express their love for God. Therefore, worship facilitates our transformation, because "our participation makes us part of the story."[210]

The transformative power of God's self-giving in and through liturgical action has to do with the shaping of perception, of knowing and of feeling over time. The true ethos of Christian liturgy is that web of grace through word, sacrament, and song, through eating and drinking together, and being remembered by God, whereby God's saving power in the flesh transforms and transmutes all human pathos.[211]

The elements of worship create a "web of grace," a synergistic effect. The ordo and elements of worship are not merely learned by the worshipper, but also effectively make space for transformation in the mind of the worshipper.[212] Elements of worship incite not only the human intellect, but also human emotion and volition. Tom Driver says,

> The aim of religion is not simply intellectual understanding; it is also, and primarily, transformative action, for which the principal technique is ceremonies, rites, and services. . . . A religion is a praxis, a certain way of acting or attempting to act in the world, and this is established through a certain way of acting ritually.[213]

Liturgical rituals can be "vehicles for reconnecting God's story with our human stories."[214] By practicing in the worship ceremony, the people of God remember and anticipate God's salvific works. The Word and ritual in worship not only create personal transformation, but also form the com-

---

207. Polanyi and Prosch, *Meaning*, 156.
208. Smith, *Desiring the Kingdom*, 27.
209. Baillie, *Theology of the Sacraments*, 54.
210. Chan, *Spiritual Theology*, 108.
211. Saliers, *Worship as Theology*, 38.
212. Chan, *Liturgical Theology*, 87.
213. Driver, *Liberating Rites*, 169.
214. Anderson and Foley, *Mighty Stories*, ix. Regarding the power of narrative, see Ibid., 4–5. They insist on "the narrative form of human existence itself."

munity and give meaning.²¹⁵ Furthermore, each person, through interaction with society and culture, is impacted by social messages and receives impressions for transformation. According to Randall Collins,

> The central mechanism of interaction ritual theory is that occasions that combine a high degree of mutual focus of attention, that is, a high degree of intersubjectivity, together with a high degree of emotional entrainment—through bodily synchronization, mutual stimulation/arousal of participants' nervous systems—result in feelings of membership that are attached to cognitive symbols; and result also in the emotional energy of individual participants, giving them feelings of confidence, enthusiasm, and desire for action in what they consider amorally proper path.²¹⁶

Therefore, experiencing ritual "creates new symbolic objects and generates energies that fuel the major social changes."²¹⁷ Through liturgical practice, participants are aroused not only cognitively, but also emotionally. Therefore, liturgical participation creates a context for transformation. Continuity and repetition are powerful factors in transforming both individual and community. According to Levi-Strauss, "The real function of ritual is . . . to preserve the continuity of lived experience."²¹⁸ Agamben elaborates further, describing the purpose of ritual as a way to reconcile "mythic past and present," bringing them together in physical time and space.²¹⁹ Therefore, ritual guarantees continuity and synchronicity. Ritual allows people to participate in the original event. According to Gerd Theißen, the strict regularity of rites that transcend time and space helps facilitate people's transformation and change of mind; through the rite, people experience the presence of eternity in this place and this time.²²⁰ Rites and rituals vividly deliver feelings and the experiences of their ancestors of faith, as well as sharing the messages that have been encoded in the liturgy. As I mentioned in the last chapter, according to Roy Rappaport, the canonical message in the rituals requests resolution for participation. In this respect, a ritual has transformative power.²²¹ So, liturgical practice connects original event and present, so that make congregation as participants of original event. In other

215. Driver, *Liberating Rites*, 172.
216. Collins, *Interaction Ritual Chains*, 42.
217. Ibid., 42–43.
218. Agamben, *Infancy and History*, 77.
219. Ibid., 141.
220. Theißen, *Die Religion*, 172.
221. Anderson and Foley, *Mighty Stories*, 19.

words, by practicing liturgy, participants are faced with original message of God more vividly. This message request human transformation consistently and efficiently.

James Smith's recent work gives further attention to the transformative power of ritual. He writes,

> Our corporate worship should be aimed at constituting us as disciples who are countercultural agents of redemption. Communion and confession, foot washing and economic redistribution are ways of practicing what it means to be citizens of the kingdom. And such practices inscribe this telos of the kingdom into our character.[222]

Worship is a sort of discipline to train the people of God; through it, people are reminded of the Word of God, and make a resolution to embody the love of God by loving their neighbor. According to Smith, people are "noncognitive, affective creatures." Therefore, rather than doctrine and proposition, "the vision of the good life moves because it is a more affective, sensible, even aesthetic picture of what the good life looks like."[223] In this way, liturgy is a sort of tool for discipline of faith. First, it helps people to memorize God's will in the body. Then, it forms the foundation for transformation. Through liturgy and ritual in the worship, memory "makes something or someone present for us in an instant, once our brains can make the connections," keeping events of the past current for us, including "their significance and meaning."[224] Memory enhances the possibility of transformation in that it makes the human mind more vivid and enables persons to stand in the presence of God. In light of this, habit or repetition is very important; "patterns of body use become ingrained through our interactions with objects. . . . Postures and movements which are habit memories become sedimented into bodily conformation. Actors can mimic the impressions, doctors can examine the results."[225] That is to say, ritual and ceremony are efficient because they are implanted in the body.[226] Habit forms human thought.[227] This formation is not merely cognitive, but impacts the mind and its desires.

---

222. Smith, *Desiring the Kingdom*, 107.

223. Ibid., 53.

224. Atkins, *Memory and Liturgy*, 64.

225. See Connerton, *How Societies Remember*, 94.

226. Smith, *Imagining the Kingdom*, 95.

227. Merleau-Ponty says, "Puisque la sensation est une reconstitution, elle suppose en moi les sediments d'une constitution prealable, je suis, comme sujet sentant, tout plein de pouvoirs naturels dont je m'etonne le premier." Merleau-Ponty, *Phenomenologie*

Therefore, practice as an embodiment of thinking is very important because, through practice, formation occurs. Real transformation of human beings depends on the work of the Holy Spirit, and the wisdom gained through ritual opens the mind, body, and heart to the Holy Spirit's guidance. Since the early days of the Church, people have called on the name of the Holy Spirit to evoke the presence of God in worship.[228] This presence is the reason transformation can take place in worship. James Torrance asserts, "This work of memory, of realizing our participation and fellowship in the suffering of Christ, is the work of the Holy Spirit. He brings these things to our remembrance and interprets to us the meaning of the events."[229] God has given us Jesus Christ and the Holy Spirit, because humans are imperfect and cannot grasp this meaning without help. Depending on the work of Holy Spirit does not mean setting aside liturgical practice. Rather, the Holy Spirit uses human participation and liturgical practices to help human weakness.

---

de la perception, 249. According to him, a person senses with the ability he or she has formed habitually.

228. Zizioulas, *Being as Communion*, 160.

229. Torrance, *Worship, Community*, 86.

4

Participation of Children and Persons with Cognitive Challenges in Church Life

UP TO THIS POINT, we have studied the formative function of liturgy in the process of faith formation. In general, reason—i.e., verbal communication with cognitive ability and understanding—has been considered the most important criterion in demonstrating spiritual status and faith. Traditionally, the church has limited the full inclusion of children and cognitively challenged persons into the sacrament and public worship because of their perceived lack of cognitive ability and understanding.[1] However, we find that human faith cannot be explained only in the dimension of learning and cognition; recognition and religious understanding can also be enhanced by action and participation. To show that liturgy as action can impact faith formation and overcome the limits of cognition and articulation, we must look at some examples in the worship and the church.

Is the cognitive ability of children and cognitively challenged persons truly characterized by a lack of ability to understand and recognize God and the truth of the Bible? What level of rational functioning do they have? Is it rather a matter of lack of communication ability and skill, not of thought and cognitive ability? Is it really possible to learn the Christian faith not by instruction, but by practicing the liturgy?

---

1. Brock, "Introduction," 1–7.

Currently, in response to progress in cognitive development theory and special education, some Presbyterian and Reformed churches in America—for example, the Presbyterian Church USA (PCUSA), the Christian Reformed Church (CRC), and the Reformed Church in America (RCA)—have begun efforts to include children and cognitively challenged persons in public worship and sacraments. These denominations, having considered the priority of God's grace in sacramental practice, the inclusiveness of covenant, and the possibility of faith in children and cognitively challenged people, now include them in public worship. Following this example, the Korean Church has also begun theological reflection about including them.

NORTH AMERICAN INFLUENCES ON KOREAN CHURCHES AND SOCIETY

North American churches have impacted not only the theology of the Korean Church, but also the practice, due in part to the North American missionaries who delivered the Gospel into Korean Society.[2] These early missionaries had varied denominational and theological backgrounds, but they were all raised in the evangelical character of nineteenth-century North American Protestantism.[3] According to Ryu's studies, it was the early missionaries' evangelical Protestant character that particularly shaped the Korean Presbyterian Church.[4] North American theology, patterns of worship, and practices became the textbook of the Korean Presbyterian Church. Because there had been no theological tradition at that time, the Korean Church absorbed their puritan, Calvinistic theology.[5] Mark Noll explains the similarity of the North American and Korean churches as follows: first, evangelicalism is related to personalism rather than to the fellowship of believers and, therefore, emphasizes personal sacrifice and devotion. Second, these churches were shaped by the revival meeting, which developed church growth and facilitated evangelism, but made people devalue God's works in the past and present. Emphasizing the mandate to transform culture,

---

2. Park, *Worship in the Presbyterian Church*, 31–34. From 1884 to 1945, there were 1,529 missionaries working in Korea; of those, 1,059 (69.3 percent) were American, 199 (13 percent) were English, 98 (6.4 percent) were Canadian, and 85 (5.6 percent) were Australian. Kim and Park, *Comprehensive Survey*, 4.

3. Lee, "McCormick Seminary Graduates," 6.

4. Ryu, "Origin and Characteristics," 371–99.

5. Brown, *Mastery of the Far East*, 540.

Korean churches focused on worldly blessing and success rather than concern for poor and marginalized people.⁶

The impact of early American missionaries can also be found in the church law and worship directory that is the core structure of the Korean Church. In 1922, the Korean Presbyterian Church published a constitution composed of five parts that generally followed the American Presbyterian Church's constitution.⁷ A worship directory was created following that of the Southern Presbyterian Church in the USA.⁸

The North American churches also influenced educational systems in the Korean Church. Korean Sunday Schools for teaching adults started in 1888.⁹ In 1900, the wife of Pastor W. A. Noble started Sunday school for children.¹⁰ The school started with 200 children between the ages of 5 and 15, taught by twenty teachers. Until 1905, Korean Sunday schools tried to teach the Bible and doctrine without the aid of curricular resources. However, after 1905, they introduced "a uniform lesson" from the North American Church¹¹ emphasizing memorization of Bible verses, catechism, singing, and evangelism.¹² Two students memorized the New Testament, except the book of Matthew, and three memorized four thousand Bible verses.¹³

Historically, North American churches have Sunday school systems to nurture children and adolescents; "the American Sunday School Union was founded in 1824. Where public schools had not been established, the Sunday school . . . taught reading and recitation."¹⁴ From the nineteenth century to now, the system has been the representative educational institution in the Protestant Church and has significantly affected religious education. With a fervor for salvation, these schools emphasized conversion, and also contributed to the education of society so they could successfully make

---

6. Noll, "What can the Korean Church Learn," 253–56.

7. Those are as follows: "(1) the Confession of Faith, (2) the Westminster Shorter Catechism, (3) a Form of Government, (4) a Book of Discipline, and (5) a Directory of Worship." See Joo and Kim, "Reformed Tradition in Korea," 488.

8. Kim, "Reformed Tradition in Korea," 118–23.

9. Scranton, "Woman's Work in Korea," 5.

10. Sohn, "Early Sunday School Education," 161. Gangel and Benson say that "a uniform lesson" started at "the fifth national convention in Indianapolis in 1872" had a great impact on the world "wherever British and American missionaries were working." See Gangel and Benson, *Christian Education*, 286–87.

11. Chang, "History of Christian Education," 48.

12. Sohn, "Early Sunday School Education," 163.

13. Noble, "Some Personal Reminiscences," 94.

14. Gangel and Benson, *Christian Education*, 285.

contact with non-Christian children and adults.[15] Of course, some persons and institutions, such as *Life* magazine, criticized Sunday school as "the most wasted hour of the week."[16] Although Sunday school taught children and adolescents how and what Protestants believe and do, with respect to worship and the sacraments, the Sunday school system has caused some problems.

One of the most important of these problems is the separation of children and young adolescents from public worship and sacrament. Age-appropriate separation has merit in that it educates children according to their developmental abilities; however, this creates a gap between children's church experiences and adults' worship and church traditions. The Sunday school's emphasis on teaching and memorizing also unwittingly hampers the natural transmission of faith, which can be obtained by intergenerational communication.

NORTH AMERICAN ATTITUDES TOWARD THE COGNITIVELY CHALLENGED

Historically, neither the church nor society has shown a deep concern for the issue of the cognitively challenged, and although concern is increasing, it does not have a long history.[17] Early church attitudes were shaped by their Greco-Roman context, in which people commonly discarded infants born handicapped, a custom that lasted until the fourth century.[18] Plato and Aristotle espoused negative opinions of the cognitively challenged as well.[19] In Rome, the mentally handicapped could not inherit an estate or participate in "legal activity."[20] Some who escaped tardocide (the killing of those considered to be "idiots") became "objects of display and amusement

---

15. Lynn and Wright, *Big Little School*, 155.

16. Shrader, "Our Troubled Sunday Schools," 110.

17. It seems that the first known description of cognitively challenged persons was in 1500 BC. See Grossman, *Classification in Mental Retardation*. Regarding the historical study of the cognitively challenged, see Scheerenberger, *History of Mental Retardation*. Amos Yong points out the problem that arises when people try to find a biblical foundation for inclusion of the cognitively challenged is that "the Bible talks about the blind, the deaf, and the lame, among other impairments and impeding conditions, but not about 'Down's Syndrome' or even about 'disability.'" See Yong, *Theology and Down Syndrome*, 20–21.

18. Winzer, *History of Special Education*, 14; Scheerenberger, *History of Mental Retardation*, 11–20.

19. Taylor, et al., *Mental Retardation*, 3.

20. See Gardner, *Being a Roman Citizen*, 160.

for the rich."[21] They were "lacking understanding, similar to children," with no "legal capacity."[22]

From the Middle Ages to the Reformation, the mentally handicapped were sometimes misunderstood as "practitioners of witchcraft"[23] or "changelings."[24] Until the eighteenth century, "the concept of intellectual disability, regardless of the term used to describe it, was enigmatic to a world that did not have a sophisticated knowledge base with which to understand it."[25] In America in the eighteenth century, people again accused the mentally handicapped of being witches; they were subject to persecution and sometimes death.[26] In the early 1900s, the American eugenics movement claimed that the cognitively challenged threaten society.[27] Even worse, in 1907, the "first compulsory sterilization law" for cognitively challenged people was passed in the state of Indiana.[28]

However, in the mid-twentieth century, attitudes toward the cognitively challenged began to transition. In the 1950s, "a significant number of legislative acts provided support for individuals with disabilities."[29] In 1963, President John F. Kennedy instituted the Division of Handicapped Children and Youth and tried to enhance "public awareness of mental retardation."[30] In 1976, the Education of All Handicapped Children Act was passed so that cognitively challenged children could have the opportunity to receive an education.[31] And, in 1990, the Americans with Disabilities Act upheld the rights of "people with disabilities in employment, transportation, public

---

21. Evans, *Lives of Mentally Retarded People*, 33.
22. Covey, *Social Perceptions of People*, 130.
23. Evans, *Lives of Mentally Retarded People*, 35.
24. Covey, *Social Perceptions of People*, 239.
25. Beirne-Smith, et al., *Mental Retardation*, 5.
26. See Hickson, *Mental Retardation*.
27. See Beirne-Smith, et al., *Mental Retardation*, 16.
28. Crane, *Mental Retardation*, 52. Crane says, "It was 1968 before the Nebraska legislature repealed a law that mandated sterilization for women before they were discharged from state institutions (Perske, 1981), and it was 1972 before the last operation was performed at the Central Virginia Training Center (Smith & Nelson, 1989)."
29. Taylor, et al., *Mental Retardation*, 14.
30. Ibid., 16.
31. During the eighteenth and nineteenth centuries, there was a movement concerning the education and protection of the mentally handicapped. Representative scholars were Jean Marc Gaspard Itard (1774–1838), Johann Jacob Guggenbuhl (1816–1863), and Edward Seguin (1812–1881).

Participation of Children and Persons with Cognitive Challenges

accommodation, communications, and governmental activities,"[32] making public services more accessible and fostering inclusion in ordinary life.

THE CHURCH'S ATTITUDES TOWARD PERSONS WITH COGNITIVE CHALLENGES

Despite this, it is hard to find any theological argument in church history for their participation in the sacrament and public worship.[33] The KJV translates Paul as saying in 1 Thes 5:14, "Comfort the feebleminded." Martin Barr says this has been taken to mean the cognitively challenged.[34] However, In the Greek text, it is written, "παραμυθεῖσθε τοὺς ὀλιγοψύχους"; the word "ὀλιγόψυχος" appears one time in the New Testament. F. F. Bruce insists that "ὀλιγόψυχος" means "inadequate and diffident" in contrast to "self-sufficient and self-confident."[35] Gregory Beale translate this phrase as "encouraging the timid" based on the fact that "uses of the word *oligopsychos* (noun and verbal forms) in the Greek Old Testament refer to a lack of patience, endurance or confidence."[36] Gordon Fee points out the error of the KJV translation, and insists that this admonition points to "the disheartened" in the faith community.[37] So, it is not certain whether Paul intended to mention the cognitively challenged. Saint Nicholas Thaumaturges historically insisted on the necessity of "recognizing and tenderly caring for the idiot and the imbecile" in the fourth century.[38] Evans also insists "the word 'cretin' is derived from the French 'chretien' (Christian) and is testimony to the fact that in early times the severely handicapped were cared for by monastic communities."[39]

By the fourth century, due to the impact of Christianity, "edicts against infanticide and the selling of children into slavery were issued by Roman Emperors Constantine (in AD 315 and 321); Valentinian, Valens, and

---

32. United States Department of Labor, "Americans with Disabilities Act," http://www.dol.gov/dol/topic/disability/ada.htm (accessed August 9, 2013).

33. There is no mention of a guideline for inclusion of the cognitively challenged in the Bible. Many studies on this topic have the tendency to focus on the matter of the physically handicapped. See Kokaska, "Disabled People in the Bible," 20–21.

34. Barr, *Mental Defectives*, 24–25.

35. Bruce, "1 & 2 Thessalonians," 123.

36. Beale, "1–2 Thessalonians," 165.

37. Fee, *First and Second Letters*, 210.

38. Barr, *Mental Defectives*, 25.

39. Evans, *Lives of Mentally Retarded People*, 35.

Gratian (AD 367); Valentinian, Theodosius, and Arcadius (AD 391)."[40] The church's value of children and the disabled helped "the afflicted became a sign of strength instead of weakness."[41]

Although mention of these issues is sparse, there are some references in Augustine, Aquinas, Martin Luther, and in Micron's *Shorter Catechism* (1552). Augustine emphasizes catechesis in Christian formation in his sermons and writings.[42] In *De catechizandis rudibus*, which contains Augustine's thoughts on faith education and especially on evangelization, there is no direct mention of the cognitively challenged. However, in the second chapter, we find important clues for upholding cognitively challenged persons' participation in the sacrament. He says,

> For I desire my hearer to understand all that I understand; and I feel that I am not speaking in such a manner as to effect that. This is so chiefly because intuition floods the mind, as it were, with a sudden flash of light, while the expression of it in speech is a slow, drawn-out, and far different process, and while speech is being formed, intellectual apprehension has already hidden itself in its secret recess; nevertheless, because it has stamped in a wonderful way certain imprints upon the memory, these endure for the length of time it takes to pronounce the words; and from these imprints we construct those audible symbols which are called language.[43]

Augustine sees a severe gap between our verbal expressions and our understanding. Even an adult of average intelligence has trouble delivering to the hearer the exact idea that has occurred in the mind. Expression never precisely reflects level of understanding.

Augustine cites a story of a "simpleton" named Moriones who revered Christ in order to refute the thought that all "feeble-minded" persons were sinful in previous lives, and to show that even a person with a low level of understanding can still be receptive to God's grace.[44] Moriones, ridiculed by intelligent people, was "imbued with Christian feeling" and protested to non-Christians when they blasphemed against God.[45] Through this story Augustine affirms the possibility of faith among the cognitively challenged in the context of anti-Pelagian controversy. It is difficult, however, to find

40. Scheerenberger, *History of Mental Retardation*, 19.
41. Ibid., 20.
42. See Harmless, *Augustine and the Catechumenate*.
43. Augustine, *First Catechetical Instruction*, 15.
44. Augustine, "Anti-Pelagian Works," 1:32–33.
45. Ibid.

any other direct mention of the faith development of persons who are cognitively challenged.

Aquinas emphasizes reason in receiving the sacrament, and expresses concern about persons who are cognitively challenged; "The intellect which is the principle of intellectual operation is the form of the human body."[46] According to him, "God is intelligent,"[47] and intellect is related to spiritual development.[48] Each person has "a principle of knowledge, namely the light of the active intellect, through which certain universal principles of all the sciences are naturally understood."[49] This does not mean that Aquinas demeans the value and necessity of experience. Intelligent recognition is "derived from certain separate forms or substances."[50] Understanding and intellect come from participation through "corporeal matter."[51] However, "faith is a habit of the mind" and requires "intellect assent."[52] It resides in the intellect, because "to believe is an act of the intellect, inasmuch as the will moves it to assent."[53] He recognizes the role of will in the process of faith formation, and believes intellect is the gift of the Holy Spirit; however, he says "intellective knowledge penetrates into the very essence of a thing."[54]

Considering his emphasis on reason and intelligence, let us study his sacramental theology. When he dealt with the matter of baptism, he insisted on the priority of God's grace and the faith of the community. However, in the case of the Lord's Supper, he insisted on the necessity of reason. What, then, is the relationship between understanding and receiving sacrament to Aquinas? Sacrament functions *ex opere operato* because "the sacraments derive their power from Christ's passion."[55] Regarding sacramental character, "the sacraments of the New Law produce a character" which "signifies a certain spiritual power ordained unto things pertaining to the divine worship."[56] According to him, "a character is a distinctive mark printed in a man's rational soul by the eternal Character."[57] This transforms us into a

---

46. Aquinas, *Summa Theologica*, Pt. 1, Q. 76. Art. 1 (370).
47. Aquinas, *Compendium of Theology*, 31.
48. Aquinas, *Summa Theologica*, vol. 1, Pt. 1, Q. 84. Art. 2 (422).
49. Ibid., Pt. 1, Q. 117. Art 1 (569).
50. Ibid., Pt. 1, Q. 84. Art. 4 (425).
51. Ibid.
52. Aquinas, *Summa Theologica*, vol. 3, Pt. 2-2, Q. 4. Art. 1 (1184).
53. Ibid., Pt. 2-2, Q. 4. Art. 2 (1185).
54. Ibid., Pt. 2-2, Q. 8. Art. 1 (1198).
55. Ibid., vol. 4, Pt. 3, Q. 62. Art. 5 (2353).
56. Ibid., Pt. 3, Q. 63. Art. 2 (2356).
57. Ibid., Pt. 3, Q. 63. Art. 3 (2357).

version of Christ's priesthood, and we receive "Divine gifts" while participating in "Divine worship."[58] The most important sacraments are baptism, confirmation, and ordination, which cannot occur repetitively.

Whenever Aquinas discussed baptism and the Lord's Supper, he emphasizes the role of reason; however, in the case of baptism for the cognitively challenged, he considers their special situation. Aquinas says:

> In the matter of madmen and imbeciles, a distinction is to be made. For some are so from birth, and have no lucid intervals, and show no signs of the use of reason. And with regard to these it seems that we should come to the same decision as with regard to children who are baptized in the Faith of the Church.[59]

Aquinas intended to deal with the matter of the cognitively handicapped in the same category as young children. He seems to have considered those who are cognitively challenged as lacking reason, but upholds the possibility of their baptism. He writes that "imbeciles who never had, and have not now, the use of reason, are baptized, according to the Christian's intention, just as according to the church's ritual, they believe and repent; as we stated above of children."[60] His foundation is in the context of faith and liturgical worship. He also insists upon the infusion of God's grace.[61]

Regarding sacrament for persons who are cognitively challenged, Aquinas says,

> Men are said to be devoid of reason in two ways. First, when they are feebleminded as a man who sees dimly is said not to see; and since such persons can conceive some devotion towards this sacrament, it is not to be denied them. In another way men are said not to possess fully the use of reason. Either, then, they never had the use of reason, and have remained so from birth; and in that case this sacrament is not to be given to them, because in no way has there been any preceding devotion towards the sacrament: or else, they were not always devoid of reason, and then, if when they formerly had their wits they showed devotion towards this sacrament, it ought to be given to them in the hour of death.[62]

---

58. Ibid., Pt. 3, Q. 63. Art. 3 (2356).
59. Ibid., Pt. 3, Q. 68. Art. 12 (2402).
60. Ibid., Pt. 3, Q. 68. Art. 12 (2402).
61. Ibid., Pt. 3, Q. 69. Art. 6 (2407).
62. Ibid., vol. 5, Pt. 3, Q. 80. Art. 9 (2490–2491).

He separates the two cases according to whether a person has used reason. In the Lord's Supper, "Christ's body, according to the mode of being which it has in this sacrament, is perceptible neither by the sense nor by the imagination, but only by the intellect, which is called the spiritual eye."[63] A person baptized as an infant but unable to reason as an adult must show "devotion towards this sacrament," because without it, receiving a sacrament would profane the body of Jesus Christ.[64]

Many scholars who study the history of the mentally handicapped mention the contents of Luther's *Table Talk* and insist that he had a negative opinion of the cognitively challenged.[65] The most commonly cited passage is as follows:

> In Dessau there was a twelve-year-old boy like this: he devoured as much as four farmers did, and he did nothing else than eat and excrete. Luther suggested that he be suffocated. Somebody asked, "For what reason?" He [Luther] replied, "Because I think he's simply a mass of flesh without a soul. Couldn't the devil have done this, inasmuch as he gives such shape to the body and mind even of those who have reason that in their obsession they hear, see, and feel nothing? The devil is himself in their soul. The power of the devil is great when in this way he holds the minds of all men captive, but he doesn't dare give full vent to the power on account of the angels.[66]

Luther saw this boy's acts in a spiritual perspective—as a matter of demonization. But it is hard to think that Luther's *Table Talk* reveals his whole theological stance, because *Table Talk* was not intended as a theological article, nor was written it by Luther himself.[67] In Luther's other writings, written over forty years, many passages show love and sympathy for neighbors and the weak.[68] He was also a child of the sixteenth century, when children and cognitively challenged persons did not receive concern and respect: "A child was not believed to be truly human by birthright; he was a creature in

---

63. Ibid., Pt. 3, Q. 76. Art. 7 (2454).
64. Ibid., Pt. 3, Q. 80. Art. 4 (2483).
65. See Kanner, *Care and Study*, 164.
66. Luther, *Luther's Works*, 397.
67. Miles, "Martin Luther," 20.
68. Luther, *Luther's Works*, 127–29. Also, he considers children the holders of the Kingdom of God. See Luther, *Luther's Works*, 55, 120. In his lectures on Galatians, he insists that even though the deaf cannot hear the Gospel, it does not mean they cannot know God's Word. See Luther, *Luther's Works*, 247–49. Also see Martin Luther, *Luther's Works*, 110. In fact, Luther's personal assistant, Wolfgang, who lived with Luther's family for a long time, was a mildly disabled man. See Luther, *Luther's Works*, 158.

search of humanity—unpredictable, capable of animal indolence, selfishness and savagery."[69]

The only Reformed confession that mentions participation of the cognitively challenged is *Micron's Shorter Catechism*, circa 1552, made for the Dutch refugee church in London.

> Q: Why was faith and its oral profession not equally demanded from the children of the church prior to baptism?
>
> A: The Church has far surer confirmation of its salvation from the Word of God than from the profession of adults. And congenital illness, as a result of which some persons can neither believe nor make profession, is not counted against them for Christ's sake, in whom they are blessed—that is, regarded as holy, righteous, clean, and faithful—no less than are other adult believers. The same must be thought with respect to the baptism of adults of the church who are deaf or mentally handicapped.[70]

This catechism considers young children, the cognitively challenged, and deaf persons in a special situation. Rather than requiring a profession of faith, the Dutch church permitted reception of baptism by those who belonged to the faith community. Above all, the church depended on "salvation from the Word of God." Although there is no additional explanation of that church's practice, this shows deep consideration based on the grace of God about persons of all cognitive levels who belong in the faith community.

THE CURRENT SITUATION IN THE NORTH AMERICAN CHURCHES

Currently there are some endeavors to include cognitively challenged persons in public worship and the sacraments. Brett Webb-Mitchell writes:

> In many Protestant churches, young children are welcome in the sanctuary for the first fifteen minutes of worship, up to the point clearly marked in the bulletin as the children's sermon, and then they are dismissed to go elsewhere in the building . . . Not only are children excluded from worship, but so are people with mental retardation, because they are perceived as being unable to understand and enjoy the intellectual breadth of the liturgy,

---

69. Ozment, *When Fathers Ruled*, 138. Also, Miles discusses Luther's *Works on Galatians* (1535) and surmises that Luther considered the possibility of a demon's impact on the boy at Dessau. See Miles, "Martin Luther," 190.

70. See van't Spijker, *Church's Book of Comfort*, 142.

especially the singing of hymns, the reading of Scripture, the preaching, and the recitation of creeds and prayers in unison.[71]

Children and those who are cognitively challenged have been deprived of opportunities to become accustomed to liturgy and public worship, which should be enjoyed from an early age. Protestant emphasis on understanding has not left room for the participation of these groups. Virginia Thomas points out that Presbyterian worship has also focused on the intellectual aspect; even their focus on the centrality of God's Word has remained "abstract words and profound concepts."[72] Because of this, "Sunday school made instruction in and performance of the Christian faith more an act of the mind, as the individual strove to accumulate and memorize certain sets of knowledge (e.g., the creeds, confessions, and prayers of the church)."[73] In the community, faithful attitude and character alone have been looked down upon.[74]

When churches begin to consider inclusion for young children and cognitively challenged individuals, there are two major considerations. First, that of breaking the calm, holy mood of worship by inviting noise; second, distrust of the understanding and cognitive ability of children and the cognitively challenged.[75] However, this is too myopic a view, and a shallow understanding of worship and of participation.

In many churches, there is well-intentioned concern about special worship service for specific ages, and a nursery system to ease the burden of parents in the public worship, but families are deprived of worshipping God together in the Sunday public worship. As we have seen, participation in public worship is not only an encounter with God, but also a Christian discipline, and loss of participation creates a bigger problem when young children become adults not accustomed to adult worship. Darwin Glassford points out that separated worship impacts the form and contents of public worship itself:

> Hugh Koops, in 1967, observed not only that the practice of providing alternative services for children was increasing, but also that he believed that this increase could be attributed to the reality that worship was increasingly viewed as a teaching service for adults. He asserted that the sermon had become the major instrument for adult education rather than a proclamation of

---

71. Webb-Mitchell, *Dancing with Disabilities*, 3.
72. Thomas, "Children at Worship," 122.
73. Webb-Mitchell, *Christly Gestures*, 163.
74. Ibid., 3, 160, 163.
75. Beckwith, *Postmodern Children's Ministry*, 144–45.

what God has done in Jesus Christ; the sanctuary had become a classroom for adults rather than worship for all generations, and consequently children found themselves in the wrong classroom on Sunday morning. This shifting view of worship combined with new insights from developmental psychology that emphasized teaching for learning, rather than preaching for response created a fertile environment for fostering alternative worship services for children.[76]

Even though separated worship for children helps Sunday school teach according to age, it makes worship itself merely a lecture or Bible study. Because separating groups was originally aimed at teaching, separated worship became a place of education; people began to pursue knowledge rather than gathering to celebrate and adore the blessings of the Trinity. Of course, in a separated situation, children and adults can learn doctrine and Bible according to their development and cognitive abilities, but lack of shared experience in public worship create severe generational gaps that deprive all congregants of opportunities to learn the worship practices themselves, and to experience the transmission of Christian faith gained by living and worshipping together.

Regarding the current situation in the church, Ivy Beckwith offers this critique:

> The bias at most churches seems to be that real church is for adults only. The norm is to segregate families by age so that parents and children are never together once they walk in the front door. So it should come as no surprise that parents leave the church building each week with few tools to help them care for the souls of their children.[77]

Early participation of children and cognitively challenged persons is crucial, and North American churches have begun theological reflection for broader inclusivity, a matter that has been debated in North American and European churches since 1970. The Presbyterian Church in the United States of America (PCUSA), The Christian Reformed Church (CRC), The Reformed Church in America (RCA), The Orthodox Presbyterian Church (OPC), and The Presbyterian Church in America (PCA) studied this and published a denominational report.[78] Based on the studies, PCUSA, CRC,

---

76. Glassford, "Fostering an Intergenerational Culture," 76.
77. Beckwith, *Postmodern Children's Ministry*, 103.
78. Moon, *Korean Presbyterian Church*.

and RCA have argued the inclusion of children in the sacrament and public worship.

However, until now, the participation of cognitively challenged persons has not received much attention from North American churches.[79] The PCA has made no reference to the subject at all in their denominational minutes; neither has the OPC begun to include cognitively challenged persons in the denominational dimension. However, we can draw some conclusions from their constitution: "The official process for receiving persons into church membership—which would include baptism for the previously unbaptized—and admitting them to the Lord's Table are addressed in the *Book of Church Order*'s 'Directory for the Public Worship of God, IV' and 'Book of Discipline II, B.'"[80] These sections say that any adult who comes to baptism or the Lord's Supper has to make a profession of faith. However, we can also note that each church has the responsibility to conclude for itself whether the profession is valid; no exacting rules for this are set. Likewise, each has the power to modify membership vows to make them clearer to the person taking them. Both matters fall under the presbytery's supervision. Thus, if a person is so cognitively challenged as to be incapable of communication, including a profession of faith, that person cannot be admitted to baptism or the Lord's Table.

The CRC and RCA, which both hold to the Dutch Reformed tradition, have founded a special institute for ministry to the cognitively challenged.[81] In the only major paper on disabilities the RCA has produced, "Spirituality and Hospitality: What the Church Can Learn by Welcoming Persons with Disabilities," they insist:

> The church must welcome persons with disabilities, not just because persons with disabilities need to be welcomed; the church must welcome persons with disabilities because, without such welcome, the church will not fully discover the unspeakable riches of its life in Christ.[82]

79. Yong, *Theology and Down Syndrome*, 69.

80. See Orthodox Presbyterian Church, "The Book of Church Order," http://www.opc.org/order.html (accessed December 29, 2011).

81. Reformed Church in America, "Breaking Barriers," https://www.rca.org/sslpage.aspx?pid=7239 (accessed December 29, 2011). For practical guidelines and resources for including people suffering from various sorts of disabilities, see Christian Reformed Church and Reformed Church in America, "Inclusion Handbook: Everybody Belongs, Everybody Serves," http://www2.crcna.org/site_uploads/uploads/disabilityconcerns/disability_inclusionhandbook.pdf (accessed February 21, 2014).

82. Reformed Church in America, "What the Church Can Learn by Welcoming Persons with Disabilities," https://www.rca.org/page.aspx?pid=4994 (accessed December 29, 2011).

The CRC has also shown an affirmative attitude toward baptism of cognitively challenged people, readily baptizing those who are part of a covenant family. The church considers them members of God's covenant regardless of cognitive capabilities, and that they are recipients of God's grace just as we all are. In the past twenty years, the church has been more open to including cognitively challenged individuals who make a profession of their faith, expecting them to express and testify to their faith only at the level to which they are capable in an ability-appropriate profession.[83] As a result, many persons with cognitive disabilities now come to the Lord's Table.[84] To help develop their faith, the CRC, in cooperation with the RCA, has started the Friendship Series, a curriculum for instruction and nurturing the faith of those with cognitive disabilities to be used in local congregations and outreach ministries while also educating a congregation's children about the special needs of mentally handicapped church members.[85]

The PCUSA has shown the most interest in inclusion of cognitively challenged persons. In 1988, the 200th General Assembly approved a policy that officially included people with serious mental illness in the church.[86] Later, in 2000, the PCUSA published the official document, "A Celebration of All That May Enter," which recommends all members' inclusion in worship. In 2008, the PCUSA published "Comfort My People," which was approved by the 218th General Assembly of the Presbyterian Church, which provides extensive guidelines on how pastors, members, and future church leaders should be prepared to include cognitively handicapped persons into the life of the church.[87] For example, pastors should to prepare sermons and Bible studies about mental illness issues; churches should care for and encourage families with cognitively challenged members; and churches should connect with professional or local institutions for mental health

---

83. I borrowed the term "ability-appropriate" from the Christian Reformed Church's guidelines for children at the Lord's Supper. See Christian Reformed Church, "Frequently Asked Questions," http://www.crcna.org/ministries/initiatives/faith-formation-committee/frequently-asked-questions (accessed February 21, 2014).

84. Christian Reformed Church, "Persons with Disabilities and Profession of Faith," in *Agenda for Synod 2011* (Grand Rapids: CRC Publication, 2011), 561.

85. Faith Alive Christian Resources, "Disability Resources," http://www.faithaliveresources.org/Products/CategoryCenter/DMDR/disability-resources.aspx (accessed December 29, 2011).

86. Presbyterian Church in the United States of America (Hereafter PCUSA), *Minutes of the 200th General Assembly* (Louisville, KY: Published by the Office of the General Assembly, 1988), 444.

87. PCUSA, "Comfort My People: A Policy Statement on Serious Mental Illness," http://www.pcusa.org/resource/comfort-my-people-policy-statement-serious-mental-/ (accessed November 12, 2013).

care. In 2011, the PCUSA published "Inclusion from the Inside Out: Welcoming God's Children of All Abilities," which includes practical guidelines for welcoming all God's children under the any circumstances.[88] "Disability is redemptive because it opens up our human vulnerability and dependence upon each other and God."[89] In the weakness of humanity, people can see the wholeness of God. In particular, the document comments on confirmation and church membership by pointing out the importance of inclusiveness of covenant and the "covenantal relationship"[90]: "When a parent requests church membership for their son or daughter with a disability, the session, pastor, parents, and the confirmed can enter into a covenant agreement to nurture, mentor, and support one another in church membership."[91] Verbal confession is important, but if someone lacks verbal ability, the church community can open an alternative way for the person to be included. With an open mind, they try to include the cognitively challenged in the public service and provide guidelines for local church pastors and leaders.

In 1979, the Catholic Church in America National Apostolate with Mentally Retarded Persons (NAMRP) passed the following resolution at its yearly meeting: "[It is recommended that the] NAMRP provide national leadership to work toward obtaining an official statement of approval for handicapped persons, regardless of the nature of severity of their disabilities, to celebrate the Sacrament of Christian Initiation as full, participating members of God's Church."[92] However, this has not been done as of 2013.

Protestant denominations have also made efforts to incorporate persons with cognitive challenges in their worship experiences. The Christian Church (Disciples of Christ), the CRC, the Evangelical Lutheran Church in America, the Lutheran Church Missouri Synod, the Presbyterian Church in the United States, the United Church of Christ, and the United Methodist Church have all tried to include the cognitively challenged beginning in the late 1980s. Some have proposed denominational resolutions for including the cognitively challenged in the public worship and sacrament.[93] For

---

88. Presbyterians for Disability Concerns, "Inclusion from the Inside Out: Welcoming God's Children of All Abilities," http://www.phewacommunity.org/images/disability-inclusion-packet-2011.pdf (accessed November 11, 2013).

89. Ibid.

90. PCUSA, "2011 Disability Inclusion Resource Packet," http://www.pcusa.org/resource/2011-disability-inclusion-resource-packet/ (accessed July 20, 2013).

91. Ibid.

92. Foley, "Introduction," 5. While such had been recommended, it had not in fact been done.

93. Regarding the specific contents, see Pathways to Promise Ministry & Mental Illness, "Faith Group Statements on Mental Illness," http://www.pathways2promise.org/

example, the CRC adopted a "Resolution on Disabilities" in 1985, which mentioned inclusiveness of covenant to permit "full participation in the church by people with disabilities."[94] They write, "We pledge ourselves to be the caring community according to 1 Corinthians 12, paying special attention to the needs and gifts of people with physical, sensory, mental, and emotional impairments."[95] They also published a resource guide to enhance local churches' ability to help all handicapped people.[96] The CRC Synod in 2000 encouraged local churches "to establish a network of disability-concerns consultants and congregational contacts to work in cooperation with the office of Disability Concerns."[97] In 2013, the CRC adopted a recommendation to "encourage all Christian Reformed churches to adopt a church policy on disability and to appoint at least one person in the congregation to serve as a church disability advocate."[98]

The Evangelical Lutheran Church in America (ELCA) passed a resolution in 1989 in which they decided to serve those with mentally handicaps and illnesses by preparing "material to educate congregations about mental illness and to improve the church's ministry to the mentally ill and their families."[99] In 1991 the church-wide assembly affirmed the 1989 resolution and renewed their commitment with the social policy resolution "Ministry with Persons with Disability."[100] Again, in 2011, the ELCA adopted the document, "A Social Message on . . . The Body of Christ and Mental Illness," in which they strongly insist on the role of the church to include and help persons with mental illness and their families.[101] The document considers that the mentally ill persons' "willingness to be present as vulnerable is a gift and is itself a form of service, and a reminder to the church that true freedom is found in service."[102] The ELCA believes church can be the best place

---

pdf/resolutionsoffaithgroups.pdf (accessed August 31, 2013).

94. Christian Reformed Church, "A Resolution on Disabilities," 703.

95. Ibid., 702.

96. Christian Reformed Church of North America, *Opening Doors*.

97. Christian Reformed Church of North America, *Acts of Synod 2000*, 620.

98. Ibid., 612.

99. Evangelical Lutheran Church in America (Hereafter ELCA), *Reports and Records*, 985.

100. ELCA, "Ministry with Persons with Disability, Social Policy Resolution CA91.07.101," http://download.elca.org/ELCA percent20Resource percent20Repository/Ministry_Disabled_PersonsSPR91.pdf (accessed December 11, 2013).

101. ELCA, "A social message on . . . the Body of Christ and Mental Illness," http://download.elca.org/ELCA percent20Resource percent20Repository/Mental_IllnessSM.pdf (accessed December 11, 2013).

102. Ibid.

for helping people with mental illnesses and disabilities, and says points out that clergy have been historically expected to serve as "psychologists or psychiatrists."[103] In 2012, the ELCA published "A Message on . . . People Living with Disabilities."[104] They insist on the validity of full participation of "all people as baptized members of the body of Christ."[105] Their foundation is that the human is the creation in the image of God.[106] They recommend "alterations to worship practice," "accessibility of worship," and that congregations "plan for and include both children and adults with disabilities."[107]

The Lutheran Church Missouri Synod affirmed in the document of "Ministry to People with Mental Illness and their Families" that "Our pastors and congregations will be gateways to reaching out and accepting people with mental illness into their midst. Our vision is that families living with mental illness/brain disorders are full participants in the life and ministry of the church."[108]

At the General Conference of the United Methodist Church (UMC), a representative proclaimed the necessity of helping, teaching, and supporting those who are "retarded."[109] In 2012, the UMC affirmed a resolution on "The Church and People with Mental, Physical, and/or Psychological Disabilities," declaring the necessity of including them in worship and church life from the example of Jesus' ministry in the world. The UMC insists, "the body of Christ is not complete without people of all areas of life, including people with all types of disabilities."[110] The UMC emphasizes accessibility, small meetings, worship, and sacrament, and also calls for awareness among both people and clergy about how to help and care for persons with disabilities more wisely. Pastors, seminarians, and church leaders should be trained to teach and serve handicapped people, and adequate resources should be developed for them.

---

103. Ibid.

104. ELCA, "Mental Illness," http://www.elca.org/en/Faith/Faith-and-Society/Social-Messages/Mental-Illness (accessed January 30, 2014).

105. ELCA, "A message on. . .People Living with Disabilities," http://download.elca.org/ELCA percent20Resource percent20Repository/People_with_DisabilitiesSM.pdf (accessed December 11, 2013).

106. Ibid., 2.

107. Ibid., 8.

108. Lutheran Church Missouri Synod, "Ministry to People with Mental Illness and their Families," http://www.lcms.org/Document.fdoc?src=lcm&id=436 (accessed February 21, 2014).

109. The United Methodist Church, "Journal of the General Conference (1972)," 466–67, cited in Herzog, *Disability Advocacy*, 78.

110. The United Methodist Church, "Church and People," 494.

In spite of these actions by several of the mainline Protestant denominations and the Roman Catholic Church in America, "in many churches, numerous barriers hinder the meaningful involvement of people with disabilities in the experiences and activities where faith is born."[111] Church does not provide an opportunity for those who are cognitively challenged to have "shared experience" or "relationships and belongings."[112] Current statistics on the participation of those with cognitive challenges in worship clearly shows these barriers still exist in American religious life.

The overall percentage of cognitively challenged persons in the United States is close to 3 percent.[113] It is estimated that of this group, only about 15 percent need extensive support—and of these, about 10 percent fall within the moderate range, 3 percent in the severe range, and only 2 percent in the profound range.[114] What percentage of cognitively challenged persons join Sunday public worship? If we apply these population-wide statistics to the specific numbers of the church,

> in a congregation of 400 people, you might expect as many as 12 children and adults with developmental disabilities to be in attendance. If your congregation is one of the growing numbers of faith communities with over 1,000 people in attendance, you might expect 30 or more people with developmental disabilities to be present.[115]

In reality, however, it is rare to see cognitively challenged persons in public worship: "Hayden and colleagues (1992) reported that almost one-third of children and adults with intellectual disabilities living in small

---

111. Carter, "Exchanging Gifts," 129.

112. Ibid., 133–35.

113. See *The Arc Q&A*. Regarding the ratio of the population with cognitive disabilities, as surveyed by the American Psychiatric Association, see Beirne-Smith et al., *Mental Retardation*, 295. According to Centers for Disease Control, "One in 150 individuals in the United States is diagnosed with an Autism Spectrum Disorder, resulting in a new diagnosis every 20 minutes." Boutot and Myles, *Autism Spectrum Disorders*, 5. Sousa says, "The Centers for Disease Control and Prevention in 2006 estimated that ASDs affect as many as 1 in 166 children." Sousa, *Special Needs Brain*, 179. According to Edelson's research, 75 percent of ASD children have a "cognitive disability." See Boutot and Myles, *Autism Spectrum Disorders*, 9. Autism is the "third most common developmental disability—more common than Down's Syndrome." See Yust, "World Apart, 68–79.

114. See American Psychiatric Association, *Diagnostic and Statistical Manual*, 43–44.

115. Carter, *Including People with Disabilities*, 54.

foster or group homes 'practically never' attended religious services."[116] This shows a severe gap between theory and practice.

The American Sunday School played a significant role in evangelism and social participation throughout the twentieth century. What, then, is the current state for children in public worship among North America's representative Reformed and Presbyterian denominations? The PCUSA emphasizes parental and church responsibility in faith formation for children.[117] They insist, "Worship in the church school is not to be a substitute for participation in the worship of the whole congregation on the Lord's Day."[118] In 2013, they suggested detailed guidelines for including children in public worship, based on the following statement of understanding:

> Children bring special gifts to worship and grow in the faith through their regular inclusion and participation in the worship of the congregation. Those responsible for planning and leading the participation of children in worship should consider the children's level of understanding and ability to respond, and should avoid both excessive formality and condescension. The session should ensure that regular programs of the church do not prevent children's full participation with the whole congregation in worship, in the Word and Sacrament.[119]

When baptized, children want to join in the Lord's Supper, and, under the guidance of the Session, they are welcomed.[120] The PCUSA also try to welcome those who are cognitively challenged into the sacramental life of the church.

The PCA also emphasizes participation of children in public worship. Their *Book of Church Order* points out that public and private worship must be differentiated, "in that in public worship God is served by his saints united as his covenant people, the Body of Christ. For this reason the covenant children should be present so far as possible as well as adults. For the same reason no favoritism may be shown to any who attend."[121] However, because the PCA does not permit the participation of children and the cognitively challenged in the Lord's Supper, it does not, in fact, promote an environment of public worship that is kindly and welcoming to these groups.

---

116. Ibid., 7.
117. PCUSA, *Book of Order*, Part II, 94.
118. Ibid., 114.
119. Ibid., 101–02.
120. Ibid., 119.
121. Presbyterian Church in America, *Book of Church Order*, 47–7.

The OPC, emphasizing God's covenant, insists on the necessity of participation of covenant children; "In public worship, God's people draw near to their God united as his covenant people, the body of Christ. For this reason, covenant children should be present as well as adults. Because God makes his covenant with believers and their children, families should be taught and encouraged to sit together as families."[122] In particular, the OPC emphasizes "public confession of faith:"[123] "Baptized children ordinarily shall be received as non-communicant members when their parents are received as communicant members."[124] Their emphasis and situation is similar to PCA.

The CRC puts forth the idea of "faith nurture:"

> each church shall minister to its children and youth—and to the children and youth in the community who participate—by nurturing their personal faith and trust in Jesus Christ as Savior and Lord, by nurturing their faithful participation in the Lord's Supper, by preparing them to profess their faith publicly.[125]

The CRC considers the Lord's Supper necessary to Christian nurture. However, the CRC tries to balance this participation with learning the Bible and confessions of the church. With no clear guideline for participation of cognitively challenged persons in the sacraments and public worship, the CRC still holds that "all baptized members who come with age- and ability-appropriate faith in Jesus Christ are welcome to the Lord's Supper and called to obey the scriptural commands about participation in an age- and ability-appropriate way under the supervision of the elders."[126] To permit the possibility of "age and ability appropriate faith" means faith is possible for people of different ability and maturity, opening to inclusion of any people at any circumstance.

THE CURRENT SITUATION IN THE KOREAN CHURCHES

In Korea, concern about the cognitively challenged started late compared to Western societies. Cho and Kim's studies argue the starting point of "social services for individuals with disabilities" was approximately 1445.[127] How-

---

122. Orthodox Presbyterian Church, *Book of Church Order*, 126.
123. Ibid., 139.
124. Ibid., 157.
125. Christian Reformed Church, *Church Order and Its Supplements 2012*, 90.
126. Ibid., 88.
127. Cho, "History of Korean Special Education," http://www.chohongjoong.com/

ever, this service was for the blind, not the cognitively challenged. Until 1894, a Korean caste system separated all persons by social rank. Furthermore, Korea was oppressed by Japan from 1910 to 1945, and the Korean Civil War happened during 1950–1953. Because of these long periods of difficult political and economic situations, Koreans have not been motivated to help marginalized and handicapped people more systematically.

However, there have been changes in recent times. In 1961, Reverend Youngsik Lee founded a special school for those who are mentally handicapped.[128] In 1977, the Act for the Promotion of Special Education for the Handicapped was enacted. And in 1981, the Disabled Persons Welfare Act was enacted. These acts aimed to rehabilitate the handicapped and improve welfare, but the efforts were not enough. The act has remained a proclamation without legal binding. It can be considered a sort of recommendation, but does not overcome discrimination against persons with cognitive challenges.

It has been a good starting point, however, to arouse public concern about persons who are mentally handicapped. This legislation set the objective bases for helping the handicapped. According to Ryu's study, "in the 1990s, the inclusion movement became a topic in Korean special education."[129] Furthermore, "only 11.6 [percent] of students with disabilities were receiving special education services in inclusive classrooms."[130] A survey conducted in 2007 by the Ministry of Education and Human Resources Development found a total of "144 special schools: 5 national, 50 public, and 89 private. About 62 [percent] of special schools were private, serving 53 [percent] of the special school students . . . schools for children with intellectual disabilities comprise 61.8 [percent] of special schools."[131] Even though efforts have been insufficient, Korean society has a desire to help those who are cognitively handicapped become educated and adapt in society.

Given these national trends, how is the Korean Presbyterian Church helping cognitively challenged persons? The church has experienced enormous growth, but the percentage of cognitively challenged people in the Korean churches is drastically less than in Korean society. As of 2008 there were only about 350 congregations with special programs for the cognitively

---

zboard/view.php?id=research01&page=1&sn1=&divpage=1&sn=off&ss=on&sc=on&select_arrange=headnum&desc=asc&no=18 (accessed November 12, 2013); Kim, "A Historical Study," 171.

128. Ibid., 168.
129. Ryu, "Special Education," 125.
130. Ibid.
131. Ryu, "Special Education," 133.

challenged. Considering the number of churches in South Korea, this result is shocking.[132] It shows that the Korean Church is not sufficiently concerned with outreach to this group. Fortunately, two representative denominations in the Korean Presbyterian Church have prepared pastoral guidelines for their inclusion in the sacraments. The Korean Presbyterian Church (Tonghap), following the example of the PCUSA, permits practice of sacrament among cognitively challenged persons under the guidance of the local church committee and with the parents' help. The Kosin Church affirms the possibility of baptism for cognitively challenged persons, but has not dealt with the matter of full participation in the Lord's Supper.

The Tonghap Church, published the denominational document "Guidelines for Baptism of the Mentally Handicapped" in 2005, a fresh impression for the Korean Church. It was very much a first step and did not explore deep theological reflections, but was enough to assert the necessity of baptism for the mentally handicapped. Also, in 2009, the Korean Handicapped Ministry Institute, supported by the Sarang Presbyterian Church (Hapdong), published "Guidelines for Sacraments for the Developmentally Handicapped" written for church leaders, teachers, and the parents of children with cognitive challenges on the potential of these persons to communicate with nonverbal methods and have knowledge of Bible basics.[133] It suggests three ways to include the cognitively challenged in the sacraments. One is for cognitively challenged persons who can communicate verbally, and involves several sample questions for assessing and helping their profession of faith. The second is for people who need non-verbal methods to communicate, and includes pictures that portray God, Jesus, and the church. By pointing to the pictures, or using true/false questions, church leaders and parents can assess faith. Using pictures or other multimedia can be an alternative for the non-verbal and a way to honor their traits. The third is for those who are severely cognitively challenged, and permits parents, who know the religious mind and faith of their child more than anyone else, to communicate and confess faith for their child. This does not undermine the importance of personal confession, but considers special circumstances.

Another South Korean denomination, Kosin, one of the most conservative Protestant denominations in the nation, is trying to make a denominational report on baptism of the mentally handicapped.[134] Although the Kosin Church emphasizes a believer's confession based on Reformed

---

132. Kim, *Cognitively Challenged*.

133. Kim, *Developmentally Handicapped*.

134. Korean Theological Seminary Faculty, "Baptism for Cognitively Challenged," 180–86.

theology, it also affirms the possibility of baptism based on covenant theology. They cautiously consider baptism for cognitively challenged persons similar to their perspective on infant baptism. According to their logic, even though baptism itself cannot be considered as *ex opere operato*, it can be based on the confession of parents and the church community; similarly, those who are cognitively challenged can also receive baptism, considering God's sovereignty.

Although the various Korean denominations have begun to feel the necessity of including persons with cognitive challenges in public worship, there have been few theological documents supporting the possibility of sacraments for this group of people.

The Korean Presbyterian Church's Sunday school has experienced enormous growth. The KPC has systematized education by considering the developmental abilities of the participants and presenting content that surpasses culture; this has impacted the church itself and the larger Korean society.[135] Students born into non-Christian families have merged well into Sunday School as their families join the church.[136]

However, this Sunday school unwittingly separates children from public worship with adults, and deprives them of important opportunities and experiences.[137] Baptized children are confirmed around fourteen, and can then join the Lord's Table. However, participation in public worship has not been emphasized by either parents or the church; moreover, much Korean public worship is preaching-centric and does not focus on the Lord's Supper.[138] Many people consider the Sunday public worship for mature adults, believing that children should remain in Sunday school until their college years.

Among the representative denominations in the Korean Presbyterian Church—Hapdong, Tonghap, and Kosin—each has their own stance on confession and participation. Hapdong does not mention participation of children in public worship. They uphold infant baptism and permit confirmation after the age of fourteen; for non-baptized adults, only a public profession of faith is required.[139] Those who cannot understand doctrine cannot participate in the Lord's Supper.[140] According to their logic, chil-

---

135. Kang, "Christian Education in Korea," 323.

136. Ko, "Crisis and Task," 350.

137. Ibid., 354–55.

138. Kim, *Church and Worship*, 74.

139. The General Assembly of the Presbyterian Church in Korea (Hapdong), *Constitution*, 199, 252.

140. The Presbyterian Church of Korea (Tonghap), *Constitution*, 254.

dren and the cognitively challenged are excluded from the Lord's Supper on principle.

On the other hand, Tonghap does not directly mention participation of children in public worship, but insists that Sunday school be understood as worship in the church community; children should participate in public worship as soon as they possibly can.[141] Kosin stipulates that from middle-school-age on, students should participate in Sunday public worship. For elementary-school-age children, an elder or pastor should lead a separate worship.[142] However, these children's participation in public worship depends on the parents' decision or the senior pastor's ministry philosophy. Participation of cognitively challenged persons in public worship depends on the local church's situation, but generally, churches who have the help of volunteers and a minister will have a separate worship service. Separate worship and sacramental participation results in a lack of concern for cognitively challenged church members, and unwittingly hampers the opportunity to learn through participation and experience.

SUMMARY OF RESEARCH: WHAT DOES IT SHOW?

Recently, there has been positive movement in the Korean and North American churches based on the studies of scholars such as John Swinton, Brett Webb-Mitchell, Amos Yong and others regarding the potential for cognitively challenged people to participate in the congregation and the role of community in developing faith.[143] Webb-Mitchell draws on his extensive experience with cognitively challenged persons to offer assurance about the possibility of rich faith development among them. He insists that an enculturation model of education, rather than a schooling model, can be more effective for both children and those who are cognitively challenged. By participating in the faith community, persons of varied ages and cognitive abilities can learn Christly gestures; through liturgical participation, people can learn the Christian faith, and Christian character can be developed, as practice and acting contribute to the development of *phronesis*.[144] According to Webb-Mitchell, "liturgy is the best place to integrate those who are

---

141. Ibid., 387.

142. The General Assembly of Presbyterian Church in Korea (Kosin), *Constitution*, 253.

143. Webb-Mitchell, *Christly Gestures*; Yong, *Theology and Down Syndrome*; Eiesland, *Disabled God*; Swinton, *Critical Reflections*.

144. See Webb-Mitchell, *Christly Gestures*, 172.

mentally retarded into the life of faith communities."[145] Because ritual and liturgy do not depend on human intellect, they make it possible for these people to know God.[146] Webb-Mitchell insists on the necessity of full participation in the sacraments, because people can learn while experiencing and participating in these activities; "one needs to be engaged by celebration of the sacraments before one can understand them."[147] Refuting the idea that intellect is a necessary element for participation in the sacrament, Webb asserts that "nowhere in scriptures is it written that one has to be able to do certain things in order to worship God, or that one must have a specific IQ ... God's banquet table is big enough for all who were invited to sit at it and enjoy the meal."[148]

Amos Yong insists that people with disabilities are made in the image of God, and hence, non-disabled people must see them without bias and prejudice.[149] He writes that "disabilities are not necessarily evil or blemishes to be eliminated."[150] His intention is to retrieve the meaning of weakness and inclusive ecclesiology through studying biblical texts. He explores "how people with the full range of physical and cognitive disabilities can participate in the catechisms, sacraments, and liturgies of the church."[151] According to him, the "Holy Spirit creatively empowers our full humanity in relationship to our embodied selves, to others, and to God, even in the most ambiguous and challenging of situations."[152] The work of the Holy Spirit can be the most important reason to welcome the cognitively challenged into worship. Yong also notes that "the soul remains in relationship with God even when our brains deteriorate and our minds are lost."[153]

John Swinton develops his thoughts on disability with the concept of friendship. Criticizing the Aristotelian concept of friendship, Swinton insists that the church should show fellowship with the disabled just as Jesus showed fellowship to all the people he met.[154] The church has often connected "spirituality" with "cognition."[155] But Swinton insists that, as God

---

145. Webb-Mitchell, *Dancing with Disabilities*, 7.
146. Ibid., 8.
147. Ibid.
148. Webb-Mitchell, *God Plays Piano*, 46.
149. Yong, *Bible, Disability, and the Church*, 13.
150. Ibid.
151. Yong, *Theology and Down Syndrome*, 17.
152. Ibid., 191.
153. Ibid., 190.
154. Swinton, *Resurrecting the Person*, 45–47.
155. Swinton, *From Bedlam to Shalom*, 1.

revealed himself through incarnation and accommodation, not through abstract ideas, God "accommodates Himself in the communication of love to people with profound learning difficulties through the loving relationships of friendship."[156] Since God shows grace to human beings before "any potential response," it is necessary to include persons who are cognitively challenged in the church community.[157] Although Swinton uses qualitative research methods while observing and spending time with cognitively challenged persons, he considers them not merely "objects of research," but "subjects and co-researchers."[158] From empirical research, he concludes that religious ability and learning is possible for the cognitively challenged.[159]

SUMMARY AND ASSESSMENT OF PRACTICES AND IMPLICATIONS

While researching representative Korean and American Presbyterian and Reformed denominational documents, I found most churches have given consideration to the inclusion of children in public worship, but many are reluctant to permit full inclusion, placing limitations on participation in the Lord's Supper. And while children have often been the subject of discussion and decisions, cognitively challenged people have not been the subject of much concern in these denominations until recently. The creation of separate worship services for these two groups has been one way to address the unique developmental abilities of these persons. One of most important reasons cited for these separate services is belief that a certain degree of cognition is needed to participate truly and faithfully. Of course, understanding and cognition are essential factors, but cognitive agreement is not directly connected to a faithful relationship with God. Overemphasizing cognitive ability and considering childhood merely a period of preparation deprives children and cognitively challenged individuals of the experience of the sacraments and public worship. A separate worship environment does not equip parents to nurture the spiritual development of their children. If there is no frequent family worship at home, the separation between adults, children, and the cognitively challenged exists until graduation from Sunday school, and unfamiliarity between the generations is only deepened. Public worship should include people of every generation, age, and ability while being mindful of balancing the additional needs of special groups.

156. Ibid.
157. Ibid., 31.
158. Swinton and Mowat, *Practical Theology*, 228.
159. Ibid., 230.

5

Cognitive Ability and Religious Concepts

The most important reason adults often do not permit children and cognitively challenged individuals to participate in public worship and the Lord's Supper is their distrust in the cognitive ability and understanding of these two groups. In general, because children and the cognitively challenged may not be able to understand the Bible stories and confessions the same way adults do, it is often believed that they cannot participate in the worship meaningfully, and that they may disrupt the piety and calm mood of public worship.[1] So, there are two important problems in studying "the

---

1. In this section, I set an age boundary for children and the cognitively challenged from two to eleven. This is difficult to do when studying the relation between cognition and religious concepts, because each person has a different potential and their process of development is different. Even though Fowler and Erikson developed the stages of faith and human development, they did not specify an age period. Therefore, I start from the Piagetian categorization of development. According to Barbel Inhelder, the mildly handicapped can develop until Piaget's "concrete operational period," or seven to eleven years. The severely handicapped cannot "outgrow the sensory-motor compositions (previous to language)." Inhelder, *Diagnosis of Reasoning*, 293. Therefore, in case of cognition, the mildly cognitively challenged child's development can keep up with the average child's until around the age eleven, even though they need more help. Also, in the case of the severely handicapped, even though the Piagetan theory finds their development to halt around two years old, I will show that even though they often have low verbal ability, they also have religious ability and the possibility of using alternative communicational methods. I believe that from ages two to eleven, children and the cognitively challenged can be studied at the same time, while recognizing and honoring their differences.

growth of knowledge" among children. The "impossibility of sloughing off adult modes of thought in trying to get into the child's mind; another is what is indeed perhaps the absolute impossibility of giving anything like a complete account of child thought in adult terms"[2] contributes to an adult-centric perspective.

While the cognition of children and persons who are cognitively challenged may not be as mature or as fully developed as that of adults without cognitive limitations, both groups may well have their own systems of logic and understanding. After all, adults develop understanding from their own early childhood experiences. Experience is equally necessary for children and the cognitively challenged.

As Ivy Beckwith points out, "if we are to minister to . . . children and their families, we have to understand their way of thinking and change our ways of doing things."[3] Generally, theologians and seminary-trained pastors study this matter only with respect to systematic and biblical theology. These approaches are important, but the Bible does not give direct guidelines for worship and sacrament for children and the cognitively challenged, or for anyone else.[4] We must learn from educational and psychological perspectives to understand their capacity for faithful expression and religious understanding.

THE RELATIONSHIP BETWEEN COGNITIVE ABILITY AND RELIGIOUS CONCEPTS

Is a high level of cognitive ability necessary to grasp a religious concept? Of course, to have a deep, complex understanding of religion, the answer is yes. The faith development of children is related to intellectual development.[5] Two studies on the understanding of the image of God according to age show that even though young children can know God, they need time to develop a more delicate and biblical concept of God.[6] But there is more to

---

2. Hamlyn, *Experience*, 91.
3. Beckwith, *Postmodern Children's Ministry*, 29.
4. Yong, *Theology and Down Syndrome*, 21.
5. Beckwith, *Postmodern Children's Ministry*, 51.
6. Rizzuto says, "The first conscious God representations appear between the ages of two and three." Rizzuto, *Birth of the Living God*, 178. In early childhood, parents, grandparents, kinderschool, and environment have a great impact on the image of God. Grün, *Kinder Fragen nach Gott*, 171–72. Therefore, "interpersonal experience causes the build-up of a richness of images." See St. Clair, *Human Relationships*, 7. St. Clair insists, "The child's experiences of relationships that generate image of self and others begin with the parents and end with the child's creation of an inner representation of

forming faith and religious concepts than reason and intellect.[7] Humans cannot explain it, but God's grace governs origin and maturation of faith. This grace may work through actions, messages, music, or participation.

Let us think about the doxology. It is not an objective article, but the subjective character of response from an individual who sees the glory of God in the worship.[8] As LaCugna points out, "doxology affirms God as the object of our praise. But doxology also accedes to the greater reality of God where self is let go in the process. In the gesture of praise, preoccupation with how well our speech is or is not doing is relinquished; God is given the glory."[9] To meet God in worship transcends human cognition. As Yust defines it, "faith is not a set of beliefs; nor is it a well-developed cognitive understanding of all things spiritual. It is an act of grace in which God chooses to be in relationship with humanity."[10] Faith does not equal understanding. If faith is restricted to the dimension of "cognitive understanding," then the status of any individual's faith would be determined by that person's intellectual ability and amount of biblical knowledge.[11] But if grace is emphasized, it makes it apparent that children are "fully religious beings from birth."[12] Therefore, Yust says, "Receiving faith becomes something different from acquiring a particular understanding of who God is or what God is doing in the world. Instead, God's gracious gift of faith comes to us and to our

---

the divinity long before the child becomes exposed to institutional aspects of religion." See Ibid., 11. According to him, "children bring their own God, the one each has assembled, to this official religion, which encounter really only occurs after the image of God has been formed. Now the God of official religion and the God of the child face with other and, through the child's reshaping and rethinking, there is a blending and a second birth of God." Ibid., 23.

7. As Krych points out, it is evident that God's people contain an intelligence factor. I do not downplay the role of human cognition in the process of faith formation. While being careful not to reduce the Gospel to an intellectual thesis, I want to focus on the dynamic of religious experience. See Krych, *Teaching the Gospel Today*, 16.

8. It is important to note Berryman's point: "Studies of theological cognition cannot be controlled in the way that studies about knowledge of the natural world can be controlled," because "in the theological cognition God is the ultimate variable." See Berrymann, *Godly Play*, 58.

9. LaCugna, *God for Us*, 361.

10. Yust, *Real Kids, Real Faith*, 4.

11. Downs says, "Unfortunately, Christianity experienced a highly 'scholastic' period when faith was reduced to a series of intricate theological philosophical propositions that were to be memorized, mastered, and argued." Downs, *Teaching for Spiritual Growth*, 59.

12. Yust, *Real Kids, Real Faith*, 6.

children through all our senses and experiences."[13] This transcends cognition and personal understanding.

How can it be proved that intelligence and cognitive ability are in fact needed in the formation of religious concept, but not exclusively? Studying cognitively challenged children has shown that religious experience can overcome limitations in intelligence and cognition. An IQ score does not tell us enough about religious mind and possibility. In fact, IQ tests do not evaluate the various layers of children's intelligence, but only their language and logical abilities.[14] According to May Beirne-Smith, James Patton, and Shannon Kim, "Binet himself was concerned that the instrument that he helped develop might be misused."[15] Binet's test mainly focused on showing lack of intelligence, which could be misconstrued as a signal of inferiority, and does not show the difference between ordinary people and cognitively challenged people's character of cognition.[16] Furthermore, the tests can be inaccurate, and it is difficult to determine what score should be considered "normal." James Flynn and Keith Widaman say that "a group only average on the 1972 norms (with a mean of 100) would score at about 107.50 on the 1947–1948 norms, for a rate of gain of 0.3 points per year (7.50 divided by 25 years = 0.3). This means that the IQ an individual receives is like a lottery, with the outcome dependent on when he or she was tested, what test was administered, and in what year that test was normed."[17] A person's IQ can also change according to circumstances and maturity.[18] Furthermore, the test undervalues the ability for achievement among cognitively challenged persons.[19] They may have difficulty in traditional school systems, but outside school they often show strong ability for adaptation.[20] For example, Cromer reports some cases in which children demonstrated having "quite complex language" and syntax structure despite having what was considered low intelligence.[21]

With respect to IQ scores, even children categorized as moderately or severely sub-normal or cognitively challenged can become accustomed

---

13. Ibid.

14. Gardner, *Frames of Mind*, 337.

15. Beirne-Smith, et al., *Mental Retardation*, 14.

16. Baumeister, "Methodological and Conceptual Issues," 2. Also, this cannot measure their "capacity" or "potential." Tylenda, et al., "Assessing Mental Retardation," 34.

17. Flynn and Widaman, "Flynn Effect," 123.

18. Tylenda, et al., "Assessing Mental Retardation," 34. Therefore, Tylenda insists on the necessity of frequent and various sorts of examinations. Ibid., 39.

19. Rosenberg and Abbeduto, *Language and Communication*, 14.

20. Baumeister, "Methodological and Conceptual Issues," 16.

21. Cromer, "Differentiating Language and Cognition," 114.

to ordinary life. Many can speak and perform everyday activities, and can learn and have relationships with others based on "common interests."[22] When testing cognitively challenged children, a multi-lateral approach that accounts for environment and lifestyle should be considered.[23] Many elements constitute an individual's level of cognitive functioning. A person may have a particular limitation, but they may have strong points in other realms.[24] Whenever we are dealing with and educating the cognitively challenged, we must observe them for a long time to estimate their potential for further development. James Flynn notes,

> The criterion of an IQ of 70 or below has no intrinsic rationale. Its selection is probably best thought of as an implicit agreement between professionals and policy makers that only a relatively small percentage of persons who exhibit the most extreme impairment on tests of intelligence ought to receive services under the rubric of MR. Therefore, the criterion is more a matter of sociology and social engineering than a precise indicator of the level of impaired reasoning that persons with IQs of 70 or below exhibit. It is, of course, not an entirely arbitrary choice. It is also supposed to signal the likelihood of impaired adaptive behavior.[25]

Howard Gardner insists that intelligence is not restricted to the realm of logic, but consists of musical intelligence, bodily-kinesthetic intelligence, logical-mathematical intelligence, linguistic intelligence, spatial intelligence, interpersonal intelligence, intrapersonal intelligence, and naturalist intelligence.[26] Intelligence is dynamic and multilateral. Gardner clarifies his use of the term "intelligence" as follows: "Intelligences should be thought of as entities at a certain level of generality, broader than highly specific computational mechanisms while narrower than the most general capacities, like analysis, synthesis, or a sense of self."[27] His concept of intelligence tries to include the multi-dimensional aspects of intelligence and potential.

This important theory can help explain the possibility of including young children and the cognitively challenged in the public worship and the sacrament, which consist not only of God's Word, but also of other materials

22. Beirne-Smith, et al., *Mental Retardation*, 297.
23. Tylenda, et al., "Assessing Mental Retardation," 27–28.
24. Drew and Hardman, *Intellectual Disabilities*, 19–20; Tylenda et al., "Assessing Mental Retardation," 90.
25. Flynn and Widaman, "Flynn Effect," 128.
26. Gardner, *Multiple Intelligences*, 8–18.
27. Gardner, *Frames of Mind*, 72.

(for example, water, bread, and wine), music, artistic ornament, and bodily participation. According to the theory of multiple intelligences, the elements of the sacraments give stimulation to more types of intelligence than strictly the logical. And although the linguistic expression of children and those who are cognitively challenged may be limited, other sorts of intelligence, such as kinetic, musical, spatial, and interpersonal, still work in their brains and bodies. Adults should not underestimate a child's intelligence because of an inability to articulate conceptual understanding, but remember that a child's religious concept can be developed by music, movement, and encounter with other people.[28] As Jerome Berryman asserts, "The religious life of the child is to be respected."[29] Of course, children and adults have differences in their perception. As Krych says, "The child cannot analyze the human situation philosophically and theologically."[30] But this does not mean a child cannot "embrace with much depth the reality of connectedness and its impact in a specific situation."[31] Children can experience God's love and God's story when that love and that story are related to their experience and their own situation.[32]

According to Edward Robinson's research on children's religious experiences, some children have a profound experience at age four or five, and its impact lasts throughout life.[33] In his interviews, it is clear that religious experience from childhood remains with people throughout their lives. It is often assumed that very young children cannot benefit from participation in worship or the deeper aspects of religious practice. Robinson's research suggests that this is an important period in a person's faith formation, and that greater inclusion of children in the worship is important to both their faith formation and their cognitive development.

---

28. John Westerhoff says, "Our personal encounter with that ultimate mystery which is God is nurtured, expressed, and communicated through dance, music, drama, poetry, painting, sculpture, and film, through the stimulation of the imagination and our visual, oral, and kinetic senses." See Westerhoff, "Introduction," xii.

29. Berryman, *Godly Play*, 143. Beckwith says, "I believe the spiritual formation of the child begins at birth, at the very earliest (see Psalm 139)." Beckwith, *Postmodern Children's Ministry*, 44.

30. Krych, *Teaching the Gospel Today*, 78.

31. Champagne, "Children's Inner Voice," 379.

32. Krych, *Teaching the Gospel Today*, 78. Robert Coles shows that children can think theologically. Coles, *Spiritual Life of Children*.

33. Robinson, *Original Vision*, 32–33. However, we must also see Downs: "Children of three or four years of age may make some kind of commitment to Christ, which may or may not be a true salvation experience." See Downs, *Teaching for Spiritual Growth*, 215.

Gesell's studies uphold this thought; he points out that even five-year-olds can be aware of God's presence, sometimes even fearing that "he sees what they do."[34] He relates the story of a six-year-old who loves hearing Bible stories and participating in a kind of "mock" worship service.[35] Each person experiences a faith development differently, but even young children can have religious abilities, understanding, and religious sensitivity.

This ability to have experience faith and comprehend religious imagery is also possible for those who are cognitively challenged. David Hay and Rebecca Nye say,

> Stage theories have their uses. The major problem is their narrowness, coming near to dissolving religion into reason and therefore childhood spirituality into nothing more than a form of immaturity or inadequacy. If cognitive development is central, it also puts out of court the work of Henri Bissonnier, who writes about the profound spiritual awareness he has observed in people who are mentally deficient.[36]

Children and others who cannot fully express their thoughts do not necessarily lack religious conceptualization.[37] Reason and religious conceptualization have a close relationship, but we arrive at religious concepts via various methods and routes. As Westerhoff says, "Our knowledge of God is prior to our conceptualizations of God."[38] It is evident that children understand background objects and events. However, as Anselm Grün points out, their knowledge has a hole, and they compensate for it with images.[39] Shellie Levin also believes children use "metaphoric logic," a different kind of logic from adults .[40] Children acquire spirituality and religious concept by experience.[41]

34. Gesell, *Child from Five to Ten*, 78.

35. Ibid., 124.

36. Hay and Nye, *Spirit of the Child*, 57–58. Jaspard insists that ritual can be an important method for mediating spiritual awareness for the cognitively challenged. See Jaspard, "Comprehension of Religious Rituals."

37. Hay and Nye, *Spirit of the Child*, 60. Krych reports, "As early as five years of age, children respond therapeutically to transformational narrative." Krych, *Teaching the Gospel Today*, 78. That is to say, it is important to note the difference between adults' and children's methods of expression of faith. According to Yust, expression is impacted by "physical, cognitive emotional, and social development." Yust, *Real Kids, Real Faith*, 10.

38. Westerhoff, "Introduction," xii.

39. Grün, *Kinder Fragen nach Gott*, 103.

40. Levine, "Children's Cognition," 126.

41. Merleau-Ponty says, "Thus, contrary to the negative account, the child's consciousness is not identical to the adult's in everything except for its incompleteness

PROCESSES OF LEARNING AMONG CHILDREN AND PERSONS WHO ARE COGNITIVELY CHALLENGED

How do children and cognitively challenged persons learn, understand, and acquire knowledge? According to Barbel Inhelder's study, cognitively challenged children grow according to the same developmental stages and sequences as children without cognitive challenges; their ultimate stage depends on their individual degree of potential. Severely retarded children can reach sensorimotor stages, and mildly retarded children can develop until the "concrete operation" stage.[42] However, in contrast to this, Crane reports, "children with developmental disabilities have different, rather than simply delayed, development."[43] Children and the cognitively handicapped are not identical with respect to structure and processing information.[44]

These two representative approaches have been debated among scholars. First, the "developmental approach" does not see "substantive differences in cognitive functioning" between ordinary persons and persons who are mentally retarded.[45] But Edward Ziegler's studies found that when a person who is mentally retarded is raised in the "cultural-familial" environment, that person's cognitive level can be developed like that of an ordinary person.[46] Although the speed of development is slower, the "sequence of stages of cognitive development" will be the same.[47] Also, Weisz insists the difference in cognitive processing is related to "extracognitive factors" such as motivation, personality, and support from teachers, parents, classmates, and siblings.[48]

However, the "difference approach" sees "major deficits in cognitive functioning related to IQ" in persons with cognitive challenges.[49] According to this approach, a person who is mentally handicapped is qualitatively

---

and imperfection. The child processes another kind of equilibrium than the adult kind; therefore, we must treat the child's consciousness as a positive phenomenon." See Merleau-Ponty, *Child Psychology and Pedagogy*, 131.

42. Inhelder, *Diagnosis of Reasoning*, 285, 293. Regarding who supports this opinion, see Kail, "General Slowing of Information-Processing," 333–41; Ziegler, "Individual with Mental Retardation," 1–16; Tomporowski and Tinsley, "Effect of Target Probability," 688–703.

43. Crane, *Mental Retardation*, 32.

44. See Ellis and Dulaney, "Further Evidence," 613–21.

45. Cole, "Developmental Versus Difference," 379.

46. Ziegler, "Developmental Versus Difference," 551.

47. Ziegler, "Individual with Mental Retardation," 3.

48. Weisz, "Cultural-Familial Mental Retardation," 158–64.

49. Cole, "Developmental Versus Difference," 379.

different from one with ordinary mental capabilities.[50] Based on "slowing of information-processing," Robert Kail supports the difference approach, because it shows "the difference may be global rather than one that is specific to particular tasks."[51]

In fact, the cognition of mentally handicapped people is generally more rigid than that of more ordinary people, and utilization of learning strategy and is less rigid.[52] But this does not mean those with cognitive challenges have no potential to learn. Rather, it shows that new teaching strategies are needed. The developmental approach has merit in describing "how to help people with mental retardation to utilize their intellectual capacity optimally," even though it cannot be a perfect remedy.[53]

HOW DO CHILDREN LEARN?

Daniel Stern says, "During the first six months of life the infant begins to lay the foundation of one of his most highly developed areas of expertise, namely, 'reading' the signals and expressions of other people's behaviors."[54] Infants have remarkable perception and the ability to imitate.[55] Their cognitive development is closely related to language and relationships with other people.[56] According to Piaget and Inhelder, "The sensorimotor structures constitute the source of the later operations of thought"; logic comes from action.[57] Development proceeds through interaction between body and environment, and in this process, the basic patterns of thinking are formed.[58]

50. Tomporowski and Tinsley, "Effect of Target Probability," 689.
51. Kail, "General Slowing of Information-Processing," 333.
52. Ellis and Dulaney, "Further Evidence," 614.
53. Ziegler, "Individual with Mental Retardation," 12.
54. Stern, *First Relationship*, 40; Gardner says, "By the end of the first year of life, most children are always capable of mundane symbolization." Gardner, *Extraordinary Minds*, 20. He insists, "A history of the first year of life can also be written in terms of the initial operations of specific intelligence." Gardner, *Frames of Mind*, 320. Regarding the study of the cognitive potential of infants, see Spelke and Newport, "Nativism, Empiricism."
55. Bower, *Perceptual World of the Child*, 30–31.
56. Herzfeld, "Human and Artificial Intelligence," 123.
57. Piaget and Inhelder, *Psychology of the Child*, 28, 154–157. Meltoff and Brooks insist that infants get information through experience and observation, and that forms an "abstract framework." See Virji-Babul and Weeks, "Perception, Cognition, and Action," 161. Jerome Bruner says, "Nor is it surprising that they know as much as they do." See Bruner, *Acts of Meaning*, 83.
58. Dykstra, "Faith Development Issues," 78.

Hence, the "ontogenetic dimension" and "social dimension" of development are both important.[59]

Infants acquire new knowledge through imitation.[60] According to Piaget and Inhelder, "at the end of the sensorimotor period the child has acquired sufficient virtuosity in the mastery of the imitation thus generalized for deferred imitation to become possible."[61] Repetition plays a great role in gaining new knowledge. This has some implications for children's liturgical participation. Even children as young as six months are able to imitate; by imitating liturgical action, children are exposed to its encoded meaning. By repetition and weekly participation, children are more likely to grow in Christian understanding and memory. Above all, a child's potential to learn lies in their attitude of activeness and openness about learning. Scottie May, et al., say, "Three-, four-, and five-year-old children are on the move. They are looking for answers to their questions. They are learning to play and they are playing to learn."[62]

Even at the young age of two years, children can recognize causal relationships and draw independent conclusions.[63] And by three years, "children represent . . . routine activities in the form of scripts, which are knowledge structures that describe the way that events usually go."[64] Around the age of five, children recognize other people as having their own minds and opinions, and are able to quickly and routinely interpret new experiences on their own based on their own knowledge and past experience.[65]

This is not to say that because of their cognitive potential, children are mature in their thinking. Children at this stage do not grasp such things as irony and complex arguments.[66] Also, young children are generally unable to verbalize inner thoughts and feelings.[67] These points contribute to adults' mistrust of children's thinking and ability. It is therefore required to study the process of a child's learning in more detail.

One of the most important people to contribute to the theory of child cognitive development is Jean Piaget. According to him, "the

---

59. Piaget and Inhelder, *Psychology of the Child*, 157.
60. Siegler and Wagner Alibali, *Children's Thinking*, 5.
61. Piaget and Inhelder, *Psychology of the Child*, 56.
62. May, et al., *Children Matter*, 78.
63. Siegler and Alibali, *Children's Thinking*, 442.
64. Ibid., 260.
65. Gardner, *Extraordinary Minds*, 25.
66. Ibid., 23.
67. May, et al., *Children Matter*, 220. Therefore, it is difficult to confirm whether children understand a certain abstract concept or not. See Keely, "Worship and Faith Development," 36.

basic mechanisms that produce all cognitive changes are assimilation and accommodation."[68] He believes that what we call intelligence is in essence a balance or "equilibrium" between assimilation and accommodation.[69] Assimilation is defined as "the transformation of perceptions in such a way as to render them identical to one's own thought, that is to say, with prior schemes. To assimilate is therefore to conserve and in a certain sense to identify."[70] On the other hand, accommodation is "an activity; although the modification of assimilatory schemas is admittedly brought about by resistance of the objects, it is not simply dictated by the object but rather by the subject attempting to overcome this resistance."[71] The interaction between accommodation and assimilation results in intelligence. According to Piaget, intelligence is not fixed, but develops according to stages of development; yet, a person's "previous experience" and "social milieu" play an important role in "hastening or delaying the appearance of a stage."[72] This is important in relation to children's liturgical participation. Worship and sacrament can be the "social milieu" for helping develop faith formation among children and the cognitively challenged. Worship and sacrament are public, and construct a social worshiping community.

Piaget demonstrates that children's thinking is different from adults not only in quantity but also in quality. This is in line with the idea that children's thinking is categorically different from that of adults, not merely inferior to that of adults.[73] Piaget's studies give valuable information about children's stages of development, and the process of the development of human intelligence. However, they also have some weak points.

Piaget focuses on the limitations of preoperational-period children,[74] a period in which children have "symbolical function in its various forms: language, symbolic play."[75] Through experiencing the world around them, children build foundational "logical structures."[76] True independent logical thinking only becomes possible at about age seven.[77] Before this stage,

---

68. Siegler and Alibali, *Children's Thinking*, 9.
69. Piaget and Inhelder, *Psychology of the Child*, 58.
70. Inhelder, *Diagnosis of Reasoning*, 31.
71. Ibid., 31.
72. Ibid.
73. Schweitzer, *Lebensgeschichte und Religion*, 38; Downs, *Teaching for Spiritual Growth*, 82.
74. Crain, *Theories of Development*, 150.
75. Piaget, *Child and Reality*, 57.
76. Ibid., 94.
77. Ibid., 58.

children are given a large amount of information, but they do not know it until they develop sufficiently.[78] Young children and the cognitively challenged are categorized in this pre-operational developmental stage that lacks logical thinking and understanding, in addition to being characterized by egocentric tendencies; because of this, he insists that they cannot attain a level of thinking comparable to that of an adult. However, as Siegler and Alibali point out, this may not be entirely accurate. "There seems little doubt that young children often behave more egocentrically than older ones. Labeling an age group "egocentric" is too strong, though."[79] However, children develop a sense of the numinous through role-play; by participation, children can not only experience social relationships and development, but also acquire religious understanding that, while not matching that of adults, is valuable in and of itself.

This is supported by Erik Erikson's work. His concept of "basic trust" and "ritualization" can be an alternative to the weak points of Piagetian theory. Erikson considers development a life-long process, with each stage having its own value.[80]

He thinks basic trust starts from the relationship with the mother, as the origin of faith and hope. In a trustful relationship with the caregiver, "by face and by name," the "mutuality of recognition" is developed.[81] This trust can be an important foundation for development in religious development as well. As times goes on, through "ritualizations of everyday life," learning is periodically strengthened by participation in the community, and a person learns right from wrong.[82] Eventually, everyday ritual engenders "formation of a set of behavior patterns."[83] Children come to use "cognitive patterns" and exercise personal judgment.[84]

Erikson proposes eight steps of ritualization. The first stage starts from infancy, when the infant experiences a sense of the numinous and first experiences transcendence. This early experience is absorbed into the personality and renewed in later stages. At this time, the child is also learning basic

---

78. Piaget, *Construction of Reality*, 357. Regarding some critics who point out that Piaget portrays children in a disproportionately negative light, Piaget insists that young childhood has affirmative factors in the development of stages. See Piaget, "Piaget's Theory," 705–06.

79. Siegler and Alibali, *Children's Thinking*, 61. Jerome Bruner has the same opinion. See Bruner, *Actual Minds*, 109.

80. Erikson, *Identity*, 94.

81. Erikson, *Toys and Reasons*, 87.

82. Ibid., 77–78.

83. Ibid., 81.

84. Ibid., 82–83.

trust, an important lesson in how to live and believe. Ritualization bridges personal development and social development; children are shaped socially and ethically.[85] And children do not learn these foundational principles only after fully developing logical ability.[86]

Erickson helps us to see that children have more potential than Piaget believed, and that their learning and thinking can be enhanced with the help of various sorts of teaching methods.[87] It does not signify a lack of reasoning itself when children cannot explain their reasoning with verbal methods and logic.[88] Children—and, in some cases, cognitively challenged individuals—can understand at any developmental stage if the teacher uses the proper method.[89] This recalls Gardner's multiple intelligences—a child who cannot understand a difficult topic through words alone may understand according to their potential through visual or aural methods or bodily movements.

Piaget's and Bruner's opinions have been debated, and a clear conclusion is difficult. As Perry Downs points out, it is certain that "concrete learning is necessary for later abstract thinking," and that children can understand the abstract to some extent if the teacher uses a concrete method.[90] They may not have the same abstract-thinking ability as an adult, but it cannot be said that they do not have any ability. Therefore, Piaget's idea that abstract thinking appears only after structural development is too limited a view.[91] As Sousa notes, "emotional attention comes before cognitive recognition."[92] Emotional response can come prior to cognitive function, so that trust and religious affection can be experienced independently from abstract learning and memory.

HOW DO THE COGNITIVELY CHALLENGED LEARN?

There are many types of cognitively challenged persons, all with unique and individual degrees of personal development, and all living in different environments. It is not easy to generalize learning and development among them. They have both limitations and great possibilities at the same time.

85. Erikson, *Dimensions of New Identity*, 105.
86. Erikson, *Identity: Youth and Crisis*, 103.
87. Siegler and Alibali, *Children's Thinking*, 60.
88. Ibid., 55.
89. Bruner, *Process of Education*, 33.
90. Downs, *Teaching for Spiritual Growth*, 91–92.
91. Hamlyn, *Experience and the Growth*, 139.
92. Sousa, *Special Needs Brain*, 160.

First, we must examine the limits of the cognitively challenged in learning and cognitive ability.[93] Jerome Bruner points out that the autism spectrum child has a lack of understanding of narrative or story.[94] Laura Hall points out that "students with autism spectrum disorders have difficulty generalizing new skills to new context."[95] People with severe intellectual disabilities have difficulty learning new functions and applications to real life.[96] The delay in the development of language also makes it more difficult to learn new information.[97] Cognitively challenged persons need more time to learn new semantic form, and have difficulty following new sentences.[98] They also often have difficulty concentrating.[99] They sometimes have trouble with systematic learning, and learn instead by imitation and incidental learning: "Individuals with severe disabilities have limited ability to synthesize information and skills in an organized, useful way and may fail to see the relationships among bits of information."[100] Campione and Brown point out, "Even when training results in enhanced performance, there are problems in themes of maintenance and generalization of the strategy."[101]

Nevertheless, many studies show that the cognitively challenged can learn and have possibilities for development. According to Vygotsky, mental retardation has been seen as a research object or set of symptoms to be cured.[102] He believes it should instead be considered "a process."[103] He insists that "the mentally retarded child does not consist of gaps and defects alone; his organism as a whole is restructured. The personality as a whole is balanced out and compensated for by the child's developmental processes."[104] He argues for the similarity between children's and cognitively challenged

---

93. Taylor, et al., *Mental Retardation*, 150.

94. Bruner, *Culture of Education*, 177.

95. See Hall, *Autism Spectrum Disorders*, 85.

96. Beirne-Smith, et al., *Introduction to Intellectual Disabilities*, 298.

97. Therefore, as Abbeduto insists, it is certain that linguistic communication has close relationship with intelligence factor. Rosenberg and Abbeduto, *Language and Communication*, 8.

98. "The ability of Down's children to understand speech is much closer to normal than is their ability to speak themselves." See Edgerton, *Mental Retardation*, 26.

99. Taylor, et al., *Mental Retardation*, 172. Regarding deficiency of concentration and the matter of "long-term deficiencies in intellectual development" in children with Down's Syndrome, see Landy, et al., "Responsive Parenting," 31, 33.

100. Taylor et al., *Mental Retardation*, 172.

101. Campione and Brown, "Memory and Metamemory Development," 402.

102. Vygotsky, *Collected Works*, 2:122.

103. Ibid.

104. Ibid., 125.

persons' development, and believes the development of cognitively challenged children is closely related to "cultural development."[105] Interaction with others and the environment is essential; development is related to the use of function, not strictly to structure. Experience and practice are essential for development, and the cognitively challenged need more experiential opportunities to learn effectively.

The cognitively challenged person also has strategies for memory and learning. Kwong's research found that a mildly mentally handicapped adolescent used learning strategy and metacognition for memory.[106] Systematic teaching and support can improve their ability to learn and understand complex ideas.[107]

Those with "moderate mental retardation" can also develop their learning ability. Barbara Tylenda, Jacqueline Beckett, and Rowland P. Barrett say, "With the support of specific education services, individuals in this category may acquire academic skills similar to a second- to fourth-grade student, usually by the period of late adolescence."[108] Developmental speed and ultimate functional status is relatively low, but cognitive development among this group is similar to that of an ordinary young child.[109]

Persons who are mildly mentally retarded are distinctly different from those who are moderately and severely mentally retarded, especially "in the nature of their problems in adaptation, which are the outward manifestation of their intellectual impairment."[110] Even though these groups have impaired cognitive ability in common, their degrees of adaptation and expression are different and should be considered. Though not universally successful, more repetition is necessary for moderately cognitively challenged persons' development and achievement than for mildly cognitively

---

105. Ibid., 133.

106. Kwong, "Memory Strategy," 122–28. "Metacognition refers to one's ability to understand not only how one thinks or learns, but also to understanding one's limitations and strengths relative to knowing." Boutot and Myles, *Autism Spectrum Disorders*, 26.

107. Taylor et al., *Mental Retardation*, 171. The number of mildly mentally retarded people is estimated to be 85 percent of the mentally handicapped population, and I. Q. ranges are 55–70. Tylenda, et al., "Assessing Mental Retardation," 31.

108. Ibid., 33. Also see Taylor et al., *Mental Retardation*, 171; Edgerton, *Mental Retardation*, 27.

109. "According to the results of a study by Sperber, Davies, Merill, and McCauley (1982), differences in such processing between mildly mentally retarded and non-disabled persons tend to disappear on lexical-semantic tasks when such persons are matched on MA (Wechsler Scale or Stanford-Binet)." Rosenberg and Abbeduto, *Language and Communication*, 74.

110. MacMillan, et al., "Children with Mild Mental Retardation," 210.

challenged persons.[111] June Downing notes that, "although non-readers, ... [moderately challenged] students were able to gain literacy skills, such as opening a book, pointing to text, responding to comprehension questions, learning new vocabulary, turning pages in the book, and identifying initial sounds of words."[112] Even with slower communication and developmental speed, enrichment and development are possible.

There are many examples that show the potential of cognitively challenged individuals to adapt to ordinary life, sometimes through artistic types of expression:

> "The mentally deficient," [Volmat] writes, "draw clumsily and with difficulty, but they are sometimes capable of delightful works, akin to the popular arts, in striking contrast with their weak mental level, and their lack of other means of expression. Thus, the case presented in No. 45 shows a striking contrast between the deep mental backwardness and the plastic quality of the paintings. We have published (1952) three observations of mentally defective artists. Two of these were original works: harmony and play of colors, sense of constructing a scene, and of the marvelous, richness of ornamentation."[113]

Brett Webb-Mitchell also discusses the artistic gifts of the cognitively challenged, such as art, music, and dance.[114] It is not uncommon for cognitively challenged individuals to show musical talent. Henri Bissonnier says, "Rhythm, sometimes difficult to acquire, can often be manifested as very faithful. Creativeness here is not without variety and originality. Tiring quickly is generally a common feature, but the mental deficient is capable of persevering to the end of his or her powers."[115] Even without fully developed language skills, a person with cognitive challenges can still communicate emotion and will. This is of critical importance. Cognitively handicapped individuals may have trouble with linguistic communication, but it does not signify inability to communicate; they communicate with other sorts of methods.[116] About these methods, Bissonier says, "The paths of thought and

---

111. Downing, *Academic Instruction*, 21.

112. Ibid., 19. Cf. Browder, et al., "Training Teachers," 206–19. "Studies have provided strong evidence that language and cognition thought are separated in the brain." See Sousa, *Special Needs Brain*, 75.

113. Bissonnier, "Religious Expression," 146. "Individuals with ASD are visual learners." Hall, *Autism Spectrum Disorders*, 153.

114. Webb-Mitchell, *Beyond Accessibility*, 45–48.

115. Bissonnier, "Religious Expression," 147.

116. Boutot and Myles, *Autism Spectrum Disorders*, 16, 22. "Research by D. R. Price-Williams says individuals may be capable of participating in well-structured,

speech being difficult for them, gesture, colour, music, being of more intuitive and affective order, would be all the more used by them to enter into contact with others, within the measure that this desire for communication has been aroused."[117] People who surround the cognitively handicapped should have patience, and try to understand and communicate with them using various non-verbal methods.

Mary Fulkerson says, "Individuals with severe disabilities communicate (like infants) at the presymbolic (perlocutionary) level and can communicate with other people."[118] Even those who cannot speak have the ability to communicate meaningfully, using different methods of non-verbal communication at different speeds. Sheldon Rosenberg and Leonard Abbeduto say, "A number of studies revealed that persons with mental retardation are able to utilize their knowledge of word relatedness in word-recognition tasks, although more slowly than nondisabled persons."[119] And cognitively challenged individuals can communicate and gain knowledge, even if it is not concise or logical.[120] For example, children with autism sometimes display echolalia, which "was once thought to be nonfunctional; however, it is now recognized that echolalia may in fact be the child's way of speaking."[121] Despite developmental disadvantages in their thinking and expression, persons with cognitive challenges learn about the relationship between themselves and a listener in the process of decision-making in order to express themselves.[122] Being with other people is an opportunity to exercise how to think, communicate, and learn—so it is crucial to permit these opportunities and to understand what makes each individual unique. Even cognitively challenged individuals categorized in the same ability level may have very different development in areas such as speech and language.[123] It is necessary to spend time with them and directly observe their behavior patterns

---

successful communicative interactions, in spite of their articulatory deficit. Their study also suggests that learning sign language may be of particular benefit for individuals with severe speech problems." Edgerton, *Mental Retardation*, 28.

117. Bissonnier, "Religious Expression," 147. To Vygotsky, drawing is "a unique graphic speech, a graphic story about something . . . more speech than representation." Vygotsky, *Higher Mental Functions*, 138.

118. Fulkerson, *Places of Redemption*, 41.

119. Rosenberg and Abbeduto, *Language and Communication*, 79. Amos Yong insists that even though children and Down Syndrome children have trouble delivering abstract concepts, it is possible to use communication methods in practice. Yong, *Theology and Down Syndrome*, 69.

120. Rosenberg and Abbeduto, *Language and Communication*, 162.

121. Boutot and Myles, *Autism Spectrum Disorders*, 16.

122. Rosenberg and Abbeduto, *Language and Communication*, 147.

123. Beirne-Smith, et al., *Mental Retardation*, 301.

in order to understand them, and to "take seriously the importance of the fragments of truth that [these cognitively challenged] people offer."[124]

Cognitively challenged people learn through various methods—not only traditional lecturing, but visual and tactile media and cooperative learning with others. In a study of people with Down syndrome, Von Hofsten has shown that visual information is the most dominant sensory input between the ages of 5 and 6; integration of visual, tactile, and proprioceptive information occurs some time after the age of 8.[125] Carmeli and Carmeli report that visual media are often more effective than auditory for the cognitively handicapped.[126] In light of this, the most important task is to set a curriculum that considers the character of the cognitively challenged student, and to provide a special educator who can help the student proceed while controlling the level of difficulty. As Crane writes, "Those with MR [mental retardation] usually do not use memory strategies spontaneously."[127] Sometimes, cognitively challenged students are reluctant to ask questions, because they know how they are perceived.[128] However, "when they are taught specific strategy use, their memory performance does improve."[129] Krupski points out that "individuals with mental retardation might also attend to the person presenting a task or stimulus rather than to the cues in the specific stimulus or task."[130] A qualified teacher can increase attention level of the learner by incorporating novelty and other methods.[131]

Cognitively challenged persons also have potential to develop in the community. Vygotsky explains the idea of the Zone of Proximal Development as "the distance between the actual developmental level as determined by independent problem solving and the level of potential development as determined through problem solving under adult guidance in collaboration with more capable peers."[132] A student's mental development may vary to a high degree according to the teacher's guidance. Through "interacting with people in the environment," internal developmental processes are awakened; if this process is internalized, it can "become part of the child's independent

---

124. Swinton and Mowat, *Practical Theology*, 239–240.
125. Virji-Babul and Weeks, "Perception, Cognition, and Action," 154.
126. Carmeli and Carmeli, "Teaching Jewish Mentally-Retarded," 124.
127. Crane, *Community Integration Approach*, 136.
128. Ibid., 135.
129. Crane, *Community Integration Approach*, 136.
130. Taylor et al., *Mental Retardation*, 154.
131. See Zeaman and House, "Role of Attention," 159–223.
132. Vygotsky, *Mind in Society*, 86.

Cognitive Ability and Religious Concepts 141

developmental achievement."[133] Vygotsky insists that "what a child can do with assistance today, she will be able to do by herself tomorrow."[134] Learning helps mental development; learning is not development itself.[135] In the same vein, Vygotsky writes:

> A teaching system based solely on concreteness—one that eliminated from teaching everything associated with abstract thinking—not only failed to help retarded children overcome their innate handicaps but also reinforced their handicaps by accustoming children exclusively to concrete thinking and thus suppressing the rudiments of any abstract thought that such children still have.[136]

A school or community should endeavor to help those with cognitive disabilities think and act by themselves and to develop deficient areas, rather than merely making them imitate and repeat.[137] This can be applied to the matter of worship. Due to the impact of developmentalists such as Piaget, people tend to think that children or cognitively challenged individuals cannot know or experience beyond their stage of development. But liturgical participation can do more. By participation and interaction with other believers in the church community, children and the cognitively challenged can have experience beyond their limitations. It is beneficial for them to belong to a peer group or integrative class, so that they can have as many experiences as possible with other people.

Based on this, it's clear we should nurture cognitively challenged church members systematically from an early age and help them overcome learned helplessness, which is often related to "repeated criticism and low expectations."[138] When a teacher or parent points out and encourages their

---

133. Ibid., 90.

134. Ibid., 87. "The ZPD is not limitless; a child cannot always be taught any given thing at any given time. Assisted performance is the maximum level at which a child can perform today. Children cannot be taught skills or behaviors that exceed their ZPD." Bodrova and Leong, *Tools of the Mind*, 43.

135. Vygotsky, *Mind in Society*, 90.

136. Ibid., 89.

137. Vygotsky, *Collected Works*, 2:131–33. However, this does not identify the necessity of using concrete objects in the learning process. "Students with severe cognitive impairments or who have poor memory, or who do not understand abstract symbols may need to use systems that are constant in visual or auditory form." Hall, *Autism Spectrum Disorders*, 186.

138. "Individuals with MR may also look to adults to see what to do, even in situations where they know the correct behavior." Crane, *Community Integration Approach*, 132. Therefore, excessive intervention should be avoided. Downing, *Academic Instruction*, 8.

successful deeds, they can develop confidence in their effort and ability.[139] Above all, we cannot underestimate the importance of experience in the community, the patience of caregivers, and friendships with others. The L'Arche Community stories compiled by Jean Vanier show how the cognitively challenged can express piety and learn faith by participating in communal life. These stories are not academic studies, but they do contain first-hand accounts of the cognitively challenged and their faith that can help us open our minds to the possibility of faith formation and inclusion in the faith community.

IMPORTANCE OF EXPERIENCE FOR THE GROWTH OF UNDERSTANDING

Children do not grasp reality through logical intelligence; by direct seeing and experiencing, they come to understand the world and God.[140] Cognitively challenged persons also develop understanding ability and cognitive development through "motor and sensory stimuli."[141] Therefore, the most important factor in these groups' religious development is experience. Jerome Berryman says, "Primary experiences shade into an awareness of the experience and then into the awareness of the paradox that binds our experience of God."[142] Without this continuing experience, teaching mystical knowledge is impossible.[143] Experience helps foster the growth of understanding.[144]

However, people tend to distrust the role that experience plays in faith formation, particularly the extent to which subjective experience is trustworthy, and the risk of misconstruing personal experience as new revelation. However, John Swinton writes:

> Taking human experience seriously does not imply that experience is a source of revelation. Experience and human reason cannot lead us, for example, to an understanding of the cross and the resurrection. Rather, in taking experience seriously,

---

139. Crane, *Community Integration Approach*, 132. "Retraining children's beliefs about their chances to succeed with effort is best accomplished before their attitudes become deeply entrenched; it is especially important to begin when children are young." Ibid.

140. Schweitzer, *Das Recht des Kindes*, 92.

141. Carmeli and Carmeli, "Holiday Awareness Through Symbols," 124.

142. Berryman, *Godly Play*, 150.

143. Yust and Anderson, *Taught by God*, 136.

144. Hamlyn, *Experience and the Growth*, 12.

Practical theology acknowledges and seeks to explore the implications of the proposition that faith is a performative and embodied act.[145]

Experience is important not as revelation, but to understand a deeper, wider dimension of faith through embodiment and the dynamic of faith. In this dimension, Clair says, "Religious experience involves this compounding of subjective and objective, where there can be a compounding that is not merely subjective nor exclusively objective."[146] Through experience, the objective of faith is an interaction with the subjectivity of the faithful; these impact each other to form a personal faith.

What, then, is the merit of experience? Above all, "children learn first and most profoundly through experience."[147] This does not mean habits form by rote repetition, but that repetitive experiences fix and stabilize the vestige of memory.[148] This is supported by Gadamer's idea of "fore-understanding," which is gained from experience and informs a person's interpretation of the world; this can be called a "history of effect."[149] Therefore, "prior knowledge, along with incoming information, provides data on which the change processes operate."[150] Based on fore-understanding and knowledge, people determine response and action; experience implies meaning. By participation, this meaning flows into the cognitive system.[151] John Swinton says, "The ways in which we practice and the forms of practice in which we participate are therefore filled with deep meaning, purpose and direction. Put slightly differently, the forms of practice that we participate in are theory-laden."[152] In the action and experience of humanity lies wisdom and meaning.

Experience, then, which is important in the formation and development of a person, should be incorporated from the earliest stages of life. Furthermore, Reformed theologian Herman Bavinck insists on the importance

---

145. Swinton and Mowat, *Practical Theology*, 5.

146. St. Clair, *Human Relationships*, 14.

147. May et al., *Children Matter*, 141.

148. Mullino Moore, *Teaching from the Heart*, 64–65; "Children below age 6, in particular, tend to be more suggestible than older children, in the sense that their recall of events can be greatly influenced by experiences." Siegler and Alibali, *Children's Thinking*, 228. "Children are more accurate at reporting events that they directly participated in than events that they observed or heard about." Ibid., 231.

149. Gadamer, *Truth and Method*, 299–300.

150. Siegler and Alibali, *Children's Thinking*, 440.

151. Grün says, "Fur Kinder stellen korperliche, kognitiv-abstrakte und spirituelle Erfahrungen eine Einheit dar." Grün, *Kinder Fragen nach Gott*, 48.

152. Swinton and Mowat, *Practical Theology*, 19.

of children's experience in Christian education. According to him, through early experience of religion, children grow accustomed to it.[153] Children cannot conceptualize God by themselves, but images of God are created through participation and experience in a religious family and community; early experience with a worshipping congregation is very important. Regarding this, Gardner says,

> What recent research has shown, virtually incontrovertibly, is that whatever differences may initially appear, early intervention and consistent training can play a decisive role in determining the individual's ultimate level of performance. If a particular behavior is considered important by a culture, if considerable resources are devoted to it, if the individual himself is motivated to achieve in that area, and if proper means of crystallizing and learning are made available, nearly every normal individual can attain impressive competence in an intellectual or a symbolic domain.[154]

For children, early education and intervention is important for appropriate maturation. A person raised in the Christian mood with proper methods from earliest childhood will grow up to consider Christian faith itself very important. This is supported by study findings that early childhood education strongly supports brain development.[155]

Early education and intervention are also important for those who are cognitively challenged. Geraldine Dawson and Julie Osterling insist that through early intervention, degree of mental handicap can be ascertained as soon as possible, which informs how the child's behavior will be molded.[156] Susan Landy shows that a "responsive parenting style" starting from an early age greatly impacts the development of special-needs children.[157] Guralnick also insists that early education can help foster intellectual development

---

153. Bavinck, *De Opvoeding*, 154–55; Rizzuto's opinion is similar to Bavinck's. She says, "The fact that parents mention him frequently to the child, send the child to Sunday or Hebrew school, and beyond that, worship such a being themselves, produces a profound impression on the child, for whom his parents are the biggest visible beings." See Rizzuto, *Birth of the Living God*, 50. Regarding the importance of early experience of sacrament, see Kane, "Drama, Liturgy, and Children," 119. Schweitzer insists that the root of religious experience is located in the early experience of infancy. See Schweitzer, *Das Recht des Kindes*, 41.

154. Gardner, *Frames of Mind*, 322–33.

155. Landy et al., "Responsive Parenting," 28.

156. See Dawson and Osterling, "Early Intervention in Autism," 307–26.

157. Landy et al., "Responsive Parenting," 29.

among cognitively challenged children.[158] And Clifford Drew and Michael Hardman insist that "language development during the early years is directly influenced by learning and social-experiential factors for children with intellectual disabilities."[159] Proper education and early intervention nurtures full development of cognitively challenged persons.

Age of intervention has been found to relate to treatment outcome for autism spectrum students: "children who received intensive behavioral intervention prior to 60 months of age were more likely to live with their parents [rather than an institution] and attend public classes compared with students who began attending school after age 5."[160] But experience itself cannot guarantee developmental effectiveness. Something more than mechanical participation is needed. Webster says, "Experiences are not meaningful for persons who simply have them, but gain meaning from persons engaging with them, and making choices as to how the elements of the experience are to be meaningful."[161] Experience is effective when it is related to meaning; if it does not include the process of thinking and making choices, it is not helpful in gaining knowledge.[162] Cognitively challenged persons must have opportunities not only for participation and education, but for acting by themselves. A person must be "in a position to make use of the experience if knowledge and further understanding are to emerge from it; and that implies prior understanding of some kind or other. Perception and experience thus logically imply understanding in the sense that they presuppose understanding of some kind."[163] Creating a web of meaning through experience and participation is essential. At the same time, to have an efficacious experience, recognition of causal relationships is necessary.[164]

So, what happens when such recognition is beyond the cognitive capacity of a person? While some cognitively challenged persons may not understand causality, this does not signify total inability to understand. Repetitive experiences and interaction with other people can still enhance understanding and create responsive patterns. When permitted experience and repetition, cognitively challenged individuals have an opportunity to make logical connections for themselves. Along these lines, Champagne says, "Perception and experience need to be integrated and adapted, reframed

158. Guralnick, "Effectiveness of Early Intervention," 319–45.
159. Drew and Hardman, *Intellectual Disabilities*, 209.
160. Hall, *Autism Spectrum Disorders*, 59.
161. Webster, "Personal Identity," 5–16, 9.
162. Hamlyn, *Experience and the Growth*, 6.
163. Ibid., 72.
164. Ibid., 124.

inter-subjectively, in order for the individual to realize and actualize his or her relation to reality. Individuals creatively integrate what they have heard or read according to their uniqueness."[165] Young children and cognitively challenged individuals may not have fully developed logic or recognition of causative relations, hence caregivers and teachers must, with patience, try to offer enough opportunities for them to grow in these areas.

CHILDREN, COGNITIVELY CHALLENGED PERSONS, AND EXPERIENCE

We have seen that experience is an essential factor in the growth of development and understanding for children and those who are cognitively challenged. Room for thinking is made through experience, both in and out of a worship setting; hence, worship experience is necessary for children and cognitively challenged persons to form religious knowledge and faith. Liturgy and experience in worship form a contact point between humans and God, and the sequence and contents of worship accumulate like sediment. Through this, people experience the works of God. Worship is the place of communication between humans and God, the place where God's power is shown.

Children and cognitively challenged persons learn fellowship with God through worship and fellowship in the church. This begins in early childhood. According to Perry Downs, "Two and three year olds are primarily having attitudes shaped to learn that church is a good place to be."[166] Through this recognition, children acquire the flavor of the church experience. The joy gained through this experience makes people want to repeat it, and it forms a habit, which engenders a sort of affection. Experience, habit, and religious affection have a logical connection empowered by the hospitality of the church:

> Pleasurable experiences are a fundamentally necessary part of the child's acquaintance with the church. They are necessary because, since satisfaction in any act tends toward the repetition of it, they help toward habit formation. Training is most effective when it takes place in a pervasive atmosphere of cheer, amiability, and happy expectancy.[167]

---

165. Champagne, "Children's Inner Voice," 375.
166. Downs, *Teaching for Spiritual Growth*, 150.
167. Coe, *Social Theory of Religious Education*, 89.

If the church permits the participation of children and cognitively challenged persons in public worship, and attempts to harmonize worship and education with love and hospitality, it can be the most important help for these individuals' faith formation.

How, specifically, do worship experiences help personal faith formation? Howard Gardner says, "Individuals may learn through the exploitation of linguistic codes, of kinesthetic or spatial demonstrations, or of interpersonal bonds. Even as various intelligences can be exploited as means of transmission, the actual material to be mastered may itself fall squarely within the domain of a specific intelligence."[168] Applying this assertion to worship, the experience of praise, movement of body (liturgy), and communal fellowship can be effective acts that impact the whole person. In the same vein, Perry Downs says, "God has designed people to learn in a variety of ways, and it would be foolish to limit our teaching only to words."[169] Through participation in worship, people deepen understanding with the help of various methods and media.[170]

Repetition and participation are especially necessary for cognitively challenged members of the church. Henri Bissonnier reports, "They like to repeat and act over again what they have seen and experienced: liturgical acts (mass, incensation, reading from the Missal), celebrations, for example, or just a visit to the church, a sacrament received or given to others in their presence (Baptism, Confirmation, Holy Eucharist)."[171] Various sorts of communication and teaching methods should be considered for those who lack full cognitive abilities; preaching and didactic teaching cannot give full understanding.

Even though the cognitively challenged may have difficulty understanding sermons, there are other, different methods of communicating with them in the worship. Yust asserts that children and cognitively challenged persons have difficulty learning things they have not experienced; "Children are terrific imitators of those around them, but they cannot imitate what is outside their experience. Participating regularly in the worship life of a community of faith provides exposure to religious language that they (and we) can imitate as one aspect of learning to be bilingual."[172] Through participation and imitation, they become accustomed to the mood of Chris-

---

168. Gardner, *Frames of Mind*, 350.

169. Downs, *Teaching for Spiritual Growth*, 156.

170. Schweitzer points out that it is an illusion that adults deliver the truth of religion on their own initiative. See Schweitzer, *Das Recht des Kindes*, 23.

171. Bissonnier, "Religious Expression," 149.

172. Yust, *Real Kids, Real Faith*, 71.

tianity.[173] Faith can be got through experience; when children frequently hear the story of God, their experience is intertwined with the concept of God.[174] Experience itself is formative. Experience cannot directly guarantee faith formation, but without it, formation is difficult.

Craig Dykstra says, "These symbolic actions have a way of training us and shaping us at preconscious levels so that over time their order becomes imbedded in us. In worship, we see and sense who it is we are to be and how it is we are to move in order to become."[175] Worship is not restricted to logic and reason. Worship has formative power beyond intelligence, recognition, or explanation. Like mist clinging to a garment, the contents and sequence of worship cling to the minds of the congregation. This is closely related to Aristotle's virtue philosophy, that by acting and practicing—in other words, the effect of habitus—virtue is formed.[176] Experience and repetition is important to the formation of virtue and piety. According to the World Council of Churches,

> Sometimes people "hear" or comprehend God's Word, and know the mystery and majesty of God's presence in their lives through a sensory experience: perception of light or color, a picture or sculpture, a whiff of incense, silence, music, dance, a procession, a hug, or clasped hands around a circle. This sensory experience in liturgy is important to all of us, but especially to children, elderly people and persons with disabilities. It should be considered in our planning of corporate worship and its setting. Many elements of worship are non-verbal, and we can be more intentional about how we incorporate them to enhance the service for everyone. There is the movement of dance, drama, hands clasped in prayer or raised in blessing, making the sign of the cross, handshakes and hugs, lifting the eyes, bowing the head, offering gifts, and passing the bread and cup. There are tactile elements of anointing, baptism, laying on of hands, foot-washing, touching, and vesting. We can smell the incense, wine, flowers, and candles, and taste the bread and wine or

---

173. Even though knowledge does not come from experience, we cannot deny that experience can be a catalyst for knowledge. Hamlyn, *Experience and the Growth*, 29.

174. Ibid., 42.

175. Craig Dykstra, *Vision and Character*, 106; Holmes insists that regular participation in baptism and the Eucharist fosters faith formation. According to him, by repetitive participation, "symbolic images" are engraved in "our memories." Therefore, experience of sacrament is important for the faith formation and spirituality. Even though young children do not have logical minds, practice enhances their intuitive thought and memory. Holmes, *Spirituality for Ministry*, 112–13.

176. Aristotle, *Aristotle's Nichomachean Ethics*, 26–27.

juice. Besides words, we hear music, clapping, bells, sights, and breathing. Centuries ago when many did not know how to read or have access to printed material, churches well filled with visual renditions of the Bible stories.[177]

Of course, due to personal differences, it is hard to determine to what extent children or cognitively challenged individuals are able to grasp Christian faith and religious concepts. However, as Schweitzer points out, children do not have clear concepts about their religious experience, but such experiences do imprint upon them. Church worship composed of stories, music, pictures, and so on creates a web of meaning.[178]

Learning via the body, which can compensate for impaired cognitive ability, supports participation by children and the cognitively challenged in the worship. Mary Elizabeth Moore says, "Learning involves the whole person—cognitive and affective, mental and physical."[179] The body can be a tool for learning.[180] Thomas Groome insists,

> Our bodies are the space we occupy, and through our bodies we receive the 'raw material' of everything we know. Our bodies carry the traces of past experiences and the wisdom we learned from them long after our minds may have forgotten. In a sense, the body "forgets" nothing but stores our biography for us—literally, what is written (graphia) on our living cells (bios).[181]

Experience is inscribed in the body, and through the participation of the body, is inscribed in the memory. In this process, "there is in a sense a growth of understanding in all learning."[182] This argument is not merely philosophical, but biblical. Perry Downs says, "The Old Testament's stress on feasts and rituals was specifically an educative device for the children. The action of the parents (who had experienced the reality of God's works in their lives) was designed to teach the children (who had not experienced

---

177. World Council of Churches, "Church of All and for All," 79.

178. This can be connected in a sort of Gestalt method. See Moore, *Teaching from the Heart*, 63. Also, this is a sort of "esthetic knowing." James Loder says, "Esthetic creation as a knowing event that exhibits transformational logic with emphases distinctly unique to the arts." Loder, *Transforming Moment*, 49. Perry Downs insists, "Our worship services also speak volumes about how we approach God and how we think about him." Downs, *Teaching for Spiritual Growth*, 148.

179. Moore, *Teaching from the Heart*, 67.

180. Groome, *Educating for Life*, 106–07.

181. Ibid., 106.

182. Hamlyn, *Experience and the Growth*, 128.

God's miraculous interventions firsthand)."[183] For instance, the Passover feast served an educational purpose for children over and above merely testing logic and memorization. Through participation in the feast, children could become accustomed to the biblical narrative and Christian celebration, ask questions, and hear the explanations. Similarly, participation in church worship, sacraments, and feasts today can be important educational tools for children and persons who are cognitively challenged.

Noreen Herzfeld shows that cognition is not merely related to logical thinking, but also to human emotion. She says, "Recent research has shown that emotions, far from getting in the way of thought, are actually necessary for cognition. In *Descartes' Error*, Dr. Antonio Damasio notes that patients who have had a brain injury to the parts of the brain that govern the ability to feel emotions also lose the ability to make effective decisions."[184] In learning various elements are interrelated—for example, logic, reason, and emotion. Participation is an opportunity to learn with the help of the senses, atmosphere, and affection. Prior to the development of logical thinking, other sorts of thinking exist in a child's mind, and an image inscribed on the mind at this stage can take on a permanent role in the formation of religious thinking.[185] Faith has a close relationship with experience; they support and fortify each other.[186]

The participation of children and cognitively challenged persons in the worship is generally decided according to their perceived cognitive abilities and expression of faith. However, Robert Keely points out that "adults in our congregations will also represent varied levels of faith development."[187] Adults of "ordinary" cognitive abilities still differ in understanding of faith, religious maturity, and depth of recognition from case to case. This raises serious questions about restricting participation of children and cognitively challenged individuals based on measures of cognition and expression. Childhood is often characterized by a lack of religious education or opportunity for religious experience, and this places religious development in danger.[188]

---

183. Downs, *Teaching for Spiritual Growth*, 147.

184. Herzfeld, "Human and Artificial Intelligence," 124, referring to Damasio, *Descartes' Error: Emotion, Reason, and the Human Brain* (New York: Putnam, 1994).

185. Holmes, *Spirituality for Ministry*, 113.

186. Schweitzer, *Das Recht des Kindes*, 80; *Lebensgeschichte und Religion*, 241.

187. Keely, "Worship and Faith Development," 52.

188. Schweitzer, *Das Recht des Kindes*, 43.

6

Why Children and Cognitively Challenged Individuals Should Fully Participate in the Sacraments

WE HAVE SEEN THAT although young children and cognitively challenged individuals are different from adults, they have their own learning strategies and cognitive abilities. The cognitive abilities of severely mentally challenged individuals may not meet "adult" criteria, maintaining a child's level or below. Even so, children and those who are cognitively challenged should be able to join public worship and the sacraments. They, too, have religious abilities and bear the image of God. Like all church members, regardless of cognitive ability, their faith depends on the work of the Holy Spirit, communion with the Trinity, and the impact of the church community on faith formation. The character of sacrament itself is inclusive, and all should be welcomed.

RELIGIOUS ABILITY

Faith is more than merely recognizing the contents of religion; it includes personal response and fellowship with God.[1] Every person has the capac-

---

1. "A personal relationship with God is possible at every age, including childhood." Derroitte, "Towards a Catechesis," 428.

ity for religious experience.² The attributes of recognizing God's existence and depending on God are innate in each and every person's mind.³ Hay and Nye discuss "a notion of spirituality as something biologically built into the human species, an holistic awareness of reality which is potentially to be found in every human being."⁴ It is a relatively common opinion that spirituality is a fundamental characteristic of all people regardless of religion, gender, ability, or age.⁵ Kevin Lawson notes, "Spirituality is not something that happens later in life but is a part of human experience throughout our lives, and should be taken seriously at all ages."⁶ Even young children can believe and confess to God. Religious faith is not restricted by a person's level of intellectual or religious development; at any stage of life, people can experience God.⁷ Lawson insists that "children have an inherent spiritual awareness and genuine spiritual experiences."⁸ Of course, children's concept of faith, maturity, and refinement of expression of faith can be different from that of adults, but the core belief in God is the same.

Let us think of John Westerhoff's metaphor: "Faith grows like a tree."⁹ There are differences between an old tree, which has many annual rings, and a young tree, which may have only one. However, "a one-year-old tree is truly and completely a tree."¹⁰ Faith is similar: "One stage of faith is not better or more truly faith than another."¹¹ There is no doubt that concept and expression of faith is different for adults than children. But the core of faith in both children and adults is the same in the eyes of God.

> Who can say when, in a child, the dance with God begins? No one . . . And the beginning, specifically, cannot be remembered because in the beginning there are no words for it. The language to name, contain, and to explain the experience comes

---

2. Calvin, *Institutes*, I.iii.1.
3. Butter, "Where Do Children," 372.
4. Hay and Nye, *Spirit of the Child*, 63.
5. Coles, *Spiritual Life of Children*, 277–305; Berryman, *Godly Play*, 151.
6. Lawson, "Growing in Wisdom," 141.
7. Schweitzer, *Lebensgeschichte und Religion*, 242.
8. Lawson, "Growing in Wisdom," 141.
9. Westerhoff, *Bringing up Children*, 24.
10. Ibid.
11. Ibid. Cornelius van Til says, "You may say that children are at most dormant personalities. This is true in a sense, but it is also true that before God there are no dormant personalities. Before God our children are personalities from and before their birth." See van Til, "Faith," 93.

afterward. The dance, then, the relationship with God, faithing, begins in a mist.[12]

The time of meeting with God is different for every person. Some children born in a Christian family may experience it before developing verbal skills. The memory of first experiencing God may dim as one grows to maturity, but it is possible in early childhood. Scottie May says, "Even little ones—two- and three-year-olds—can sing, praise, and give thanks. They also can show reverence on their own."[13] And with the proper opportunity and environment, older children can show their faith in the same way.[14]

> By the age of one year, the child who is regularly participating in worship will recognize the sights, sounds, smells, taste, and feel of worship. By age two, children will be imitating many of the things seen and heard: children may imitate the priest censing or carrying the gospel book, the choir director directing the choir . . . The child of three or four now looks for the new or occasional things that happen in Church: a baptism, the visit of a bishop, the blessing of fruit or palms, or a special feast day.[15]

Children, even young ones, nurtured in a Christian mood and environment learn to properly participate in the worship.[16] As Ivy Beckwith writes, "Let us never underestimate the ability of children to understand in meaningful ways what is happening in our corporate worship! Participation in the communal worship of God is a crucial piece of human spiritual formation."[17]

The case of cognitively challenged people can be considered very similar to that of children. Frequently, their expressions and communication—awkward language, gestures, and impulsive acts—lead people to doubt the work of faith in their minds. But this is only because people do not understand the traits of the cognitively challenged. God knows the hearts of children and cognitively challenged people. As with everyone, he looks into a person's mind and helps them in their weakness.

---

12. Wangerin, *Orphean Passages*, 20.
13. May, et al., *Children Matter*, 219.
14. Ibid., 219.
15. Tarasar, "Taste and See," 52.
16. Even young children can respond to the Bible story in worship. James Loder says, "As early as age five, and perhaps before, children can respond therapeutically to transformational narrative." Loder, *Transforming Moment*, 130.
17. Beckwith, *Postmodern Children's Ministry*, 141.

Spirituality can play an important role in the lives of cognitively challenged people.[18] Webb-Mitchell has seen and reported that they can express religious thoughts and emotions.[19] Furthermore, the charter of the communities of L'Arche says, "People with a mental handicap often possess qualities of welcome, wonderment, spontaneity, and directness."[20] In the same vein, John Huels writes:

> Many persons with developmental disabilities, like very young children, can apprehend the sacred on a symbolic, "pre-conceptual" level. They perceive through the conduct of their families and others around them that special behavior is expected in church. When they pray together with their family or another caring group, they have an awareness of the sacred on a primitive level and they have religious feelings.[21]

A sense of the sacred can be seen in their "primitive" level of expression. For example, in their studies of Jewish mentally handicapped people, Varda and Eli Carmeli show that although the mentally handicapped may not know the meaning of Jewish holidays logically, they can know the religious symbols of these holidays, which help their cognition and understanding to grow.[22]

The core of the problem, however, is that leaders in the church evaluate children and the cognitively challenged according to their own adult criteria and logic, and hence these groups are not invited to participate in public worship and the sacraments. "Staying together" can help overcome this perception—consciously working to widen intercommunication and understanding. Many adult believers have produced church polity or theological reflection with little intergenerational experience or time spent with the cognitively challenged. Therefore, the church has only given superficial consideration to the matter. However, with the development of cognitive science and psychology, people can better understand children and the cognitively challenged, and hence, investing time and building

---

18. Swinton and Mowat, *Practical Theology*, 230. Also, regarding qualitative studies on the religious ability and concept of faith of the cognitively challenged, see Pickett-Cooper, "In My Own Words."

19. Webb-Mitchell, *God Plays Piano*, 11. Regarding studies of spirituality among adults with mild and moderate intellectual disabilities, see Shogren and Rye, "Religion and Individuals," 29–53.

20. L'Arche Internationale, "Charter of the Communities of L'Arche," http://www.larche.org/en/resources/official_documents/charter_of_the_communities_of_larche (accessed December 11, 2013).

21. Huels, "Canonical Rights," 107.

22. Carmeli and Carmeli, "Teaching Jewish Mentally Retarded," 136.

trustful relationships is important to enhance reciprocal communication and understanding.[23] A lack of this trustful relationship may contribute to the tendency to underestimate the potential of the cognitively challenged, who may not feel comfortable enough to truly be themselves after knowing someone only a short time—so, that person does not have the opportunity to understand him or her better.

Henri Nouwen, who spent many years as a caretaker for a severely mentally handicapped person named Adam, says,

> I am convinced that somewhere deep down Adam "knew" that he was loved. He knew it in his very soul. Adam was not able to reflect on love, on the heart as the center of our being, the core of our humanity where we give and receive love. He could not talk with me about the movements of his heart or my heart or the heart of God. He could explain nothing to me in words. But his heart was there, totally alive, full of love, which he could both give and receive. Adam's heart made him fully alive.[24]

Even though Adam was severely mentally retarded and could not express his thoughts with language or show his opinions logically, it was apparent to Nouwen that Adam's heart was alive and could experience love. Living alongside the cognitively challenged, people learn the unique methods they use to express and receive ideas. For example, some people with experience working with the cognitively challenged have reported that they can show awareness of the Eucharist to some extent.[25] Their level of expression is simple, but the presence of thinking and feeling can be seen.

Webb-Mitchell comments, "While the written and verbal word can be used as a form of expression by most of us, children and those people with mental retardation are also capable of expressing their thoughts and feelings through other expressive mediums."[26] Sometimes, cognitively challenged persons express feelings and opinions not only using words, but facial expressions, eye contact, nodding the head, shouting, and other gestures. Well-trained individuals or family members can easily understand what cognitively challenged children think and feel, because they have had so many opportunities to communicate with them and learn their individual communication styles. Their mode of expression is not the words other people may be accustomed to, but they can most certainly express their feelings and inner minds.

23. Webb-Mitchell, *God Plays Piano*, 15.
24. Nouwen, *Adam*, 49–50.
25. See Francis, "Celebrating the Sacraments," 91.
26. Webb-Mitchell, *God Plays Piano*, 15.

Furthermore, it should be noted that intelligence and religious ability are not proportional. Among the cognitively challenged, there is a wide range of intelligence levels and social and physical abilities. Having comparatively high intelligence does not guarantee a person has more religious ability. Henri Bissonnier points out that that intelligence does not always accompany religious ability; conversely, a low level of intellectual ability does not always mean lack of religious ability.[27] Therefore, when a person is categorized as mentally retarded, even when unable to communicate, the church should not judge their faith. How can we know their potential with a quick test? Without observing them for several years, and without the opportunity for public worship, access to the sacraments, and a non-segregated environment, judgment will be superficial.

> It is often wrongly presumed that religion requires abstract knowledge, or formal operational reasoning. Actually, the practice of religion is very concrete. If one is open to the witness of those with mental retardation who have faith according to their capacity, it is easy to see how concrete faith is. The individual who has authentic mental retardation cannot manage formal operational though processes and yet believes.[28]

Cognitively challenged church members who cannot express their faith with logical propositions sometimes still actively participate in the liturgy of the church. Although their mode of expressing faith appears very simple, people who have spent a significant amount of time with them can see and hear a response to faith in their seemingly terse reactions. Amos Yong, who had a brother with Down's syndrome, says,

> Rather than propositions constituting the best form of catechesis, perhaps images, metaphors, paradoxes, humor, ritual, and stories mediated by a diversity of approaches—such as music, artistic media, and modeling—may be better. These are certainly the more effective models of working with those with intellectual, learning, and developmental disabilities. At the same time, catechesis for Christian initiation should not neglect the content of the gospel in the cases of moderate or mild intellectual disability.[29]

People tend to think religious faith requires abstract knowledge and logic; however, the worship practice itself is not abstract, but very concrete.

---

27. Bissonnier, "Religious Expression," 152.
28. Harrington, *Place for All*, 34.
29. Yong, *Theology and Down Syndrome*, 208.

Children with Down's syndrome are often enthusiastic during hymns, clapping their hands and raising their arms. Unchallenged adults may see this as merely a reaction to the music itself. But parents of children with Down's syndrome believe this act more—a sort of religious affection. In these cases, although the children have not verbalized any deep theological reflection or proposition, who but themselves can know whether or not they praise God through music? When the church prays together, these children often join in saying "Amen." It is just a single word, but can it not also be considered a confession of faith? A more severely cognitively challenged person cannot say "Amen," but they may, for instance, nod their head as the congregation says it, showing agreement.

The Gospel is not the examination of religious intelligence, but the confession of our hearts; "We respond on a super-conscious level. Music, art, drama, and other symbolic actions in worship add a dimension to our worship experience. In the super-conscious, God's power provides spiritual awareness and new insights and inspiration."[30] In the worship practice, God's work and personal encounter with God transcend logic and language. The essence of worship is not a matter of "knowledge about God," but a matter of "knowledge of God."[31]

We must also remember that abstract doctrine came from the practice of worship, which has a formative character not only for developing theology, but also faith. The contents of faith come first from the place of worship, which is filled with people—not from the academic society of scholars. Faith, through the generations, has been conceptualized by worship, and polished by scholars and ancestors of faith. Faith itself does not differ between previous generations and now. God is the same throughout past, present, and future. If the basic ordo is, for example, praise, prayer, act—then cannot all the people of God participate in it, regardless of intelligence?[32] Webb-Mitchell points out, "Like other human beings, people with mental retardation are appropriate liturgical participants. They ought to be encouraged to bring their own unique gifts to Christian liturgy."[33] If a human being has the character of "homo adorans," cannot others have the opportunity of learning by their actions?[34] It's possible to act without mindfulness, but it is also possible that actions can help shape and nurture sincerity of the mind. For the cognitively challenged, participation with action can be an expression

---

30. Segler, *Christian Worship*, 64.
31. Ibid., 65.
32. See Webb-Mitchell, *Dancing with Disabilities*, 7.
33. Ibid.
34. Tarasar, "Orthodox Children at Worship," 44.

of faith. Furthermore, "very early experiences . . . generate awareness of and longings for an intimacy great enough to establish their value forever, so there is no fundamental age limit on when one must undergo a 'conversion' that has lifelong value."[35]

THE IMAGE OF GOD

Every person has religious ability, because every human being is created in the image of God. The Bible says, "God created man in his own image" (Gen 1:27). This has been a powerful foundation that supports the value of humanity. However, this does raise the question, in what sense was humankind created according to the image of God? Because the Bible does not clearly answer this question, there is no consensus among scholars as to what "image of God" means, and what an image of God consists of.[36]

Traditionally, the Western church has interpreted "image of God" as humankind's cognitive ability.[37] Many theologians, including Thomas Aquinas, believed that only human reason may participate in the divine *logos*.[38] This emphasis on *logos* led people to emphasize reason in the process of faith formation, which in turn led to distrust of the body, and the human need of a bodily aspect in faith formation.[39] However, this thought is closer to Greek philosophy than to biblical attitudes. For example, Plato and Aristotle both considered humankind's intellect "divine."[40] Calvin also tends to stress the role of reason when discussing the image of God. He says, "For though the divine glory is displayed in man's outward appearance, it cannot be doubted that the proper seat of the image is in the soul"; (he does acknowledge that "though the primary seat of the divine image was in the mind and the heart, or in the soul and its powers, there was no part even of the body in which some rays of glory did not shine").[41] In the traditional perspective, which emphasizes reason, the religious ability of children and

---

35. Loder, *Transforming Moment*, 126.

36. Reymond, *New Systematic Theology*, 427.

37. Migliore, *Faith Seeking Understanding*, 183; also see Swinton, *From Bedlam to Shalom*, 1.

38. Ibid. Also see Thomas Aquinas, *Summa Theologica*, vol. 1, Pt. 1, Q. 93. Art 4 (471).

39. Swinton, *From Bedlam to Shalom*, 20.

40. Anthony Hoekema, *Created in God's Image*, 39.

41. Calvin, *Institutes*, I.xv.3.

Why Children and Cognitively Challenged Individuals

the cognitively challenged becomes suspicious.[42] Amos Yong summarizes the Western church's tradition:

> The intellect has persisted in the Christian tradition as the primary feature of the *imago Dei* due to the association between the Christian doctrine of Christ as the divine logos or wisdom and the Aristotelian doctrine of human beings as a rational for reasoning creatures. Hence, "man must be rational to have fellowship with God."[43]

This tendency to elevate the rational still has a significant impact. For example, to Kaufman, "the order of knowing with respect to God" is closely related to cognitive ability.[44] He does not believe that a "raw prelinguistic experience of transcendence" is possible.[45] Like Kaufman, Lindbeck also emphasizes the role of language and symbol in faith formation. To him, "a religion is above all an external word, a *verbum externum*, that molds and shapes the self and its world."[46] Becoming religious is only possible once a person learns this system of language and symbol.[47] According to this school of thought, the language and imagery we learn as children is more important in thinking of God and learning religion than religious experience itself.[48]

Intellect is important to faith formation, but an overemphasis on intellect may cause people to overlook the dimension of volition and emotion. According to Dutch Reformed theologian G. C. Berkouwer, the Bible sees the human being as a whole person, and does not merely focus on the dimension of reason.[49] It is concerned with human beings having a relationship with God. Similarly, Claus Westermann also insists, "Humans are created in such a way that their very existence is intended to be their relationship to God."[50] Humans were created "to correspond to him [God]."[51] Humans were created according to the image of God and should embody it by being faithful to his will; the image of God is both a gift from God and a duty to God. Because of the trend in the twentieth century toward this

---

42. Swinton, *From Bedlam to Shalom*, 25.
43. Yong, *Theology and Down Syndrome*, 172.
44. Kaufman, *Essay on Theological Method*, 5.
45. Ibid., 7.
46. Lindbeck, *Nature of Doctrine*, 34.
47. Ibid.
48. Ibid., 8.
49. Berkouwer, *Man*, 205.
50. Westermann, *Genesis 1–11*, 158. Also see von Rad, *Genesis*, 58.
51. Westermann, *Genesis 1–11*, 158.

school of thought, many theologians have since come to interpret "image of God" as mankind's relationship with God and other creatures.[52]

Can we then say that children and cognitively challenged persons are also the image bearers of God? Various forms of human weakness and illness are sometimes attributed to sin or degeneration, and many still tend to see handicapped people as somehow having lost the image of God.[53] However, in John 9, Jesus explains that the blind man is not blind because of his own sins or those of his parents; rather, Jesus says, "This happened so that the work of God might be displayed in his life."[54] Not every form of human suffering is related to sinful behavior. Calvin notes,

> Paul says that we are transformed into the image of God by the gospel. And, according to him, spiritual regeneration is nothing else than the restoration of the same image. That he made his image to consist in righteousness and true holiness, is by the figure synecdoche; for though this is the chief part, it is not the whole of God's image. Therefore by this word the perfection of our whole nature is designated, as it appeared when Adam was endued with a right judgment, had affections in harmony with reason, had all his senses sound and well-regulated, and truly excelled in everything good.[55]

Calvin considers Adam's prior status before degeneration as the image of God, retrieved by the regeneration of the Holy Spirit. The New Testament tells us that Christ, not humankind, is the image of God (2 Cor 4:4). In the same vein, Calvin writes,

> Adam was at first created after the image of God, and reflected, as in a mirror, the Divine righteousness; but that image, having been defaced by sin, must now be restored in Christ. The regeneration of the godly is indeed—as we have formerly explained—nothing else than the formation anew of the image of God in them.[56]

These texts discuss the image of God in regard to God's creation of humans in the past, and the possibility of restoring this state in the future through Jesus' work for us.[57]

52. Migliore, *Faith Seeking Understanding*, 184.
53. Yong, *Theology and Down Syndrome*, 39.
54. Carson, *Gospel According to John*, 362.
55. Calvin, "Commentaries on the First Book," 94–95.
56. Calvin, "Commentaries on the Epistle of Paul," 296.
57. See Calvin, *Institutes*, I.xv.4.

Humans can be said to be the image of God in the sense of remembering the past and aiming at the future. We can also think of the image of God as something we attain through the grace of God. Torrance says, the image of God "is not that which God has put into us by nature, but that which he has put into us by grace."[58] People who are in a relationship with God are the image of God, and anyone who has this relationship, regardless of their status or intelligence, has the image of God.

This can also be applied to children and the cognitively challenged as image-bearers of God. The Bible says, "For all of you who were baptized into Christ have clothed yourselves with Christ. There is neither Jew nor Greek, slave nor free, male nor female, for you are all one in Christ Jesus" (Gal 3:26–27). All baptized people are incorporated to the body of the church. They are one, and one family. Children can be members of the family, and carry value like other members of the family. They can join their family's meal table after having been weaned. They do not need to pass a qualifying exam; as the son or daughter of their parents, they carry the image of their parents.

Generally, adults tend to view children from a standpoint of adult development. But does the image of God given to children grow according to the development of their cognitive abilities? Does their image of God become a "real" image of God only when their intellectual ability reaches an adult level? In the eyes of God, young and old alike are all sons and daughters of God; geniuses, intellectuals, cognitively challenged individuals, physically handicapped individuals—everyone. God makes a covenant with people regardless of their status and invites them into a covenantal relationship. The image of God has a close relationship with the covenant.[59]

The idea that it's possible to categorize people as a "lesser" image of God according to their level of development or maturity is humanistic and adult-centric. The Bible does not judge the essence and value of any human being with respect to growth and development. Before becoming adults, children already themselves are the image of God. Romans 8:29 says, "For those God foreknew he also predestined to be conformed to the likeness of his Son, that he might be the firstborn among many brothers." That is to say, the human being was created to imitate the image of Christ—according to the image of God, towards the image of God in Christ. When we consider this, the image of God is "both gift and charge, indicative and imperative."[60]

---

58. See Torrance, *Theology in Reconstruction*, 105.
59. Schilder, *Heidelbergsche Catechimus*, 90.
60. See Moltmann, *God in Creation*, 226–27.

Because a person participates in "Trinitarian communion" by grace of God, that person becomes a "true human being."[61]

According to Torrance, "the image anew in man" comes from the work of the Holy Spirit.[62] The Holy Spirit gives grace in order that people may acknowledge and confess God.[63] If we acknowledge the sovereignty of the Holy Spirit, then communion with God must include children and even those with profound intellectual disabilities, because communion depends solely on the grace of God extended in fellowship.[64]

It is important that personhood of children and those who are cognitively challenged is recognized in the faith community.[65] It should also be recognized that everyone has a handicap in some sense, even though the "symptoms" vary from person to person.[66] Every person depends on others, and as time passes, it may very well increase as the energy and function of the brain deteriorates—but religious ability does not vanish. God reveals himself even to these people; he has "hidden these things from the wise and learned, and revealed them to little children" (Matt 11:25, Luke 10:21). Knowledge of God is given through one's relationship with God, not from the work of humankind, and can be given regardless of age or level of intellect.

When children and the cognitively challenged are in fellowship with God, they are in the image of God.[67] The fact that they are beloved by God makes us see them as real human beings, not as inferior beings held up against the limited perspective of intellectual effectiveness.[68] We must see them as whole persons.[69]

THE WORK OF THE HOLY SPIRIT

The spirit of the human being has fellowship with the Spirit of God in worship. The reason why children and those who are cognitively challenged

---

61. Reinders, *Receiving the Gift of Friendship*, 15; Robert Reymond also insists that the image of God needs to be defined not only "in terms of *entis*" but also "in terms of *relationis*." See Reymond, *New Systematic Theology*, 429.

62. Torrance, *Calvin's Doctrine of Man*, 80.

63. Ibid.

64. Webb-Mitchell, *God Plays Piano*, 4.

65. Webb-Mitchell, *Dancing with Disabilities*, 23.

66. Bergant, "Come, Let Us Go," 29.

67. Yong, *Bible, Disability, and the Church*, 13.

68. Reinders, *Receiving the Gift*, 220.

69. Tibbatts, "Our Brother's Keeper," 103.

should participate in public worship and sacraments is that faith—for all of us—does not depend on human endeavor, but on the work of the Holy Spirit. People think of the work of the Holy Spirit within the scope of human reason and understanding—a limitation that is easily understood, as our minds are only capable of working within these parameters. However, the Holy Spirit is not in fact limited in this way. If the Holy Spirit wills, cannot young children and cognitively challenged people experience God? As Pailin insists, "Every person is to some extent limited, restricted and finite. This is what it is to be human rather than divine."[70] Every person has limits and weak points, a fragile vessel in the eyes of God. We must remember that God gives faith as a gift. A person may have superior intelligence, but with no relationship with God, their knowledge and intelligence have no ultimate benefit. However, someone who is weak and small in the world will be the most treasured in the world if he or she is beloved by God.

Taking this perspective, Robert Keely says, "Faith comes from God. Any fancy curriculum or great words on our part or the part of any teacher or adult cannot change the fact that the Holy Spirit has to work in the hearts of people to move them toward God."[71] If faith can be defined as knowledge of God, then this knowledge can only be gained through a relationship with the Spirit of God.[72] Participation in worship as a place of communion is important, and, of course, discernment and preparation of the mind is also important in public worship and the sacraments. Yet it should be kept in mind that without knowing the interior minds of young children and the cognitively challenged, using adult criteria to bar their approach to worship values human criteria rather than the work of the Holy Spirit, which is beyond the limits of human expectation. James Loder says, "The Divine Spirit dramatically and powerfully penetrates and permeates the whole person so that he is consumed by the Divine Presence. Regardless of what point in one's life span such a realization may occur, the totality of the life span from birth to death is brought under the power and purposes of God."[73]

In the eschatological perspective, God invites everyone to his table. Yong uses Jesus' parable of the eschatological banquet in Luke 14 to illustrate this. He believes this shows that God invites every person to his table, including the cognitively challenged:

> The parable reaches its height when non-disabled listeners are shocked to realize that the intimate relations around the

---

70. Pailin, *Gentle Touch*, 59.
71. Keely, *Helping Our Children Grow*, 11.
72. Loder and Neidhardt, *Knight's Move*, 47.
73. Loder, *Logic of the Spirit*, 232.

eschatological table are shared with the blind, the lame, and the impaired—just as the rich would have been against that they were eating at the banquet table with the poor, or the sociopolitical elite would have been stunned to learn that the lower-class masses were the main guests enjoying the master's accommodations.[74]

Through participation of children and the cognitively challenged, the eschatological aspect of the Lord's Supper can be revealed. In this parable, the host invites people of every class and condition into the banquet, suggesting that in the heavenly banquet, even poor, weak, and alienated people will be gathered around God. Interestingly, the model characteristic of praising God with all his invited people is found in the Lord's Supper—when we see people around the Lord's Table, we see the eschatological kingdom of God in this world. According to Zizioulas, when people see that the church is gathered in one worship place in the Eucharistic community, "it manifests the Church not simply as something instituted, that is, historically given, but also as something constituted."[75] The Eucharist makes the church. Zizioulas writes, "In the Eucharistic assembly . . . the Word of God does not dwell in the human mind as rational knowledge or in the human soul as a mystical inner experience, but as communion within a community."[76]

The Lord's Supper, as a communion within the community, is a sort of eschatological act that overcomes the differences among people seeking knowledge. At God's table, every person chosen by God may participate. Moltmann discusses texts such as Isa 25:6–8, Matt 8:11, Luke 14:14, Luke 15:2, and Mark 14:25 as support for the importance of an eschatological aspect in the Lord's Supper.[77] According to Moltmann, the image of the Messianic banquet is central to the theology of the Lord's Supper, especially in the four gospels. He also insists that Christ is present with the Holy Spirit in the eschatological dimension.[78] In the same vein, Webb-Mitchell says,

---

74. Yong, *Bible, Disability, and the Church*, 133.
75. Zizioulas, *Being as Communion*, 22.
76. Ibid., 115.
77. Moltmann, *Church in the Power*, 246–52.
78. Ibid., 250. I cannot fully agree with their opinion, because the Bible says that Jesus commanded the Lord's Supper in a special context, and that Passover was important background in its institution (Isa 52:13–15, 53:1–12; John 1:29; Rom 3:25; Heb 9:26; Rev 5:12). See Jeremias, *Eucharistic Words*; Marshall, *Last Supper and Lord's Supper*. The tendency to evaluate Jesus' Last Supper as an ordinary meal is commonly emphasized by liberation theologians. This approach has helped to recover the eschatological emphasis in the text, though it sometimes moves beyond the text and ignores the link with Passover.

"This is Christ's table. This simple declaration of whose table we gather around is key to our understanding of everything else that occurs at, and because of, this table."[79] The host of the table is God, not a pastor, theologian, or bishop. As guests, we are welcomed regardless of age or of physical or cognitive ability.

However, I do not put forth this concept of the "open table" without reservations. A confession of faith is important, but it would be unfair to request logic on an adult level for the cognitively challenged and young children in this. It is necessary to permit age- and intelligence-appropriate participation in public worship and the Lord's Supper.

In addition, if we include covenant children, we embody the corporate character of the Lord's Supper based on covenantal theology.[80] Reformed tradition permits infant baptism based on the concept of covenant.[81] Calvin insists, "The Lord is able to furnish them [children] with the knowledge of Himself in any way He pleases."[82] However, Calvin prohibits children's communion due to his emphasis on mature faith and understanding.[83] In this way, he applies the concept of covenant inconsistently in dealing with baptism and the Lord's Supper. Furthermore, Stookey points out that because a certain level of ability has been required in the Lord's Supper, it has become a privilege available only to people who appear to understand its meaning.[84]

The church should consider extending participation in the Lord's Supper to children and cognitively challenged individuals who have been baptized, and therefore belong to the covenantal community. If the church sees it as appropriate to baptize them, there is no reason to prohibit participation in the Lord's Supper based on cognitive ability. In fact, in the early church, baptism, first communion, and confirmation all occurred in a single ceremony.[85] The covenant includes all family members of the church, and its inclusiveness must be considered.

---

79. Webb-Mitchell, *Dancing with Disabilities*, Chapter 3.

80. Reisz says, "We have made questions of personal piety primary while neglecting the corporate character of the meal." See Reisz, Jr., "Infant Communion," 65.

81. Calvin, *Institutes*, IV.xvi.17.

82. Ibid., IV.xvi.18.

83. Ibid., IV.xvi.30.

84. Stookey, *Baptism*, 128.

85. Johnson, *Rites of Christian Initiation*, 245–47.

PARTICIPATION IN COMMUNION WITH THE TRINITY

Cognitively challenged persons and young children can participate in public worship because worship is the place where the Triune God is present, and God invites human beings into communion with the Trinity.[86] This is a holy place. In worship and sacrament, the almighty God fills the participant's spirit with the Holy Spirit, which leads to the place of communion with the Trinity—the foundation of fellowship between God and humans. This can be the reason for welcoming all into the worship.

As LaCugna says, "The doctrine of the Trinity affirms that the essence of God is relational, other-ward, that God exists as diverse persons united in a communion of freedom, love, and knowledge."[87] The Trinity represents the unification of three persons into one, and trinitarian doctrine takes this one step further to an "encounter between divine and human persons in the economy of redemption."[88] The Trinity is the means by which the Triune God reveals himself and fellowship with humans becomes possible; it is "the way God communicates God's personal self to human beings."[89] Zizioulas supports this idea: God is not "being-in-itself," but "being-in-relation." Human salvation means participation in God's personal existence.[90]

At this point, the most important concept is *perichoresis*: "being-in-one-another, permeation without confusion. No person exists by him/herself or is referred to him/herself; this would produce number and therefore division within God."[91] This concept, first introduced by Eastern fathers, inspires us to proceed to the place of union and relationship with God; and "just like substance, communion does not exist by itself: it is the Father who is the cause of it."[92] Communion among the Trinity makes it possible for humans to enter into the place of communion. *Perichoresis* itself means intertwining within the Trinity, a close inter-relational fellowship, which can be seen as a model for the means by which God invites humanity into fellowship with him. God's hypostasis is union through love, which can lead people into personal encounters with God. According to Zizioulas, love is "the only exercise of freedom in an ontological manner" that "makes God

---

86. White, *Sacraments as God's Self-Giving*, 24.
87. LaCugna, *God for Us*, 243.
88. Ibid., 305.
89. Haight, "Point of Trinitarian Theology," 200.
90. Zizioulas, *Being as Communion*, 49–50.
91. Ibid., 271.
92. Ibid., 17.

what He is."[93] God's sovereign love embraces people and leads people into personal communion with him.

Zizioulas believes that "the person cannot exist without communion."[94] With the help of a relationship with God, personhood can be preserved. Rather than emphasizing the image of God in the ontological perspective, the image of God can be found in a relationship with God; "Outside the communion of love the person loses its uniqueness and becomes a being like other beings."[95] Of course, to Zizioulas, this does not mean non-Christians do not have the image of God; but that the real likeness of God is restored only when people have a relationship with God, and with other people of God. However, I do not accept the separation between the image and likeness of God in the Orthodox perspective, according to which we retain the image of God after the fall but have lost our likeness of God and seek the restoration of that likeness in Christ and the Christian life.[96] These two terms—image and likeness—are parallel, not different terms. When people work for and stand in a good relationship with God, they are in his image.

In the inclusive fellowship of communion, people maintain the Christian identity and develop "a way of knowing."[97] Miroslav Volf says, "Just as a person cannot arise, develop, and live apart from her relationships with others, neither can a Christian exist as a Christian before entering into relation with other Christians."[98] Participating in communion, people learn, because "meaning is made in relationships"[99] and indwell in the place of fellowship with God, where subjectivity intercommunicates with God's objective truth. In this process, the Holy Spirit gives participants knowledge of God. Communion with God and fellowship with other Christians enable people to learn the Christian faith and maintain the Christian identity.

By participation in the fellowship, the subject comes to indwell in the object of truth, gaining knowledge through encounter with God and people in the community. This is tied to the idea of tacit knowing—the idea that "we know more than we can tell"; even though the doctrine of the Trinity cannot be fully understood and explained, people "know" it to some extent

---

93. Ibid., 46.
94. Ibid., 18.
95. Ibid., 49.
96. Heyer, ed., *Konfessionskunde*, 167.
97. James Loder says, "Conscious human existence is inevitably and irrepressibly self-relational . . . knowing is something other than a self-involving relational act." Loder and Neidhardt, *Knight's Move*, 42–43.
98. Volf, *After Our Likeness*, 178.
99. Berryman, "Rite of Anointing," 63.

through participation and fellowship.[100] Through personal participation, people are confronted with the truth of God, and that truth modulates the subjectivity of the person. Above all, this process occurs by the work of the Holy Spirit; through indwelling, people can gain knowledge of God, which itself is a gift from God.

James Loder's work on the intertwined relationship between the human spirit and the Spirit of God discusses how human subjects can come to know God. He says, "This hidden wisdom must be grasped by the spirit of the person in communion with the Spirit of God; thus wisdom is acquired Spirit to spirit; human spirit . . . transformed by the Holy Spirit of Christ becomes a human figure for the Divine reality."[101] Participation is a sort of indwelling in the presence of God; therefore, real participation in worship is necessary. Before a person enters the sanctuary, regardless of that person's feelings, God is already present in the sanctuary. Regardless of human will, God is present in the worship and sacrament.[102] God's presence makes the place a holy place. Then, people who join together there become a holy people.[103] Hence, participation and encounter with God should be emphasized. When the church repeats rite and ritual, people experience God's presence, and participants become participants in the original event.[104] As Gabriel Pivarnik says, "participation in the sacramental-liturgical experience is meant to lead the participant into ever-greater union with the divine. Liturgical participation always points to a participation in the life of the Trinity."[105] Participation in the liturgical worship is not merely "liturgical celebration," but is "centered on the transformation of the human person through grace in the medium of the church in order to bring the individual back to his or her Creator, the source of being."[106]

Mere cognitive ability cannot maintain this important relationship with God. According to Hans Reinders, people need to see other people

---

100. Polanyi, *Tacit Dimension*, 4. Of course, as Miroslav Volf points out, "Our notions of the triune God are not the triune God, even if God is accessible to us only in these notions. A certain doctrine of the Trinity is a model acquired from salvation history and formulated in analogy to our experience, a model with which we seek to approach the mystery of the triune God, not in order to comprehend God completely, but rather in order to worship God as the unfathomable and to imitate God in our own, creaturely way." Volf, *After Our Likeness*, 198.

101. Loder and Neidhardt, *Knight's Move*, 47–48.

102. Holmes, *Spirituality for Ministry*, 108.

103. Hart and Muether, *With Reverence and Awe*, 91–95.

104. Holmes, *Spirituality for Ministry*, 108.

105. Pivarnik, *Toward a Trinitarian Theology*, xxii.

106. Ibid., 5.

from the perspective of relation rather than possession.[107] Even though the world influences people to form self-images based on their possessions, the Christian reality is that human beings should be honored because of their relationship with other people and with God. A relationship with God can be maintained even if the brain ceases to function, because God is gracious and faithful to the covenant. Amos Yong argues:

> The soul remains in relationship with God even when our brains deteriorate and our minds are "lost." In an emergentist perspective, the sum of the whole (the soul) after years of conscious (cognitive) relationships with God does not just disappear when the brain dysfunctions and the mind drifts (as happens with, e.g., Alzheimer's disease). Rather, the whole is indelibly shaped by the various parts of its experience and therefore other dimensions of the whole (e.g., the affections) remain informed and engaged by those experiences even after they cease intensity).[108]

Even those who develop dementia or lose memory through an accident stay in the grace of God when they have lived in the faith community. The core of a person's relationship with God lies in God's grace and promise, rather than in the person's "worthiness" in the eyes of others. God remembers his people, and is faithful to the covenant. This also works through the faith community. Sometimes, God works through other people to help children and the cognitively challenged; sometimes, God works through children and those who are cognitively challenged to help other people. Their faith is nurtured by other people's teaching, guidance, advice, and fellowship with them, and these acts themselves nurture faith reciprocally. This fellowship maintains and empowers the image of God.

Participation in public worship and the sacraments, where God is present and encounters us, is critical. How can we meet God without it?[109] Through worship, people meet and develop a close relationship with the Triune God while learning and being disciplined by God. Rather than separating a person and permitting participation in public worship only after finishing a designated level of education, as was the educational aim of catechumen in the early church, the church now must consider the power of participation and engagement.[110] This does not undermine the necessity of catechetical instruction and the authority of the sacraments. Rather, when harmonizing participation and catechism, religious affection can be gained

107. Reinders, *Receiving the Gift*, 201.
108. Yong, *Theology and Down Syndrome*, 190.
109. Thomas, "Children at Worship," 124.
110. Ibid.

more effectively. While participating, experiencing, and understanding worship, people can proceed to greater spiritual benefit.

THE ROLE OF THE FAITH COMMUNITY AND THE CONCEPT OF COVENANT

Participation in the covenant community is also the experience of having fellowship with Triune God and people of God. Participants gain knowledge of God through communion, and it is encouraged and deepened living in the covenant community. Herbert Anderson and Susan Johnson say, "Raising children is a communal activity. Families do not and cannot do it alone."[111] Children are nurtured and inherit Christian faith while participating in a faith community. Joseph Gelineau insists, "Christian faith is ecclesiastical and communal by nature."[112] John Westerhoff, throughout several decades of work, also successfully shows how a faith community can impact faith formation of children. According to him, one of the serious problems found in the praxis of church education is that Christian faith is not transferred to the next generation; instead, the church teaches mere knowledge of biblical truth. Rather than "the schooling, instructional-training paradigm," Westerhoff insists on a "community of/body of Christ paradigm."[113] He presents the importance of participation in worship and various liturgies while stressing that the educational function of liturgy, which disappeared after the Reformation, must again be revitalized.[114] He calls this a "socialization model," and insists that by this process, which includes interaction and appropriation among the community, the shape of faith can be formed.[115] To Westerhoff, socialization means "all those formal and informal influences through which persons acquire their understandings and ways of living."[116] Participation in the community takes on the function of a "hidden curriculum"[117]; participating in communal meetings, worship, and liturgy, people learn the contents of Christian faith. Westerhoff believes we "can teach about religion," but we cannot "teach people faith."[118] If a person is

---

111. Anderson and Johnson, *Regarding Children*, 4.
112. Gelineau, "Reflections," 28.
113. Westerhoff, *Will Our Children have Faith?* xv.
114. Westerhoff, and Willimon, *Liturgy and Learning*, 55–86.
115. Westerhoff, "A Socialization Model," 80–90.
116. Westerhoff, *Will Our Children have Faith?* 14.
117. Ibid., 15.
118. Ibid., 18.

not involved in the community, he loses access to one of the primary means faith is transmitted.[119]

The transmission of community faith occurs with the help of peer groups and "interrogational experiences."[120] It is not formed by rote-style education, but continuous participation. In worship, through "imitation and repetition . . . rites, rituals, values, and perceptions of the nature of the sacred" are transmitted from generation to generation.[121]

In fact, when looking back on my own personal history of faith, I see that it was by participating in public worship and the sacraments, and by imitating other people's faithful attitudes and the repetitions of the worship practice, that I developed the habits of worship. I accepted the Christian faith by joining the church community's faithful worship and seeing the model of people I trusted.[122] Ellis Nelson says, "The major thing we must keep in mind is that faith resides in, and arises out of, a community of believers."[123] For cognitively challenged individuals, belonging to and having relationships in the faith community is critical to developing religious affection.[124] Mary Harrington insists, "We have seen that those with disabilities are quite capable of faith education, provided that there is affectivity in abundance and that there is time, space, people, and a process that can develop symbolic competence."[125] The community of faith is the soil in which faith formation grows for those who are cognitively challenged.

In particular, the sense of belonging in the community plays a significant role in forming faith. Constance Tarasar says, "The sense of belonging enables the child's inclination for worship to grow and develop. The child responds positively in situations which result in feelings of security, acceptance, and respect as a person."[126] Along these lines, James Torrance insists that our belonging decides our beliefs; "Our belonging to Christ is not conditional on our believing and repenting. . . . We believe that we belong. . . . Faith is our response to the gospel, our acknowledgement that we are not our own but are bought at a price and bought long before we were born."[127] That is to say, people do not belong to a faith community based on having

---

119. Westerhoff, "What is Religious Socialization?" 43.
120. Lawson, "Growing in Wisdom," 147.
121. Foster, *Teaching in the Community*, 36.
122. Beckwith, *Postmodern Children's Ministry*, 58–59.
123. Nelson, "Ten Righteous People," 48.
124. Harrington, "Affectivity and Symbol," 119.
125. Ibid., 128.
126. Tarasar, "Orthodox Children at Worship," 53.
127. Torrance, "Some Theological Grounds," 200.

made a decision, but by belonging to the faith community, we can learn that we are not our own, but belong to God. This is not to disparage the importance of individual confession. However, if someone cannot communicate with other persons, that person can still proceed to the presence of God with the help of the community's faith and nurturance.

Actually, as John Webster points out, confession is a "thankful, praising, self-committing acceptance of God's self-revelation in Christ . . . It lies wholly beyond our intellectual or spiritual or moral reach."[128] Therefore, we need to re-examine our understanding of the practice of confession. It is a public act that cannot be separated from the life of the faith community.

John Swinton insists the church should consider not only how to similarly recognize the salvation of cognitively challenged individuals, but also how to embrace them into the life of the church.[129] The church community makes a vow at the time of an infant's baptism to raise the child in God's Word, but there is no consistency between vow and practice if they do not include the child positively in weekly public worship.[130]

Worship is a part of the covenant renewal practiced by the Israelites in the Old Testament.[131] Deuteronomy 29:10–11 describes it thusly: "The people of Israel are standing before Yahweh in an assembly . . . it includes everyone in Israel."[132] All Israelites took the oath, and were thus led into the covenantal relationship. Similarly, in Joshua 8:35, the whole assembly participated when Moses read the law—including young children.[133] Whenever God has established or renewed the covenantal relationship with a group of people, he has commanded participation of the whole congregation. This makes these covenant renewals "intergenerational events."[134] Participation across generations means God's people could experience God more deeply and learn from each generation. For example, in Exodus 12, we see that while learning about Passover, children received religious training in a natural manner. The father tells the child of the salvific history of God at the child's level of understanding; even more importantly, the child could ask

---

128. Webster, *Confessing God*, 72.

129. Swinton, "Friendship in Community," 102–06. In the same vein, Barbara Reid says, "The capabilities of the entire community and not an individual believer are the criteria for admission." See Reid, "Whole Broken Body of Christ," 49.

130. Beckwith, *Postmodern Children's Ministry*, 148.

131. Witvliet, *Worship Seeking Understanding*, 26–30. Also see Deut 29:10–11, Josh 8:35, 2 Chron 20:13, Neh 8:3, and Ps 148:12–13. Regarding learning by intergenerational experience, see Deut 6:6–9, Ps 78: 1–8, 1 Tim 5: 1–2, and Titus 2: 1–5.

132. Currid, *Deuteronomy*, 456.

133. Woudstra, *Book of Joshua*, 150.

134. Vanderwell, "Biblical Values," 21.

questions.[135] Intergenerational events show more vividly that the salvation of God is not restricted to historical events, but happens here and now.

Such renewal occurs through public worship. God calls people through the Call to Worship, and people respond with their confession of faith. In this encounter, God's covenant is renewed and vividly penetrates the mind.[136] Therefore, it is only natural for God's young children and cognitively challenged church members to participate in the place of covenantal renewal. Covenant itself has a character of inclusiveness, which comes from God's grace. Of course, grace requires human response, but the sacraments, especially baptism, show God's generosity and inclusiveness. Stookey insists that baptism is Christ's act, not merely the church's act.[137] This generosity and inclusiveness stems from Christ's self-giving. Hendrikus Berkhof makes a similar argument concerning the inclusiveness of the baptismal covenant:

> In this washing of regeneration life is not made dependent on man's faith, but on Christ's substitution. However, only the awakened faith understands this and therefore can desire this washing. Is it therefore true that only he who consciously believes can go through this washing? However, this washing speaks of a salvation which lays the foundation for faith and transcends faith. Partnership in the covenant is broader than this faith. It also embraces the children, the mentally handicapped, the demon possessed, the despondent in slums and tenements.[138]

As we see in the cutting ceremony described in Genesis 15, the making of the covenant between God and Abraham, God gives grace rather than drawing a contract people. God himself takes the burden of covenantal responsibility; as Michael Horton says, "It is a one-sided promise."[139] Horton also draws a parallel between the cutting ceremony of Genesis 15 and the Lord's Supper. He suggests:

> It is exactly the same passing through the pieces that Jesus enacts in the Lord's Supper: "Now he offers himself to you. He says:

---

135. Swift, *Education in Ancient Israel*, 65–66.

136. Michael Horton says, "The ceremonies of the sacraments belong to this world of covenant-making. Every time we witness a baptism or receive Communion, God is shaking hands on the deal he has made with us." Horton, *Introducing Covenant Theology*, 137.

137. Stookey, *Baptism*, 16.

138. See Berkhof, *Christian Faith*, 356.

139. Horton, *Introducing Covenant Theology*, 41.

'Take, eat; this is my body. This is my blood of the covenant shed for many. Drink, all of you, of it.'"[140]

Seeing God's sacrifice in the covenantal burden shows us the character of grace. Of course, a promise requires obedience; God's calling and responsibility come first, and human responsiveness and responsibility, expressed in love and fidelity, follow.[141] It is here that we find the continuity between the Old and New Covenant.

This is why worship as a place of covenantal renewal should be inclusive. As long as someone does not intentionally interrupt and oppose the worship, the church must endeavor to include them. The person's inner mind and intention can be judged by God alone,[142] and therefore the church community must receive all with hospitality.

SUBJECTIVITY OR OBJECTIVITY?

To support the propriety of participation of children and the cognitively challenged in the sacraments and public worship, we should consider the matter of objectivity and subjectivity of sacramental efficacy. This has been debated for several centuries, and it is not my intent to give a clear answer in this short chapter or to outline all the many scholars' arguments and points. Rather, in order to gain insight about the participation of children and cognitively challenged persons in the sacraments, I will review John Calvin's sacramental theology, especially on means of grace, which has strongly impacted the Presbyterian and Reformed churches.

This matter is an important factor in American and Korean Presbyterian and Reformed churches. Descendants of the Reformed tradition, these denominations value doctrinal knowledge and confession of faith at the

---

140. Ibid., 66, citing Robertson, *Christ of the Covenants*, 146.

141. James B. Torrance says, "God's covenant love (held out in baptism and the Lord's Supper) is unconditioned by any considerations of worth or merit or good works—unconditioned even by faith and repentance. This was the Reformation insight in the interpretation of *sola gratia* and the reinterpretation of the sacraments." Torrance, "Some Theological Grounds," 201.

142. van Til says, "Moreover, I must regard all children of believers as children of God until the contrary appears to be true." van Til, "Faith and our Program," 93. Michael Horton comments, "If you are living in open rebellion against the promises of God and do not delight in his law inwardly, then the inheritance does not belong to you even if you have been incorporated visibly into the covenant community. The gospel is greater than we ever imagined, and the judgment is severe for those who reject the realities it brings into our lives." See Horton, *Introducing Covenant Theology*, 193.

expense of liturgical participation, creating imbalance between objectivity and subjectivity of sacramental efficacy.

Historically, Protestant and Catholic churches have tended to simplify each other's sacramental theology, failing to understand the depth of the matter of objectivity and subjectivity. As Stookey points out, "there is oversimplification both in the Protestant polemic that Trent embraced a magical sacramental view and in Trent's perception that Protestantism rejected outright the historic principle that the sacraments communicate the grace they signify."[143] However, as James White says, the term *ex opere operato* means that the grace of the sacrament only depends on God, and the efficacy of the sacrament is not restricted by human ability and contribution.[144] Roman Catholic scholar Edward Schillebeeckx studied *ex opere operato* not in the dimension of real transformation, but in the dimension of transsignification. To him, a personal encounter between God and human beings is more important than explaining the relationship between accidents and substances.[145] According to Schillebeeckx's explanation, God gives love to humans. It is a compelling sign. God's Word and sacrament efficiently invoke human reaction, as a firm handshake inspires one in response. In a personal encounter, the sign and efficacy of a sacrament can be joined. Therefore, we must reconsider the real meaning of *ex opere operato*.

At the same time, the Roman Catholic Church should widen their understanding about the Protestant Church's sacramental theology. Bavinck writes, "The truth of the sacrament does not depend on faith."[146] However, "though Christ is in fact objectively, truly, and seriously offered to all participants in the sacrament, as he is in the Word to all who hear it, still, subjectively, a working of the Holy Spirit is needed for them to enjoy the true power of the sacrament."[147] That is to say, the Protestant emphasis on subjectivity does not intend that God's grace is altered according to a person's decision and effort, but confession of faith and the work of the Holy Spirit are necessary. Therefore, rather than dichotomous thinking about subjectivity and objectivity, each church needs to have an open mind. Why, then, should we study the objectivity and subjectivity?

---

143. Stookey, *Eucharist*, 182.

144. White, *Sacraments as God's Self Giving*, 33. In fact, Baillie considers the idea of transubstantiation an attempt to satisfy medieval piety about a miracle of the altar among the people. It was an attempt to explain the concept of real presence; an attempt Baillie considered insufficient. Baillie, *Theology of the Sacraments*, 100.

145. Schillebeeckx, *Christ the Sacrament*, 40–45, 60–73.

146. Bavinck, *Reformed Dogmatics*, 4:578.

147. Ibid., 488.

If the objectivity of the sacrament is emphasized, in that children and the cognitively challenged cannot somehow compromise the grace of sacrament, the church can permit their full participation. However, if the subjectivity of the sacrament were emphasized (i.e., the efficacy is dependent on our action, response, and ability to respond in a particular way), the church would need to reconsider their participation.[148] Both these stances have strong and weak points; the former grants assurance and comfort to participants; the latter helps discipline people to follow God's Word and will. However, the former can weaken the importance of intention and preparation of mind among participants; the latter has potential to weaken the importance and particularity of the sacrament itself. To answer the question of participation for children and the cognitively challenged, the relationship between sacramental objectivity and subjectivity must be understood by discovering the contact point between John Calvin's thought and modern Reformed and Presbyterian church practice.

CALVIN'S CONCEPT OF SACRAMENT AND MEANS OF GRACE[149]

What is the sacrament to Calvin, and why was it given to human beings? Calvin says, "It is an external sign, by which the Lord seals on our consciences his promises of good-will toward us, in order to sustain the weakness of our faith, and we in our turn testify our piety towards him, both before himself and before angels as well as men."[150] Sacrament is a gift from God and a means of discipline given by God, who understands people's weaknesses and wants to help their faith grow. The sacrament begins with God rather than with people. Calvin says, "God uses the means and instruments which he sees to be expedient, in order that all things may be subservient to his glory, he being the Lord and disposer of all."[151] God uses the sacrament as an instrument to transform people into participants in grace.[152] In that grace, such as when the bread is eaten, the vitality of the life of God becomes

---

148. The Reformed Church recognized that promise requires response. See Kumphuis, *In dienst van de vrede*, 16.

149. The Reformed Church calls it *media gratiae*; the Lutheran Church calls it *media salutis*. See Honig, *Handboek van de gereformeerde dogmatiek*, 610.

150. Calvin, *Institutes*, IV.xiv.1.

151. Ibid., IV.xiv.12.

152. Ibid., IV.xiv.16.

Why Children and Cognitively Challenged Individuals

the life of the people.[153] At this point, Calvin understands the sacrament as not an abstract concept, but as real and vivid grace for the people of God.

CALVIN ON THE EFFECT OF THE SACRAMENT

Calvin seems to focus on the objective character of the sacrament. He insists, "I admit and hold that the power of the sacrament remains entire, however the wicked may labor with all their might to annihilate it . . . the flesh and blood of Christ are not less truly given to the unworthy than to the elect believers of God."[154] Human weakness cannot corrupt the glory and grace of God. Because the sacrament is given by God, Calvin insists, "What I have said is not to be understood as if the power and truth of the sacrament depended on the condition or pleasure of him who receives it."[155] Human beings are weak and unstable, but God's will is firm and stable, and the sacrament depends on his sovereignty alone. But God's promise requires a human response:

> Just as the rain falling on the hard rock runs away, because it cannot penetrate, so the wicked by their hardness repel the grace of God, and prevent it from reaching them. . . . They confer nothing, and avail nothing, if not received in faith, just as wine and oil, or any other liquor, however large the quantity which you pour out, will run away and perish unless there be an open vessel to receive it.[156]

Although Calvin considers God's grace rich enough for everyone, it is absorbed, like the rain, only into that mind which loves that grace. The recipient's attitude *is* important.

Calvin affirms both the objectivity and subjectivity of sacramental grace at the same time. This maintains the priority of God's grace in the sacrament while acknowledging the role of the receiver's intention. Calvin's opinion here can be understood with respect to his pneumatology. In Calvin's idea of sacrament, the most important thing is the work of the Holy Spirit; it is a means of grace, not a contributor of grace; "This ministry, without the agency of the Spirit, is empty and frivolous, but when he [Holy Spirit] acts within, and exerts his power, it is replete with energy."[157] The

---

153. Ibid., IV.xvii.5.
154. Ibid., IV.xvii.33.
155. Ibid., IV.xiv.16.
156. Ibid., IV.xvii.33; IV.xiv.17.
157. Ibid., IV.xiv.9.

Holy Spirit is that which makes the sacrament effective and meaningful, and which controls the faith of a person, forming the connection between objectivity and subjectivity.

Is the work of the Holy Spirit wholly dependent on the outward sign? Zwingli emphasizes the sovereignty of God, which surpasses the Word and sacrament; however, Luther insists on the sovereignty of God in the Word and sacrament.[158] According to Zwingli, outward things cannot impact the inward things.[159] In other words, the sovereignty of God and God's will is not bound to visible signs and means of grace.

What is Calvin's perspective on sacramental symbol and reality? To answer this, we must study the relationship between symbols in his thought.

SYMBOL AND REALITY

Calvin says, "There may be invisible sanctification without a visible sign, and, on the other hand, a visible sign without true sanctification."[160] He insists that the sign itself obtains meaning through close relationship and interaction with its contents. However, he warns against emphasizing the outward sign without the related promise. The priority lies in God's Word: "In order that you may have not a sign devoid of truth, but the thing with the sign, the Word which is included in it must be apprehended by faith."[161] But if someone cannot understand the Word, does the symbol itself have no meaning?

God's Word is central in Calvin's theology. Calvin says, "There never is a sacrament without an antecedent promise, the sacrament being added as a kind of appendix, with the view of confirming and sealing the promise, and giving a better attestation."[162] However, the symbol itself is not empty; if a symbol orients us toward Christ, the grace of God really is given with the symbol, and that "indeed, outward sign is helpful if those [outward signs] invite us to Christ, when they are distorted by other, the whole advantage of them is undeservedly overturned."[163] This does not mean symbol is evalu-

---

158. Stephens, *Theology of Huldrych Zwingli*, 179.

159. Ibid., 187.

160. Calvin, *Institutes*, IV.xiv.14.

161. Ibid., IV.xiv.15.

162. Ibid., IV.xiv.3 According to Calvin, if it were not for God's Word, the sacrament would become "no more than a cold ceremony without efficacy." Calvin, "Short Treatise on the Holy Supper," 161.

163. "et quidem adiuvantibus externis signis, quae, si nos ad Christum invitant, ubi alio torquentur, indigne evertitur tota eorum utilitas." Calvin, *Joannis Calvini*, 5:274.

ated solely according to personal or subjective understanding, but that a proper symbol leads us to the Word. To Calvin, the objectivity and subjectivity of validity are closely related, although he does not confuse the sign and the thing signified. According to Calvin, a symbol is not an empty tool, but a sort of instrument used to deliver God's will and to enhance human understanding. Participation and exposure to a symbol can be just as effective for developing people's faith as exposure to a sermon.

UNDERSTANDING CALVIN'S VARIOUS THOUGHTS ON SACRAMENTS

The difficulty in studying Calvin's perspective on sacrament lies in the discrepancies between his mention of the subject in *Consensus Tigurinus* (1549) and in other documents. In *Consensus Tigurinus*, especially in article 17, Calvin opposes the fundamental cohesion between the sacramental elements and reality.[164] While negotiating with Bullinger, he tries to separate signs from reality in order to prevent dependence on outward symbols. However, in the *Institutes* (1559), Calvin says,

> We must not suppose that there is some latent virtue inherent in the sacraments . . . They do not of themselves bestow any grace, but they announce and manifest it, and, like earnests and badges, give a ratification of the gifts which the Divine liberality has bestowed upon us . . . God, therefore, truly performs whatever he promises and figures by signs; nor are the signs without effect, for they prove that he is their true and faithful author.[165]

It seems from this that Calvin places great meaning on the sacramental symbol itself, even as he rejects its power to act on its own. How, then, can this difference be understood? Firstly, it should be determined whether *Consensus Tigurinus* can be taken as a representative document of Calvin's sacramental theology.[166] Some theologians, such as Charles Hodge, insist that *Consensus Tigurinus* encapsulates Calvin's thoughts on the Lord's Supper.[167] Many Protestants consider this a representative work of Calvin, but Francois Wendel believes the *Consensus Tigurinus* does not reflect Calvin's

---

164. Bullinger and Calvin, *Consensus Tigurinus*, 262.

165. Calvin, *Institutes* IV.xiv.17.

166. However, Hodge insists, "The *Consensus Tigurinus* is the most carefully considered and cautiously worded exposition of the doctrine of the Reformed in relation to the sacraments, belonging to the period of the Reformation." See Hodge, *Systematic Theology*, 3:517.

167. See Hodge, *Systematic Theology*, 3:631–32.

own sacramental theology because its purpose is political, intended to establish a consensus between Geneva and Zurich.[168] In the same vein, Paul Rorem says, "Completely missing from the *Consensus* were Calvin's usual references to the actual presenting ('exhibiting') of what is signified, to the sacraments as 'instruments' (although they are called 'implements'), and as that 'through' which God confers grace."[169] His "Short Treatise on the Holy Supper of Our Lord and Only Saviour Jesus Christ" (1541) enables us to see more clearly Calvin's own sacramental theology. In this work, Calvin says, "[Sacrament] is . . . symbolized by visible signs, as our infirmity requires, but in such a way that it is not a bare figure, but joined to its reality and substance."[170] He goes on to say that in all of God's sacraments, the visible signs do have "some correspondence with the spiritual things they symbolize."[171] From this, it seems Calvin recognizes the peculiarity of the sacrament itself. Calvin's own stance does seem to fall somewhere between absolute objectivism and absolute subjectivism, while leaving plenty of room to allow participation of people whose understanding and faith cannot be definitely known. Calvin's thoughts in the "Short Treatise," his "Second Defense against Westphal" (1556), in the *Institutes* (1559), and "The Best Method of Obtaining Concord" (1561) are similar, while the *Consensus Tigurinus* (1549) has some noticeable differences.

In his "Second Defense against Westphal" (1556), it is clear that Calvin opposes the Zwinglian idea of sacrament as an empty sign.[172] In the *Institutes* (1559), he also discusses the idea that a symbol given by God cannot be meaningless.

> The thing meant consists in the promises which are in a manner included in the sign . . . in the mystery of the Supper, by the symbols of bread and wine, Christ, his body and his blood, are truly exhibited to us, that in them he fulfilled all obedience, in order to procure righteousness for us, first, that we might become one

---

168. Wendel, *Calvin*, 330.
169. Rorem, "Consensus Tigurinus," 88.
170. Calvin, "Short Treatise," 147.
171. Ibid., 158.
172. Calvin, "Second Defense," 275. It is evident that there are clear differences between the *Tigurinus* and "Second Defense." Davis summarizes as follows: "The exhibiting function of the Eucharist; union with Christ; true partaking of the body and blood of Christ; the relation of sign and thing signified; the special nourishing function of the Eucharist as opposed to simple faith; the mode of communion and the nature of instrumentality and accommodation." See Davis, *Clearest Promises of God*, 56–57.

body with him; and, secondly, that being made partakers of his substance.[173]

He also explains in "Obtaining Concord" that God "performs by the secret virtue of his Spirit that which he figures by external signs, and hence on God's side it is not empty signs that are set before us, but reality and efficacy at the same time joined with them."[174] Unlike Zwingli, Calvin insists that even though the sign itself does not confer grace by its power, it is not a mere "empty promise," but bears meaning which cannot be separated from it. People are true participants who participate in *res*.

In his later writing, such as "Obtaining Concord" and "The Clear Explanation of Sound Doctrine Concerning the True Partaking of the Flesh and Blood of Christ in the Holy Supper" (1561), Calvin insists the sign of sacrament works beyond mere symbol. He says, "[The sacraments] are as truly exhibited to us as if Christ were placed in bodily presence before our view, or handled by our hands"; Christ "recommends the eating of his flesh, viz., that we are quickened by the true partaking of him, which he designated by the terms eating and drinking."[175] He also believes that partakers are "substantially fed" via the sacraments, though he rejects "the gross fiction of a local compounding."[176]

Calvin does not insist on transubstantiation and concomitance, but he expresses belief in God's grace and real presence in the symbolic act of the sacrament. His expressive imagery is eloquent and not unlike the language found in mysticism. He says, "Paul declares that we are of the members and bones of Christ . . . by the power of His Spirit, He engrafts us into His body . . . the flesh and blood of Christ are offered (*exhiberi*) to us in the Lord's Supper."[177] This differs from the Roman Catholic idea of transubstantiation or Luther's notion of consubstantiation. He says in the "Short Treatise,"

> It is a spiritual mystery, which cannot be seen by the eye, nor comprehended by the human understanding. It is therefore symbolized by visible signs, as our infirmity requires, but in such a way that it is not a bare figure, but joined to its reality

---

173. Calvin, *Institutes*, IV.xvii.11.

174. Calvin, "Best Method," 325.

175. Calvin, *Institutes*, IV.xvii.5. Calvin says, "Nor are we merely reminded that Christ was once offered on the cross for us, but this sacred union is ratified to us, by which his death may be our life; in other words, being engrafted into his body, we are truly nourished by it, just as our bodies feed upon meat and drink." See Calvin, "Obtaining Concord," 326.

176. Calvin, "Clear Explanation," 264.

177. Ibid., 210.

and substance. It is therefore with good reason that the bread is called body, since not only does it represent it to us, but also presents it to us. Hence we shall readily concede that the name body of Jesus Christ is transferred to the bread, as it is the sacrament and figure of it. But we likewise add that the sacraments of the Lord ought not and cannot at all be separated from their reality and substance. To distinguish them so that they be not confused is not only good and reasonable but wholly necessary. But to divide them so as to set them up the one without the other is absurd. Therefore when we see the visible sign, we ought to regard what representation it carries and by whom it is given us.[178]

Calvin believes that symbol and *res* are unified, but maintains a tension between them. When a person points to the moon with a finger, the important thing is the moon itself, not the finger. To Calvin, the Holy Spirit cannot be subjected to the material; we must focus on God's presence rather than the sacramental matter. The symbol itself is not an empty figure, but closely related to the *res* of Eucharist. Calvin explains this with "sacramental manner."[179] That is to say, "the figure is not put forward as an empty phantom, but taken grammatically to denote a metonymy."[180]

According to Calvin, the physical body of Christ is in the heavens, but at the place of the Lord's Supper, Christ is present "really and substantially."[181] At the Lord's Supper, the minds of believers ascend into heaven by the work of the Holy Spirit, which overcomes distance and makes the sacrament effective. Calvin says, "He testifies and seals in the Supper, and that not by presenting a vain or empty sign, but by exerting an efficacy of the Spirit by which he fulfills what he promises. And truly the thing there signified he exhibits and offers to all who sit down at that spiritual feast."[182]

In Lutheran theology, the Holy Spirit is subjected to the Word; and in Roman Catholic theology, the Holy Spirit is subjected to the material. However, Calvin's insistence on the sovereignty of the Holy Spirit attempts to overcome the shortcomings of Lutheran and Roman Catholic sacramental theology. But it's difficult to determine whether he emphasized subjectivity or objectivity when we consider his unclear use of the word *res*. Why, unlike

---

178. Calvin, "Short Treatise," 147–48.
179. John Calvin, "Obtaining Concord," 327.
180. Ibid.
181. John Calvin, "Second Defense," 280.
182. Calvin, *Institutes*, IV.xvii.10.

Why Children and Cognitively Challenged Individuals

Zwingli, does Calvin use the concept of *res* frequently in his writings on the sacrament?[183] Studying this can show Calvin's intentions more clearly.

Hans Grass gives several reasons, taking into account the latter part of Calvin's work.[184] Calvin's use of *res* emphasizes the reality that Christ is present at the Lord's Supper, and that people eat and drink the body and blood of Christ—although he opposes the transubstantiation of material itself or the idea of a purely spiritual Christ. He says, "I am not satisfied with the view of those who, while acknowledging that we have some kind of communion with Christ, only make us partakers of the Spirit, omitting all mention of flesh and blood."[185]

Calvin's thought on *res* has raised objection from scholars in the Reformed tradition such as Charles Hodge, who says,

> It has high symbolical authority in its favour. It is being clearly expressed in the *Consensus Tigurinus* the common platform of the church, on this whole subject, and in the Second Helvetic Confession the most authoritative of all the symbols of the Reformed church, and even in the Heidelberg Catechism, outweigh the private authority of Calvin or the dubious expression for the Gallican, Belgic, and some minor Confessions.[186]

Hodge refutes Calvin, writing that "while Calvin denied the real presence of the body and blood of Christ in the Eucharist . . . he affirmed that they were dynamically present . . . he held, therefore, that there was something not only supernatural, but truly miraculous, in this divine ordinance."[187] Hodge insists, "Anything is said to be present when it operates duly on our perceiving faculties . . . A spiritual object is present when it is intellectually apprehended and when it acts upon the mind."[188] To Hodge, presence is "meant [as] not local nearness, but intellectual cognition and apprehension, believing appropriation, and spiritual appropriation."[189] Hodge insists on the idea of "a presence of Christ's body in the Lord's Supper; not local, but spiritual; not to the senses, but to the mind and to faith; and not of nearness,

---

183. Gerrish says, "When relations with the Lutherans turned sour, he continued to insist on this bond and to distance himself, on the other side, from Zwingli." See Gerrish, *Grace and Gratitude*, 174.

184. Grass, *Die Abendmahlslehre*, 248–51.

185. Calvin, *Institutes*, IV.xvii.7.

186. Hodge, "Mystical Presence," 251.

187. Hodge, *Systematic Theology*, 3:628.

188. Ibid., 637–38.

189. Ibid., 641.

but of efficacy."[190] The sacraments "were appointed to . . . convey or apply, and thus to sanctify, those who by faith receive them."[191] However, Hodge's opinion is similar to Zwingli's symbolic memorialism.

John Nevin disagrees with Hodge, believing that the sacrament "is a real communion with the Word made flesh; not simply with the divinity of Christ, but with humanity also; since both are inseparably joined together in his persons."[192] He says,

> The body of Christ is in heaven, the believer on earth; but by the power of the Holy Ghost, nevertheless, the obstacle of such vast local distance is fully overcome, so that in the sacramental act, while the outward symbols are received in an outward way, the very body and blood of Christ are at the same time inwardly and supernaturally communicated to the worthy receiver, for the real nourishment of his new life.[193]

Nevin criticizes modern puritanism and rationalism, which "make the objective to be nothing, and the subjective to be all in all," disregarding forms while elevating the spirit to absolute importance.[194] He claims modern puritans and rationalists "sink the sacraments to the character of mere outward rites; or possibly deny their necessity altogether."[195] According to his analysis of the Reformed doctrine of Christ's presence,

> It asserted always a real presence, not simply as an object of thought or intelligence on the part of men but in the way of actual communication on the part of Christ—a presence not conditioned by the relations of space, but transcending these altogether in a higher sphere of life; a presence, not material, but dynamic.[196]

The critical factors are the incarnation and the relationship between symbol and signified.

Robert Letham evaluates the argument between Hodge and Nevin as follows: "The verdict of history has been that Nevin was right and that

---

190. Ibid., 643.

191. Ibid., 487.

192. Nevin, *Mystical Presence*, 58.

193. Nevin, *The Mystical Presence*, 61. However, Nevin says, "not that the material particles of Christ body are supposed to be carried over, by this supernatural process, into the believer's person." See Ibid., 61.

194. Ibid., 148.

195. Ibid., 147–48.

196. Nevin, *Mystical Presence*, 292.

Hodge had failed to grasp his own theological tradition."[197] Calvin did not exclusively value subjectivity or intelligence in sacrament. Although he opposes the idea of transubstantiation, he also believes the real presence of Christ is in the place of Lord's Supper. This cannot be categorized as objectivity or subjectivity, but can be called a third way, in that he perceives the real presence of Christ at this time, at this place, by the help of the Holy Spirit. This can be the starting point for inclusion of children and the cognitively challenged. Sacrament itself cannot produce grace, but by the presence of God, and God's use of the sacrament as tool for enhancing faith, participation in the sacrament can be the place of fellowship between God and human, which can nurture faith formation.

APPLICATION OF CALVIN'S SACRAMENTAL THEOLOGY

The Presbyterian and Reformed churches support a faith formation pattern that leads from infant baptism to confirmation. A baby born into a Christian family can always be baptized, although the parents' confession is necessary. When cognitively challenged persons reach the age of confirmation, parents and church members may be unsure whether it is proper for them to join the Lord's Supper.

Based on the idea of "recognizing the body of the Lord" in 1 Cor 11:29, the Reformed church has opposed participation of children prior to confirmation, considering them not intellectually mature enough.[198] Many scholars consider the 1 Corinthians text a universal teaching about the Lord's Supper.[199] And only one Reformed confession mentions participation of cognitively challenged persons.[200]

Calvin did not address participation of the cognitively challenged; he dealt only with infant communion. He says, "The Supper is intended for those of riper years, who, having passed the tender period of infancy, are fit

---

197. Letham, *Lord's Supper*, 2.

198. The only Reformer who insists on the validity of infant communion is Musculus. See Musculus, *Loci communes theologiae sacrae*, 471–73, in Bavinck, *Reformed Dogmatics*, 4:583. Also, the Reformed Church did not show concern about this matter. Keith A. Mathison says, "As Robert Rayburn observed in his minority report to the PCA's General Assembly, Reformed theology never gave this issue the deep exegetical and theological reflection that it gave to so many other issues." See Mathison, *Given for You*, 320.

199. See Venema, "New Testament Evidence," 24; Gallant, *Feed My Lambs*, 75.

200. The only Reformed confession that mentions the participation of the cognitively challenged is Micron's Shorter Catechism (1552). See van't Spijker, *Church's Book of Comfort*, 142.

to bear solid food. . . . If they cannot partake worthily without being able duly to discern the sanctity of the Lord's body, why should we stretch out poison to our young children instead of vivifying food?"[201] Calvin would permit the Lord's Supper only after public confession and explanation of Christian faith.[202] Right knowledge and right confession were important factors for participation in the Lord's Supper. However, in Geneva, catechetical instruction and admission to the Lord's Supper took place at about eleven to twelve years of age. Even though Calvin opposed infant communion, he did not oppose communion for more mature children.

In Calvin's thought on sacrament and means of grace, there are some expressions that can be used to uphold the possibility of sacrament for the cognitively challenged. Although he values reason and knowledge of God, he also recognizes the peculiar status of sacrament itself. He opposes *ex opere operato*, but does acknowledge the importance of participation itself.[203] He says, "For the Lord there communicates his body so that he may become altogether one with us, and we with him. Moreover, since he has only one body of which he makes us all to be partakers, we must necessarily, by this participation all become one body."[204] By participating in Christ, we all become coinheritors. Wandel says, "The Supper, for Calvin, was not external—a ceremony to be performed regularly . . . Christ is made completely one with us and we with him."[205]

It is evident that Calvin believes the grace of sacrament cannot be harmed by the shortcomings of the human beings receiving the sacrament. So, in this way, Calvin is inconsistent, arguing for a level of cognitive understanding even as he argues that human shortcomings do not harm the sacramental grace. He also emphasizes that sacrament is the tool of the Holy Spirit: "The bond of that connection, therefore, is the Spirit of Christ, who unites us to him and is a kind of channel by which everything that Christ has and is, is derived to us."[206] The Holy Spirit works both within and outside the covenant. This is the freedom of the Holy Spirit—the means cannot restrict the sovereignty of the Spirit. Sometimes the Holy Spirit works beyond the means of grace, and therefore, the means itself cannot be absolutized. So, Calvin's pneumatology opens the possibility for children and the cognitively challenged to participate in the sacrament and public worship.

201. Calvin, *Institutes*, IV.xvi.30.
202. Peter, "Geneva Primer," 138.
203. Calvin, *Institutes*, IV.xiv.14
204. Ibid., IV.xvii.38.
205. Wandel, *Eucharist in the Reformation*, 171.
206. Calvin, *Institutes*, IV.xvii.12.

Why Children and Cognitively Challenged Individuals

If the Holy Spirit wills, these groups can receive grace and enlightenment through participation.

To decide whether to include someone in the Lord's Supper and public worship based solely on cognitive ability raises issues with respect to sacramental theology. For example, if one person endeavors to test and assess another's cognitive ability for this purpose, it means a human becomes the judge of another's religious ability. As Horton says, "The Supper is a means of grace for the weak, not a reward for the strong."[207] Exclusion based on perceived intellect puts humans in control of the Lord's Supper.

If sacramental symbol is closely related to *res*, as Calvin says, it is possible that symbols work in the minds of people because they are inseparable from the contents.[208] As Horton says, "[Sacrament] brings subjective assurance because it is an objective pledge."[209] This cannot be tested by other people. What happens in the sacraments surpasses the limits of human understanding. Calvin himself says, "I will not be ashamed to confess that it is too high a mystery either for my mind to comprehend or my words to express; and to speak more plainly, I rather feel than understand it."[210] Cognition is one method that helps humans to learn, but the mind can also be opened to and by the work of the Holy Spirit, who can work using other methods incomprehensible to us.

The Holy Spirit is present wherever people gather in the name of God. The place of the Lord's Supper, where we gather to celebrate God, is a holy place because of the presence of God. The people gathered around the table are sanctified because the Holy Spirit works in their minds, bodies, and spirits. If children and cognitively challenged individuals join in the holy place, they too can enjoy sacramental grace by the will and work of the Holy Spirit, who governs very aspect of the sacrament. The part of humans in this is to help educate children and the cognitively challenged to enhance their knowledge of God and deepen the sincerity of their confession.

The sacrament is God's gift to us and cannot be corrupted by humans. The sacrament itself has peculiarity in that it is intimately related to the grace of God. Of course, the sacrament itself cannot deliver grace magically, but the practice of sacrament is a means of grace and an effective tool for faith. Concerning inclusion of children and the cognitively challenged, the critical factor is God's grace and God's giving of himself. The question

---

207. Horton, *Christian Faith*, 819.

208. Reformed theologian Michael Horton says, "A sacrament is not only the sign, but the reality signified that is joined to them." See Horton, *Christian Faith*, 815.

209. Ibid., 781.

210. Calvin, *Institutes*, IV.xvii.32.

of sacramental objectivity and subjectivity is resolved when we open our minds to the work of the Holy Spirit, which is not subject to or governed by sacramental material, sacramental word, or human intellect. The Holy Spirit works according to his sovereignty and will. Based on this and on God's faithfulness to his covenant, we can clearly see the validity and possibility of including children and cognitively challenged people who are born and raised in the covenant community into the worship.

7

What are the Benefits for Children and Cognitively Challenged Individuals?

How does a church benefit from including these groups, and how do children, cognitively challenged persons, and their families benefit? The ways are many.

DEVELOPMENT THROUGH EXPERIENCE FORMS A POSITIVE SELF-IMAGE, AND TEACHES SOCIAL SKILLS

Through experience, children and cognitively challenged persons gain power for their own growth and development. Experience is accumulated from participation, and this nurtures development of their thinking. The wisdom that grows from developed thinking makes more effective communication. Churches must extend opportunities for learning experiences to children and cognitively handicapped persons so they can learn to make "informed spiritual choices."[1] The reality, however, has been that churches have not permitted their participation. As Jean Vanier writes, "those with intellectual disabilities are among the most oppressed and excluded people in the world."[2] Their parents and families are sometimes hesitant to include them fully in everyday life, and society is often inhospitable to them.

---

1. Swinton and Mowat, *Practical Theology*, 230.
2. Vanier, *Becoming Human*, 72.

In addition, churches have not permitted their participation in baptism and the Lord's Supper for a long time.³ The case of young children is similar. In Sunday public worship, one rarely gets the impression that children are welcomed. Public worship is mostly adult worship; its contents and form are not child-friendly. Furthermore, churches tend to see a calm mood in worship as a sign of holiness. Therefore, children and cognitively challenged persons have largely been deprived of the opportunity to experience Sunday public worship and the sacraments, and the opportunity for growth that comes with participation. Given the chance to participate in worship and church life, these groups have potential for full faith development.

Faithfulness and intelligence in the worship should not be devalued, but the idea that cognitive ability is essential to being a good worshiper makes church an inaccessible environment for children and cognitively challenged persons. However, if the church includes them in the worship and life of the church, everyone in the church can benefit.

Firstly, inclusion in the community helps nurture formation of a positive self-image for cognitively challenged individuals. Duvdevany found that "physical self-concept and satisfaction with the whole self-concept were better in individuals with intellectual disabilities who participated in integrated leisure programs as opposed to segregated ones."⁴ Of course, this study is not focused on the relationship between religion and self (and worship is not a leisure activity), but does suggest a connection between self-concept and integration in a community. When people live in fellowship with other people and are received, nurtured, and cared for, they feel they are loved and their existence is precious. Vogel, Polloway, and Smith's study does focus directly on religious matters, and shows a similar impact of inclusion in a religious community on the formation of self-esteem among people with cognitive disabilities.⁵ Similarly, belonging is necessary for development of

---

3. Nouwen, *Adam*, 24. In fact, until now, the church has not been hospitable to the idea of including children and cognitively challenged persons in public worship and the sacraments. In the case of children, not only has there been concern about the propriety of infant baptism, but since the twelfth century, children have been prohibited from the Eucharistic celebrations. See Walker, *History of the Christian Church*, 274; Dalby, "End of Infant Communion," 60; Holeton, *Infant Communion*, 8; Crawford, "Infant Communion," 527, 529–30; Venema, "Paedocommunion," 28. In the case of cognitively challenged persons, it is hard to find theological reflection about their participation in the public worship. A few mentions can be found in Aquinas's *Summa Theologica*, and Luther's *Table Talk*, but it is hard to find the church's effort toward a positive attitude for their participation.

4. Taylor, et al., *Mental Retardation*, 174, reporting Duvdevany, "Self-Concept and Adaptive Behavior," 419–29.

5. Vogel, et al., "Inclusion of People with Mental Retardation," 100–11.

self-image in children. Participating in the religious community, children learn they are loved and connected to adults and friends.

Secondly, by participating in the worship and small groups, cognitively challenged persons and children are given opportunities to learn from peer groups who do not have intellectual disadvantages. Those who are cognitively challenged especially "need regular and close contact to acquire typical interactive behaviors, typical speech patterns where possible, and appropriate behaviors in general."[6] Continuing experience is crucial; repetitive exposure is needed for these individuals to assimilate information.[7] Participating in the public worship and ability-appropriate group activities weekly, cognitively challenged individuals are exposed to the contents of worship and Christian faith, and become accustomed to Christian mood and worship practice.[8] Above all, with a peer group's consideration, care, and help, cognitively challenged individuals can have an opportunity to practice what is taught by other people by themselves. This is an opportunity for self-determination; which, in turn, fortifies their potential and enthusiasm for achieving goals.[9]

Thirdly, participation in the religious community can enhance physical and mental health for the cognitively challenged. According to Patricia Pickett-Cooper, many studies show the close relationship between a lack of religious participation and increased health problems, both emotional and physical.[10] Participating in religious meetings and worship can also improve health for cognitively challenged people, because religion arouses the inner mind, and positively impacts emotions and the body.[11]

Furthermore, children and the cognitively challenged can learn and exercise social skills in the religious community. Yust says, "Welcoming persons with autism spectrum disorders and inviting them to interact with others in the faith community multiplies the opportunities for constructive social feedback required in new skill acquisition."[12] The cognitively challenged are sometimes lacking in sociability. This is partly related to their disability, but also largely related to the lack of sufficient opportunities

6. Downing, *Academic Instruction*, 11; also see Yust, "A Word Apart," 76.

7. Giangreco, "Foundational Concepts," 19.

8. Picket-Cooper's study data shows the sources of learning about God are primarily parents, church, and experience of prayer and healing. See Pickett-Cooper, "In My Own Words," 55.

9. Wehmeyer, "Self-Determination," 22–29.

10. See Pickett-Cooper, "In My Own Words," 1. Also see Jones Ault, "Participation of Families," 10–11.

11. Poston and Turnbull, "Role of Spirituality and Religion," 101–103.

12. Yust, "A Word Apart," 75.

to communicate with others. It is common knowledge that even though cognitively challenged persons often are not successful in traditional schools, they often have occupations in society. In this case, social skills are even more important, and can only be learned belonging to a group and community. If the church embraces the cognitively challenged, it can help them learn to communicate more effectively and to practice controlling themselves according to the atmosphere of the community—a great opportunity to develop maturity. Young children also may also develop social skills participating in a religious group. Social skills are learned by direct contact and engagement.

Fourth, participation in public worship and the sacraments greatly impacts Christian faith formation, which has a deep connection to the relationship between God and God's people.[13] Because of this relationship, people can know and believe in God; similarly, through relationships with people, faith is nurtured and disciplined. In worship, people encountering God personally and communally—singing hymns, listening to God's Word, and praying—and are transformed. While receiving the bread and cup at the Lord's Supper, people experience God's love more vividly. Without participation in public worship and sacraments, children and cognitively challenged persons are deprived of enough opportunities for being formed and nurtured in the body of Christ.

The verse "discerning the body" in 1 Cor 11:29 is often used to support the necessity of oral confession to receive the bread and cup, leading to exclusion of children and cognitively challenged individuals from the sacrament.[14] But Jeffrey A. D. Weima says, "Although we cannot know with certainty what led to divisions over the Lord's Supper at Corinth, it is clear that the problem involved social discrimination: the wealthy Christians celebrated the Lord's Supper in a way that despised and humiliated their poorer fellow believers."[15] The context of the text is one of "social discrimination" rather than universal instruction on the Lord's Supper. Based on this, Weima insists on the necessity of including children in the Lord's Supper.

> When children today are excluded from the Lord's Supper, there is the very real danger of committing the same sin for which Paul criticized the Corinthians: humiliating fellow believers. But, this interpretation does not automatically mean, however,

---

13. Maddix, "Spiritual Formation," 241–44.
14. Venema, "New Testament Evidence," 26.
15. Weima, "Children at the Lord's Supper," 8.

that children ought to take part fully at the communion table, nor does it remove the need for some form of self-examination.[16]

Even though this text cannot be used for upholding the necessity of children's communion directly, it is discriminatory to ban children who are born in a covenant family from the Lord's Table. Even though the Bible does not specifically mention the practice of the Lord's Supper for children and those who are cognitively challenged, the Pauline text insists that people's eyes be wide open about the matter of discrimination among groups of believers in the church. If "recognizing the body" appeals to the necessity of deconstructing discrimination and considering other bodies in the church community, cannot this problem be solved by permitting intergenerational experience and inclusion of people with a range of ability levels in church life? Children and cognitively challenged individuals, by participating in the public worship and the sacraments, gain the opportunity to reflect on their inner minds and consider other persons in the community; in this sense, inclusion can be a driving force to accomplish the real meaning of "recognizing the body."

ENCOURAGING THE FAMILY

Inclusion benefits not only cognitively challenged individuals, but also their families. It is not easy for the parents and family of cognitively challenged children to participate in public worship. When cognitively challenged persons or children make noise or trouble during the worship service, parents must endure glaring eyes from other adults. Many families experience frustration at this point.[17] According to Poston and Turnbull, some parents who have a cognitively challenged child "felt that their children were not accepted or that they did not have the support to participate fully."[18] If they cannot endure this process, they separate from worship and small groups. But if the church shows hospitality and welcomes them into full participation, families of young children and the cognitively challenged feel support

---

16. Ibid., 8. Berkouwer says, "We do not come to the Lord's Supper to testify there to our worthiness, but with the acknowledgement that we seek our life in Jesus Christ and that without him we lie in the midst of death." Berkouwer, *Sacrament*, 257.

17. Regarding the current status of cognitively challenged individuals' participation in the faith community, including a survey of hospitality in the community, see Carter, *Including People with Disabilities*, 7–8. Webb-Mitchell writes about "many stories of families with children with disabilities, who were asked to leave the church because of a child who was 'uncontrollable,' talking loudly or strolling up and down the aisle during worship." See Webb-Mitchell, *Beyond Accessibility*, 15.

18. Poston and Turnbull, "Role of Spirituality," 103.

and encouragement.[19] The religious life and feeling of being welcomed have a positive impact on the spiritual life of parents and families.[20] They can truly experience the love of God through welcome and respect from the rest of the church for their lives and the lives of their loved one, which can give them more time and energy to nurturing their disadvantaged family member's needs.

Another benefit for families is that, while participating in worship and praying together as a family, family members share together the formation of Christian faith. Parents and caregivers better understand their own faith from teaching, supporting, and encouraging children and the cognitively challenged in worship. Parents and caregivers must rethink Bible stories and other content to teach children or the cognitively challenged in ways more understandable to them. Using "baby talk" to teach children and the cognitively challenged, they begin to understand the grace and sacrifice of God and acknowledge thankfulness toward God.[21]

Praying together, family members can feel oneness and belonging together.[22] This helps create their fidelity to the Christian faith and fortifies their love for each other as fellow Christians. Hearing the prayer and basic confession of children and cognitively challenged individuals, other family members can enjoy and realize the purity of their minds in the presence of God. When families sing hymns and psalms together, faith is formed and strengthened as they consider the hymn's meaning, and intergenerational worship fortifies the process, making the whole family better worshippers.[23] Children and the cognitively challenged may not be able to think critically about hymns and psalms, but they can respond to the sounds and rhythms. Adult family members become conscious of their attitude and practice of faith in the eyes of their child, and are reminded of God's grace and patience while teaching and helping them.

WHAT ARE THE BENEFITS TO THE CHURCH?

While it may be easy to see how children and cognitively challenged persons and their families will benefit from inclusion and participation, it may be harder for other members of a congregation, who may feel the participation

---

19. Ibid.
20. Selway and Ashman, "Disability, Religion and Health," 14–15.
21. Actually, the word "baby talk" is borrowed from John Calvin. See Calvin, *Institutes*, I.xiii.1.
22. Casinos and Beckwith, *Children's Ministry*, 115.
23. Ibid.

of these groups interferes with their own opportunities to enjoy the worship and learning. However, everyone in the faith community can benefit by inclusion of children and the cognitively challenged.

Intergenerational worship that is inclusive of all ability levels

Through the inclusion of cognitively challenged persons and children, the church can have worship that includes all generations and abilities. Intergenerational worship has been an issue among Reformed churches in North America.[24] Generally, worship is separated according to culture, generation, and theological or practical appetite, and it is hard to find a church that practices intergenerational worship.[25] Such segregation contributes to narrow thinking in congregants and deprives them of the experience of oneness in the presence of God. With barriers among themselves, people cannot experience a real fellowship with God and others. People learn from one another, even children and the cognitively challenged, and fully able adult members most definitely can learn reciprocally from them. The existence of young and weak people remind us of God's Word: "I tell you the truth, anyone who will not receive the kingdom of God like a little child will never enter it" (Mark 10:15). Their presence has great meaning.

In most churches in South Korea that separate worship according to age, children may grow from toddler to college age exclusively within the Sunday school system. In addition, many parents will discourage older children's participation in public worship so they can spend more time studying for the highly competitive Scholastic Aptitude Test (SAT). So, after they become adults, they are not accustomed to public worship. Thus, many churches have suffered from a generational gap in worship, and the traditional worship pattern of the church has been confronted with the need for change.

Howard Vanderwell defines intergenerational worship as "worship in which people of every age are understood to be equally important. . . . Each generation has the same significance before the face of God and in the worshiping congregation. Each and all are made in the image of God."[26] It includes every generation and respects their differences, just as every generation joined the place of covenantal renewal in the Old Testament. Let us look at Josh 24:1 and 8:35. Joshua 24 narrates the covenant renewal at Shechem. In verse 1, "Joshua assembled all the tribes of Israel."

24. Vanderwell, "New Issue," 1.
25. Ibid., 2.
26. Ibid., 11.

This is similar to chapter 8.[27] In Canaan, Moses read God's law before the whole assembly of Israel, including "women, little ones, and sojourners."[28] Therefore, intergenerational worship is a sort of covenant renewal.[29] Every person is important, because every person bears the image of God. This is different from the concept of equality in the world. Everyone joins the worship as a covenant renewal, and therefore, intergenerational worship is a sort of "countercultural activity."[30] Each generation can learn and absorb each other's merit. Children's apparent innocence and willingness to question; adolescents' and young adults' enthusiasm, energy, and rebellion; and older generations' wisdom and theological reflection are mingled, making for a "complex learning environment."[31] In particular, a "child's spontaneity and lack of inhibitions coupled with his inherent spiritual inclinations can add a dimension to corporate worship that is not found when children are excluded."[32] Such enthusiasm and vitality makes public worship, which is easily "fossilized" in tradition, more vivid and energetic. And children and cognitively challenged persons, along with parents and caregivers, receive concern and encouragement from the other adults in the congregation.[33]

The most important thing is that reformation and transition of worship patterns in the church should fit within the church's situation and congregational assent. Intergenerational worship does not require the abolition of Sunday school; for instance, age-appropriate worship or small-group activity could be supplemental to integrated public worship. Worship that is sensitive to the traits of children, special groups, and differing developmental abilities is necessary for effective nurture.[34]

It is also necessary for children and the cognitively challenged to encounter higher stages in worship for their own development. In addition to age-appropriate learning, children and cognitively challenged individuals sometimes just need more encounters in the worship services. Vygotsky's "zone of proximal development" supports the possibility of learning among children and cognitively challenged persons with the help of teachers and

27. Vanderwell and de Waal Malefyt, "Worship as Covenant Renewal," http://worship.calvin.edu/resources/resource-library/worship-as-covenant-renewal-bible-study-/ (accessed August, 31, 2013).

28. Woudstra, *Book of Joshua*, 150.

29. Regarding worship as covenant renewal, see Witvliet, *Worship Seeking Understanding*, 25–30.

30. Glassford, "Fostering an Intergenerational Culture," 71.

31. Allen, "No Better Place," 115.

32. Beckwith, *Postmodern Children's Ministry*, 142.

33. Yust, *Real Kids, Real Faith*, 164.

34. Keely, *Helping Our Children*, 108–09.

adults.[35] Although children and the cognitively challenged may not demonstrate a certain ability now, today's experience can be tomorrow's ability.

So, I insist on the wise interconnection between public worship and age- and developmentally-appropriate worship. Regarding this, Holly Allen says:

> If children or teens are normally separated during the primary worship service, search for ways to include the children for fifteen to twenty minutes (or more) of praise in the Sunday morning worship on a regular basis (once a month, every fifth Sunday, every other week, or all the time).[36]

A church can maintain both Sunday school and public worship and gradually integrate generations through efforts to enhance mutual understanding and accommodation. When planning intergenerational public worship, the pastor and worship committee should also keep in mind that intergenerational worship is, of course, not intended for children alone, but should keep children's concentration abilities in mind while also fostering a sense of mission in adults.[37] Further, rather than dismissing children after the sermon in the preface of worship, the church may also want to prepare them for opportunities to join in reading the Bible, singing in the children's choir, and helping with special events. These all provide excellent opportunities for learning liturgy and sacrament. Arousing the educational mission for children and cognitively challenged people, a congregation makes their church a church for all people.

Friendship

The participation of children and cognitively challenged individuals in worship helps all congregants experience new and real friendship within the faith community. Because everyone is made according to the image of God, church members can develop and share real friendships, despite differences in age, intelligence, or social status.[38]

> Friendship is available to everyone, at least potentially. The tiny baby who is befriended by her mother is learning friendship. The elderly person around whom a community gathers when she is dying is capable of teaching friendship. Friendship, by its

35. Vygotsky, *Mind in Society*, 89.
36. Allen, "No Better Place," 119.
37. Ritchie, *Always in Rehearsal*, 46.
38. Swinton, *Resurrecting the Person*, 44.

nature, assumes that persons live in relationship, and that relationships are good.[39]

People can share friendship with anyone in any circumstance, because friendship is not merely for satisfying one person's needs, but for sharing and being together. It is evident that ordinary persons can enjoy friendship with cognitively challenged persons, and learn much. As Amos Yong says, those who are cognitively challenged "are conduits of the revelatory and transformative gifts of God's Spirit for those who will slow down enough to befriend them."[40] Through their existence, people can see the presence of God. Their presence in the church community is God's gift, which makes us feel God's grace and presence. John Swinton insists, "In a very real sense, truly shalomic friendship is sacramental in that it reveals something very profound about the nature of God."[41] However, this friendship requires adults of ordinary intelligence levels to develop patience and make time. Friendship with those who have profound cognitive disabilities can be especially challenging; the story of L'Arche shows real friendship is possible only after accumulating trust over a long time.[42] When Henri Nouwen first tried to care for Adam, he had trouble communicating and efficiently helping Adam. He became frustrated and thought this work was for specially trained persons. But after meeting with Adam every day for some months, Nouwen began to share a friendship with him.[43] Friendship is not innate, but can be achieved from experience and with practice[44]

Through friendship with people who are different from themselves, believers come to understand God's friendship with humanity. As God has shown friendship toward us who are weak and fragile, we realize that we are, each one of us, necessary for each other. Through friendship within the church—based on the friendship that Jesus showed for us—people who have not been cognitively challenged learn to see cognitively challenged individuals as not merely objects of healing, but as beings with their own personal existence.[45] Swinton considers it common for people to "associate

39. Swinton attributes this quote to Mary Hunt, but cites Hoekendijk, *Church Inside Out*, 105. See Swinton, *Resurrecting the Person*, 44.

40. Yong, *Bible, Disability, and the Church*, 114.

41. Swinton, *From Bedlam to Shalom*, 86.

42. Yong, *Bible, Disability, and the Church*, 114. To form a friendship, the church should intentionally make an effort to include those with cognitive disabilities in the public worship and small group activity. Parmley and Shannon, "Ministry and Persons," 16.

43. Nouwen, *Adam*, 40–45.

44. Swinton, *Resurrecting the Person*, 145.

45. Ibid., 37.

with others on the basis of likeness, utility, or social change."[46] That is to say, people in the world have a tendency toward the Aristotelian concept of friendship, which is that it exists for mutual interest and necessity: "Not everything seems to be loved but only what is lovable, and this seems to be what is good, pleasant, or useful."[47] To Aristotle, friendship is possible "only insofar as they [the parties involved] come to have something good from the other."[48] He considers ideal friendship as "friendship of those who are good and alike in point of virtue."[49] Of course, according to his opinion, friendship happens among "base people" based on similarity. However, he says, "The friendship of base people is corrupt: they share in base things and, being unsteady, they come to be corrupt by becoming like one another."[50]

If people abide by this perspective, children and cognitively challenged individuals cannot have friendship with "normal" adults. In Aristotelian friendship, as Hans Reinders points out, "since true friendship is possible only between persons of good character whose lives imply a rational principle, it must follow that persons with intellectual disabilities cannot be part of such friendship."[51] Nevertheless, he also insists, "We do not choose our friends for their virtue, that is, in order to extend acts of good will to them— particularly not when these friends are despised in the eyes of the world. We are called to be their friends."[52] To Christians, friendship is not just a social contract but a duty from God, who shows friendship for all people, none of whom are "qualified" to receive it in the Aristotelian sense. We must convey the character of friendship that Jesus Christ showed us. According to Swinton, the friendship of Jesus was not "instrumental," but personal.[53] Jesus overcame personal accomplishment in friendship, and made possible "the development of a positive sense of personhood."[54] His friendship is "inclusive, open and public."[55] Christians must overcome worldly friendship, and see their neighbors with the help of the friendship God shows to mankind.

46. Ibid., 39.
47. Aristotle, *Aristotle's Nicomachean Ethics*, 165.
48. Ibid., 166.
49. Ibid., 168.
50. Ibid., 209.
51. Reinders, *Receiving the Gift*, 358–59.
52. Ibid., 365.
53. Swinton, *Resurrecting the Person*, 142.
54. Ibid., 142–43.
55. Swinton, *From Bedlam to Shalom*, 83.

Hans Reinders says, "Friendship is our vocation."[56] It is challenging to maintain friendships by human will alone. To seek friendship with children and cognitively challenged persons, the church's starting point should be God's commandment. Stanley Hauerwas says,

> As Christians, our friendship is not made constant by an act of our own will, individual or corporate, or even by our own virtue, but rather because we and others find ourselves through participation in a common activity that makes us faithful both to ourselves and other. That activity is not, as it seems to be in Aristotle, mutual enjoyment as an end in itself, but rather it is the activity of a task we have been given. That task is nothing less than to participate in a new way of life made possible by the life of the man Jesus.[57]

Hauerwas uses the term "common activity"; surely the representative "common activity that makes us faithful" is public worship. By worshipping together, we learn that everyone in the church is part of one body. Each is a brother and sister for whom Jesus paid his blood. Christian friendship is not an interchange for the purpose of increasing each person's virtue, as Aristotle insists, but an opportunity to nurture each other's endeavor to be faithful to God's Word proclaimed in worship. This type of friendship can be called "radical" and "messianic."[58] We are required to prepare hospitality for everyone in the public worship; through this inclusiveness, we all experience real friendship with God and with all who are our neighbors.

Nurturing the spirituality and virtue of those who serve

While worshipping together and living together in a church community, those adult Christians who do not experience cognitive challenges can learn to make more concrete effort to love and honor children and cognitively challenged people.[59] Alongside the young and differently abled, "normal" adults can learn God's will and experience their faith more deeply. As Bernardin says, "A child who is profoundly disabled and cannot speak or move can still contribute to those around him or her by a loving presence."[60] The

---

56. Reinders, *Receiving the Gift*, 365, 163.
57. Hauerwas and Pinches, *Christians Among the Virtues*, 49.
58. Swinton, *Resurrecting the Person*, 39.
59. Vanier, *Becoming Human*, 27.
60. Bernardin, *Access to the Sacraments*, 7.

very existence of children and cognitively challenged people can teach love to the older or normally abled people around them.[61]

When those adults who see themselves as "normal" worship with cognitively challenged persons and young children, they may believe that they are sacrificing opportunities to gain deeper knowledge about their faith. However, sometimes these experiences actually help develop faith more fully and deeply. Cushing and Kennedy studied whether non-disabled students would fall behind when partnered to support a severely disabled classmate, and found students in this situation actually excelled.[62] This educational insight can be applied to the spiritual dimension as well. Those people who see themselves as "ordinary" do not sacrifice in spirituality and knowledge when cognitively challenged persons and children are included in the worship; quite the opposite. For example, in order to include cognitively challenged persons and children in worship, leaders must study their traits and develop an appropriate communication method. Leaders will need to re-examine the content and delivery of worship before performing it—preachers must learn to make their messages both simpler and more profound; congregations must develop more effective education. To Christians who doubt the benefit of worshiping with weak persons, Fulkerson says,

> There is still segregation of normal from non-normal in the community. However, simply worshiping together and gathering in a face-to-face way makes a difference. When members of the community take time to physically welcome one another during the passing of the peace, bodily proprieties of normality are breached in the regular Sunday service. Some in the congregation are learning a different way to be in relation to those marked as special needs members.[63]

Being together can be a great starting point for breaking barriers between handicapped and non-handicapped persons. Prejudice is strengthened by separation. By making an effort to understand each other and practicing loving one's neighbor, personal spirituality grows. New practices can sometimes arouse opposition and awkwardness, so intentional training and discipline is necessary to support a new habit.[64] Change can start from a little thing like shaking a hand, offering a hug, or doing something together.

61. Reinders, *Receiving the Gift*, 320.
62. Downing, *Academic Instruction*, 12.
63. Fulkerson, *Places of Redemption*, 124.
64. Hauerwas, *Community of Character*, 148.

Hauerwas explains says, "Aristotle and Aquinas suggest that it is through our habits that we acquire a 'second nature'; and insofar as those habits are virtuous they furnish us with a nature befitting our moral structure."[65] That is to say, virtue can be gained from practice itself. Aristotle goes on to say, "For the things which we have to learn before we can do them we learn by doing... Hence, it is no small matter whether one habit or another is inculcated in us from early childhood; on the contrary it makes a considerable difference, or rather, all the difference."[66] If the church invites children and cognitively challenged persons into the worship weekly, and all experience liturgy and sacraments together, worshippers will be trained in the "habitus of comfort with the other," and church members can extend "welcome" and "inclusion."[67]

Persons who care for children and those who are cognitively challenged often come to realize the limits of all human beings. As Hans Reinders says, those people who are accustomed to considering themselves "normal" and "ordinary" are, in fact, only "temporarily able-bodied."[68] A person can become handicapped in the body, mind, or spirit at any time. This truth, which can be very hard for an adult in full health and mature development to notice, can perhaps be best realized through fellowship with children and those who are cognitively challenged. In fellowship with those who seem to be weaker than we are, we may be fortunate enough to realize everything people have is by God's grace; this helps us to proceed with a humble mind toward God.

Stanley Hauerwas says, "To see the retarded honestly is to remind ourselves that we cannot earn significance for our lives; it is a gift from God.... I do not gain significance by trying to relieve all suffering; that would be another form of trying to establish my power.... To love the weak in Christians is to dare to free the weak from our dependency on their need."[69] Living with those whose weaknesses are more obvious in the church community, all members realize that none of us are perfect, and all need others' help. Living with Adam, Henri Nouwen found that "Adam had few distractions, few attachments, and few ambitions to fill his inner space.[70] Moreover, "[other people's] encounters with Adam often became experiences of inner renewal because he offered them an opportunity and a context to think dif-

---

65. Ibid., 123.
66. Aristotle, *Aristotle's Nicomachean Ethics*, 26–27.
67. Fulkerson, *Places of Redemption*, 124.
68. Reinders, *Receiving the Gift*, 320.
69. Hauerwas, "Christian Care of the Retarded," 133–34.
70. Nouwen, *Adam*, 30.

ferently about their lives, their goals, their aspirations. Adam offered those he met a presence and a safe space to recognize and accept their own, often invisible disabilities."[71] Serving cognitively challenged persons, people can reflect on human spirituality.

Fellowship with cognitively challenged persons and young children helps not only them, their caregivers and parents; it impacts the spirituality of an entire community:

> Children with disabilities often embody the gift of evangelism, creating a caring community around them. These children encourage congregations to find alternative ways of expressing the gospel, ways that would never have been developed if that particular child had not been in their midst.[72]

Their existence makes room in the community to care for vulnerable people, and to have concern for the matters of salvation, evangelism, and nurturance. This is not the kind of welfare offered by the worldly, but this fosters an inclusive attitude for those people to be considered full members.

Through the presence of children and cognitively handicapped persons, other people can realize that all human beings are dependent on God, and through this realization, all will be closer to God.[73] The worldly view emphasizes obtaining virtue and value by one's own exertion. Through friendship with children and handicapped persons, Christians can better realize that everything is given by God's grace, so that human beings have only to respond with gratitude, because God gave friendship to us first.

Perfecting the covenant community

The participation of children and cognitively challenged persons in worship reminds Christians that faith is not merely a personal issue. In the sacraments, the most important thing is God's grace; the starting point of sacrament is "God's self-giving."[74] This gift is given to the community, not just to individual persons. Laurence Stookey says, "Because God's action in the sacrament is bound up with the community of faith, baptism cannot be properly administered or interpreted apart from the life of that community."[75] Sacrament is closely related to communal confession and

71. Ibid., 64.
72. Webb-Mitchell, *Dancing with Disabilities*, 68.
73. Ault, "Participation of Families," 123.
74. White, *Sacraments as God's Self-Giving*, 13.
75. Stookey, "Personal and Community Faith," 76.

practice. The matter of participation of children and cognitively challenged persons is a personal one, but should be dealt with in the community through consensus and confession. This comes back to the idea that the confession of children and the cognitively challenged often does not satisfy adult and able-minded expectations. Stookey says,

> Once the community of faith exists, it cannot exclude from it those who are born into it by assuming that all forms of faith and growth in grace depend upon the attainment of a certain age or a specific level of doctrinal comprehension or ethical discrimination. Because what is proclaimed through baptism can elicit faith, the baptism of the children of the faithful is not merely appropriate but important.[76]

He first points out that once a faith community exists, persons who are born into it belong to that community because of the priority of God's grace and trust in the faith of a person, even though the person's expression and cognition may be low. According to Stookey, if young children and the cognitively challenged are raised in the church, even though they cannot clearly express with a "spoken word," they can show the existence of faith through "non-verbal" methods; therefore, they should not be excluded from the sacrament.[77]

In fact, currently many people's attitude of faith is too personalized; they focus too much on personal growth, individual growth of knowledge, and one's personal salvation.[78] They find it easy to dismiss or ignore the communal dimension of faith. Stanley Hauerwas says,

> Mentally handicapped people are reminders that belief and faith are not individual matters, but faith names the stance of the church as a political body in relation to the world. We are not members of a church because we know what we believe, but we are members of a church because we need the whole church to believe for us.[79]

That is to say, children and cognitively challenged people's existence teaches us that human vulnerability means human beings are not perfect, but all need each other's help in the community.[80] By sharing worship and the sacraments together, Christians will learn not to consider faith as some-

---

76. Ibid.
77. Ibid.
78. Stookey, *Baptism*, 72.
79. Hauerwas, "Church and the Mentally Handicapped," 184.
80. Webb-Mitchell, *Beyond Accessibility*, 40.

thing obtained through personal understanding, but remember that faith is also communally transferred, not automatically, but through the work of the Holy Spirit.

> For what the mentally handicapped challenge the church to remember is that what saves is not our personal existential commitments, but being a member of a body constituted by practices more determinative than my personal commitment. I suspect this is the reason why mentally handicapped people often are better received in more "liturgical" traditions—that is, traditions which know that what God is doing through the community's ritual is more determinative than what any worshiper brings to or receives from the ritual.[81]

People cannot know the degree of faith in the mind of those who are still children or who are cognitively challenged, and therefore may have difficulty accepting them in the public worship and the sacraments. However, when these groups of persons are considered with respect to the faith community, their existence itself can be seen as precious, because they remind us that ordinary people are an "assembly of the righteousness" (Ps 1:5) and "great cloud of witnesses" (Heb 12:1). As Brett Webb-Mitchell insists, "in Christ's body, none of us is disabled, for we are tied into and are integral to the other parts of the body tied into the mind of Christ."[82] In other words, everyone is necessary for the formation of the church.[83] Whenever adults who are cognitively unchallenged interact with children and those who are cognitively challenged, they are reminded that "salvation cannot be by knowing this or that but rather by participating in a community through which our lives are constituted by a unity more profound than our individual ends."[84] Thus, do Christians, by participating in the covenant community, receive salvation and learn the Christian faith and confession.

Of course, as I have already argued, this is not automatic, but it is possible with the help of community. If a certain person who has a problem of cognition and communication ability, if they want to join the worship experience, this person's participation itself can be the method of visible confession. By observing liturgy as communal confession of faith, even severely cognitive challenged individuals, with the help of family and friends in the community, can join public worship and the sacraments. Regarding the necessity of including the cognitively challenged, Hans Reinders says,

81. Ibid., 183–84.
82. Ibid., 65.
83. Ibid., 50.
84. Ibid., 184.

"Without their presence the church would be impoverished . . . without them the Eucharist cannot be celebrated as the communion with Christ at all."[85] Therefore, when young children and cognitively challenged persons participate in the worship, the church can first realize that our belonging to church is a gift from God, and then foster a sense of inclusiveness and faithfulness to the ideal of covenant community.[86] Through the participation of children and the cognitively challenged, people will notice that no person in the church is unnecessary, and that each one depends on each other as one body.

Charles Foster says, "For the first time children and youth are recognized officially as making a necessary contribution to the nurture of their elders."[87] That is to say, other believers benefit by the inclusion of children. Inclusion benefits the whole body of the church. In this respect, while dealing with Fairless's points on "inclusion of children in a church's weekly worship," Beckwith says, "a church that's working toward the meaningful inclusion of its youth in corporate worship is one that believes all ages are a part of the faith community."[88] Therefore, living together is not only important, but also very necessary.[89] By staying together, people can understand each other and experience real friendship. To proceed, Brett Webb-Mitchell insists that people can discover interdependence through the participation of children and cognitively challenged persons in the Lord's Supper.[90] That is to say, by sharing the meal at the table, people grow past a selfish nature and remember the calling as one body.

In conclusion, through the participation of the vulnerable, the church can visibly show that the church is in the world, but not of the world. The world does not honor weakness and difference; it idealizes the appearance of strength and material success. However, extending friendship to the weak and "different"—such as small children and cognitively challenged individuals—is the Christian's duty and vocation, for it mirrors the friendship God extends to us, who are weak and simple compared to God. By extending our friendship, we learn to see the weak, especially cognitively

---

85. Reinders, *Receiving the Gift*, 179. Brett Webb-Mitchell insists, "One of the reasons faith communities need the presence of people whom the world calls 'disabled' is because they enable or facilitate the group in becoming a community." See Webb-Mitchell, *Beyond Accessibility*, 39.

86. In that dimension, everyone is necessary for each other's growth of faith. See Hielema, "Wide and Long," 16.

87. Foster, "Intergenerational Religious Education," 284–85.

88. Beckwith, *Postmodern Children's Ministry*, 148.

89. Nouwen, *Adam*, 48.

90. Webb-Mitchell, *Dancing with Disabilities*, 24.

challenged people, as beings imbued with social value. Thus, the existence of cognitively challenged people in the church challenges church members to remember that the church's mission is love and compassion; and through the practice of love and compassion, true virtue is learned.

The Bible says God uses the weak to subvert worldly values and reveal his glory. Therefore, even the weakest member of the church is a fitting vessel for God's sacraments. For this reason, the participation of children and cognitively challenged people in public worship is necessary. In this dimension, the existence of the weak and the handicapped, makes people reflect on their existence and spiritual status, can be a "sacrament for us: outward signs of a more genuine humanity."[91]

---

91. Wadell, "Pondering the Anomaly," 63.

Conclusion

TRADITIONALLY, THE CHURCH HAS emphasized the role of cognitive ability and oral confession in faith formation. Therefore, children and cognitively challenged individuals who cannot satisfy these cognitive criteria have been segregated from public worship and sacrament. Of course, to some extent, knowledge about faith and some kind of ability to express it are necessary, but such knowledge itself cannot guarantee real faith. Real faith can be more clearly seen in a person's participation in the life of the church.

The knowledge- or confession-centered model of faith formation has emphasized the importance of preaching and catechetical education while giving little or no consideration to faith formation through the sacraments and public worship. The Protestant Church in particular, since struggling with Roman Catholic worship during the Reformation, has lost the precious liturgical tradition passed on from the ancestors of the faith. For example, the Protestant Church has not prioritized the frequent celebration of the Lord's Supper, and its preaching-centered worship, lacking sacrament but emphasizing the importance of listening, has made congregants somewhat passive and dependent on an intelligence-centered model of faith formation.

As a Protestant believer and Reformed scholar, my intent has been to argue that liturgy is not an empty sign or a meaningless act. Rather, it is through doing and participating in worship itself that people learn both the content of Christian faith and form the character of faith within themselves. In order to establish the formative power of liturgy, which surpasses human reason, I have studied the character of learning and religious thinking in children and persons who are cognitively challenged. Even though these people may not be able to eloquently and logically explain their theological thinking, they can express their religious understanding and abilities—through their actions toward others, for example, or their participation in religious music or painting. While researching the processes of development, I have showed how liturgy can touch not only cognitive knowledge, but also religious formation.

The necessity of liturgy begins with God's incarnation and accommodation to human imperfection. Just as God understands the weaknesses and limitations of human beings and, through Jesus Christ, enables people to understand and know him, God gives liturgy and sacrament to people so that we may be capable of understanding his Word. Liturgy is the channel for fellowship between God and human beings; when people participate in liturgy, they are able to worship and enjoy God. The repetitive actions of liturgy are not meaningless; just as a single droplet of water—when repeated—can make a beautiful lime cave throughout the years, it is possible for people to know and realize the meaning in worship through repeated doing and participating. Liturgy is not an empty act, but forms and delivers the meaning of the Word of God, thereby forming faith.

This does not deviate from the Reformed Church's theology, but is in agreement with John Calvin, Nicholas Wolterstorff, John Witvliet, and James K. A. Smith. Many people consider John Calvin an important Reformed scholar, but his critiques of the church's liturgy have been somewhat misunderstood. His *Institutes*, commentaries, treatises, and letters reveal that he did not have a negative opinion on the use of liturgy, and that he recognized the formative power of liturgy on faith. His proposed content and sequence of worship—for example, his use of the Decalogue and confession, his teaching on prayer, and the use of psalms in the worship—show he recognized liturgy's formative powers. Although the term "faith formation" did not exist at the time of his writing, his opinions on infant baptism, catechetical education, and the practice of the Lord's Supper, show emphasis on the roles of church and family in faith formation.

Generally, people tend to overemphasize cognitive ability and right knowledge in defining faith. Faith is not merely cognitive agreement or propositional statement, but a divine gift gained through fellowship with God that engages not just the intellect, but the whole person, including the body. Contrary to traditional dualistic opinions that separate the bodily and the spiritual, the body can be a tool for spiritual discipline and faith formation. Participating in public worship impacts cognition, metacognition, and subcognition. Of course, people gain faith by listening to God's Word; however, that faith is not perfect until it is embodied through action. The practice of ritual enhances human memory, and that memory forms identity and plays an important role in transformation. Participating in liturgy leads people to more profound kinds of knowing.

Because of this, young children and cognitively challenged individuals have as much potential as anyone else to benefit from participation in liturgy, and should be included. The theological scholarship of important church figures supports this. Augustine affirmed the possibility of faith among the cognitively challenged through the grace of God, and put the cognitively challenged in the same category as children in the matter of baptism. If the church baptizes infants, baptism for the cognitively challenged can be possible. But in regard to the Lord's Supper, Aquinas insisted that participation of a cognitively challenged individual should be related to the individual's experience of using reasoning in his or her life. Martin Luther is often represented as having a negative opinion of cognitively challenged persons, but his emphasis on children's faith and loving one's neighbor supports a more positive response. And Micron's concludes that salvation depends on God's sovereignty, and therefore, baptism for cognitively challenged should be given.

Cognitively challenged persons and young children, generally regarded as lacking logic and reasoning, can have religious thinking, even when they cannot express or articulate their faith. Though children and the cognitively challenged differ in speed of learning and ultimate development, both groups can develop their faith by participating in the faith community with the help of family, peer groups, and congregations, and can grow through participation and experience. Of course, it can be difficult to study the profoundly cognitively challenged, but for mildly and moderately handicapped people, who represent the majority of the cognitively challenged population, development in thinking and faith can be easily seen and assessed. We must give them enough time and opportunity for religious experiences; adult church members simply need to be patient.

Many scholars, including Scottie May, Brett Webb-Mitchell, and Karen-Marie Yust, have shown that children and the cognitively challenged can be religious. And many point out that everyone who has fellowship with God represents the image of God, regardless of their cognitive ability. The work of the Holy Spirit surpasses expectation and cognition. People must open their hearts to the work of the Holy Spirit not only in themselves, but in others, including children and the cognitively challenged. Furthermore, as John Westerhoff has shown, faith is transferred naturally when people participate in religious groups and worship. Of course, participation itself cannot guarantee faith, but observing and doing liturgy has the power to encourage and strengthen faith formation. Also, based on the idea that all people were welcomed in the covenantal renewal in the Bible, the propriety of including children and the cognitively challenged into the public worship becomes clearer.

Conclusion

A study of the objectivity and subjectivity of sacrament supports the idea that participating in a segregated worship is not sufficient for children and the cognitively challenged. Sacrament itself cannot guarantee grace automatically, but it is not an empty rite. Comparing Nevin's and Hodge's interpretations of Calvin's thought shows that Calvin did not consider sacrament a void ceremony, but gave great consideration to its spiritual characteristics. Rather than taking Hodge's stance, which overemphasizes the role of human reason, I concluded that Nevin's thought is more akin to Calvin's. Sacrament is an opportunity to impact the whole person's faith, for children and cognitively challenged individuals too.

Participation of children and the cognitively challenged benefits they themselves and their families and the church community. While worshipping, singing, and praying together, every church member can experience spiritual growth and encouragement from the community. The church benefits from welcoming these groups into the public worship, especially intergenerational worship. Segregated worship tends to focus on education, rather than on celebration, which is the essence of Christian worship, but intergenerational worship can help people experience communal spirituality and develop real friendships, which overcome the Aristotelian concept of friendship. As Jesus included people alienated from society in his communion, the church extends friendship by welcoming children and the cognitively challenged into the life of the church.

It is clear that, though the logic of children and cognitively challenged individuals is different from that of adults and those who are not cognitively challenged, the core of faith is not different between these groups of people. Many studies of the religious activities and expressions of children support their religious ability and potential for religious knowledge. Many researchers also testify to the existence of religion in the minds of the cognitively challenged, who may not be able to explain their faith in oral confession. In addition, there are many reports that affirm faith among the cognitively challenged from those who have spent many years with them. Rather than stand as examiners who test the validity of their faith, the church should stand as caregivers, helpers, or parents to those who cognitively challenged. Rather than depriving them of opportunities to participate in public worship and sacrament, the church would be wiser to help foster their growth and understanding through experience and inclusion.

Even though confession and knowledge about the Bible are important factors in forming our faith, people can also develop their faith while participating in worship and experiencing the sacrament. The work of the Holy Spirit sometimes uses human cognition, but sometimes transcends cognition and reasoning. I do not underestimate the value of preaching and catechetical instruction, but public worship is not merely Bible-study time. The core of worship lies in praising God and a personal relationship with God. Worship should be worshipful, and Word, sacrament, and liturgical factors, including confession, profession of faith, praise and prayer, should be harmonized.

We must remember that participation in worship is important in faith formation, even though it alone cannot guarantee faith. How can people experience fellowship with God without participating in the presence of God? By participation, people know God more deeply and their faith is matured. Therefore, the church should invite children and the cognitively challenged into public worship and the sacraments.

Bibliography

Agamben, Giorgio. *Infancy and History: On the Destruction of Experience.* Translated by Liz Heron. London: Verso, 1993.
Allen, Holly Catterton. "No Better Place: Fostering Intergenerational Christian Community." In *Shaped by God: Twelve Essentials for Nurturing Faith in Children, Youth, and Adults,* edited by Robert J. Keely, 110–25. Grand Rapids: Faith Alive, 2010.
American Psychiatric Association, *Diagnosis and Statistical Manual of Mental Disorders.* Arlington, VA: American Psychiatric Association, 2000.
Anderson, E. Byron. *Worship and Christian Identity: Practicing Ourselves.* Collegeville, MN: Liturgical, 2003.
Anderson, Herbert, and Edward Foley. *Mighty Stories, Dangerous Rituals: Weaving Together the Human and the Divine.* San Francisco: Jossey-Bass, 1998.
Anderson, Herbert, and Susan B. W. Johnson. *Regarding Children: A New Respect for Childhood and Families.* Louisville: Westminster/John Knox, 1994.
Antze, Paul, and Michael Lambek, eds. *Tense Past: Cultural Essays in Trauma and Memory.* New York: Routledge, 1996.
Aquinas, Thomas. *Compendium of Theology.* Translated by Richard J. Regan. Oxford: Oxford University Press, 2009.
―――. *Summa Theologica,* 5 vols. Translated by Fathers of the English Dominican Province. New York: Cosmo Classics, 2007.
Ariès, Philippe. *Centuries of Childhood: A Social History of Family Life.* Translated by Robert Baldick. New York: Vintage, 1962.
Aristotle. *Aristotle's Nichomachean Ethics.* Translated by Robert C. Bartlett and Susan D. Collins. Chicago: University of Chicago Press, 2011.
Assmann, Aleida. *Erinnerungsraume: Formen und Wandlungen des Kulturellen Gedachtnisses.* München: C. H. Beck, 1999.
Atkins, Peter. *Memory and Liturgy: The Place of Memory in the Composition and Practice of Liturgy.* Burlington, VT: Ashgate, 2004.
Augustine. "The Anti-Pelagian Works." In *The Works of Aurelius Augustine, Bishop of Hippo,* vol. 4, edited by Marcus Dods. Edinburgh: T. & T. Clark, 1872.
―――. *The First Catechetical Instruction.* Translated by Joseph P. Christopher. Westminster, MD: The Newman Bookshop, 1946.

Ault, Melinda Jones. "Participation of Families of Children with Disabilities in their Faith Communities: A Survey of Parents." PhD diss., University of Kentucky, 2010.

Baillie, Donald M. *The Theology of the Sacraments*. New York: Charles Scribner's Sons, 1957.

Barr, Martin W. *Mental Defectives: Their History, Treatment and Training*. Philadelphia: Blakiston's Son, 1913.

Bass, Dorothy C., and Craig Dykstra. "Growing in the Practices of Faith." In *Practicing our Faith: A Way of Life for a Searching People*, edited by Dorothy C. Bass, 195–204. San Francisco: Jossey-Bass, 1997.

Baumeister, Alfred A. "Some Methodological and Conceptual Issues in the Study of Cognitive Processes with Retarded People." In *Learning and Cognition in the Mentally Retarded*, edited by Penelope H. Brooks, Richard Sperber, and Charley McCauley, 1–38. Hillsdale, NJ: Lawrence Erlbaum Associates, 1984.

Bavinck, Herman. *De Opvoeding der Rijpere Jeugd*. Kampen: Kok, 1932.

———. *Reformed Dogmatics*, 4 vols. Translated by John Vriend. Grand Rapids: Baker, 2008.

Beale, Gregory K. *1-2 Thessalonians: The IVP New Testament Commentary Series*. Downers Grove, IL: IVP Academic, 2003.

Beckwith, Ivy. *Postmodern Children's Ministry: Ministry to Children in the 21st Century Church*. Grand Rapids: Zondervan, 2004.

Beckwith, Roger. T. "The Age of Admission to the Lord's Supper." *Westminster Theological Journal* 38 (1976) 123–51.

Beeke, Joel R. "Appropriating Salvation: The Spirit, Faith and Assurance, and Repentance." In *Theological Guide to Calvin's Institutes: Essays and Analysis*, edited by David W. Hall and Peter A. Lillback, 270–300. Phillipsburg, NJ: P & R, 2008.

———. *Puritan Reformed Spirituality*. Webster, NY: Evangelical, 2006.

Beirne-Smith, Mary, James R. Patton, and Shannon H. Kim. *Mental Retardation: An Introduction to Intellectual Disabilities*. Upper Saddle River, NJ: Pearson, 2005.

Belcher, Kimberly Hope. *Efficacious Engagement: Sacramental Participation in the Trinitarian Mystery*. Collegeville, MN: Liturgical, 2011.

Bell, Catherine. *Ritual: Perspectives and Dimensions*. New York: Oxford University Press, 1997.

———. *Ritual Theory, Ritual Practice*. New York: Oxford University Press, 2009.

Bergant, Dianne. "'Come, Let Us Go Up to the Mountain of the Lord' (Isa 2:3): Biblical Reflections on the Question of Sacramental Access." In *Developmental Disabilities and Sacramental Access: New Paradigms for Sacramental Encounters*, 13–32. Collegeville, MN: Liturgical Press, 1994.

Bergson, Henri. *Matter and Memory*. Translated by Nancy Margaret Paul and W. Scott Palmer. New York: Macmillan, 1911.

Berkhof, Hendrikus. *Christian Faith: An Introduction to the Study of the Faith*. Grand Rapids: Eerdmans, 1979.

Berkhof, Louis. *Systematic Theology*. Grand Rapids: Eerdmans, 1996.

Berkouwer, Gerrit Cornelis. *Man: The Image of God*. Grand Rapids: Eerdmans, 1978.

———. *The Sacrament*. Translated by Hugo Bekker. Grand Rapids: Eerdmans, 1969.

Bernardin, Joseph. *Access to the Sacraments of Initiation and Reconciliation for Developmentally Disabled Persons: Pastoral Guidelines for the Archdiocese of Chicago*. Chicago: Liturgy Training, 1985.

Bibliography

Berryman, Jerome W. *Godly Play: An Imaginative Approach to Religious Education.* Minneapolis: Augsburg, 1995.

———. "The Rite of Anointing and the Pastoral Care of Sick Children." In *The Sacred Play of Children,* edited by Diane Apostolos-Cappadona, 63–77. New York: Seabury, 1983.

Billings, J. Todd. *Calvin, Participation, and the Gift.* New York: Oxford University Press, 2007.

Birch, Bruce C. "Memory in Congregational Life." In *Congregations: Their Power to Form and Transform,* edited by C. Ellis Nelson, 20–42. Atlanta: John Knox, 1988.

Bissonnier, Henri. "Religious Expression and Mental Deficiency." In *From Religious Experience to a Religious Attitude,* edited by Andre Godin, 143–54. Chicago: Loyola University Press, 1965.

Bodrova, Elena, and Devorah J. Jeong. *Tools of the Mind: The Vygotskian Approach to Early Childhood Education.* Columbus, OH: Pearson, 2007.

Borg, Marcus J. *The Heart of Christianity: Rediscovering a Life of Faith.* New York: HarperOne, 2003.

Boulton, Matthew Myer. *Life in God: John Calvin, Practical Formation, and the Future of Protestant Theology.* Grand Rapids: Eerdmans, 2011.

Bourdieu, Pierre. *The Logic of Practice.* Translated by Richard Nice. Stanford, CA: Stanford University Press, 1990.

———. *Pascalian Meditations.* Translated by Richard Nice. Stanford, CA: Stanford University Press, 1997.

Bousma, William J. *John Calvin: A Sixteenth-Century Portrait.* New York: Oxford University Press, 1988.

Boutot, Amanda, and Brenda Smith Myles. *Autism Spectrum Disorders: Foundations, Characteristics, and Effective Strategies.* Upper Saddle River, NJ: Pearson, 2010.

Bower, T. G. R. *The Perceptual World of the Child.* Cambridge, MA: Harvard University Press, 1977.

Bradshaw, Paul, ed. *The New Westminster Dictionary of Liturgy and Worship.* Louisville, KY: Westminster John Knox, 2002.

Brienen, T. *De Liturgie bij Johannes Calvijn.* Kampen: Uitgeverij de Groot Goudriaan, 1987.

British Council of Churches, Consultative Group on Ministry Among Children. *Children and Holy Communion: An Ecumenical Consideration amongst Churches in Britain and Ireland.* British Council of Churches, 1989.

Brock, Brian. "Introduction: Disability and the Quest for the Human." In *Disability in the Christian Tradition,* edited by Brian Brock and John Swinton, 1–23. Grand Rapids: Eerdmans, 2012.

Browder, Diane M., Katherine Trela, and Bree Jimenez. "Training Teachers to Follow a Task Analysis to Engage Middle School Students with Moderate and Severe Developmental Disabilities in Grade-Appropriate Literature." *Focus on Autism and Other Developmental Disabilities* 22 (2007) 206–19.

Brown, Arthur J. *The Mastery of the Far East.* London: G. Bell and Sons, 1919.

Browning, Don S. *A Fundamental Practical Theology: Descriptive and Strategic Proposals.* Minneapolis: Fortress, 1996.

Bruce, F. F. *1 & 2 Thessalonians, Word Biblical Commentary Vol. 45.* Dallas: Thomas Nelson, 1982.

Bruner, Jerome. *Acts of Meaning.* Cambridge, MA: Harvard University Press, 1990.

———. *Actual Minds, Possible Worlds*. Cambridge, MA: Harvard University Press, 1986.

———. *The Culture of Education*. Cambridge, MA: Harvard University Press, 1996.

———. *Making Stories: Law, Literature, Life*. Cambridge, MA: Harvard University Press, 2002.

———. *The Process of Education*. New York: Random House, 1960.

Bucer, Martin. "De Regno Christi" in *Melanchthon and Bucer*. Edited by Wilhelm Pauck, 155–394. Philadelphia: Westminster John Knox, 1969.

———. "The Censura" in *Martin Bucer and The Book of Common Prayer*. Edited by E. C. Whitaker, 10–173. Great Wakering: Alcuin Club, 1974.

Bullinger, Heinrich and John Calvin. *Consensus Tigurinus. Heinrich Bullinger und Johannes Calvin uber das Abendmahl*. Edited by Emidio Campi and Reich Ruedi. Zurich: Theologischer Verlag, 2009.

Burgess, John P. "Reformed Explication of the Ten Commandments." In *The Ten Commandments: The Reciprocity of Faithfulness*, edited by William P. Brown, 78–99. Louisville: Westminster John Knox, 2004.

Butter, G. "Where Do Children Get Their Theology From?" In *Children's Voices: Children's Perspectives in Ethics, Theology and Religious Education*, edited by Annemie Dillen and Didier Pollefeyt, 357–72. Leuven, Belgium: Uitgeverij Peeters, 2010.

Byungha, Kim. "A Historical Study on the Pioneer of Special Education in Korea." *The Journal of Special Education: Theory and Practice* 9 (2008) 167–98.

Calvin, John. *Calvin: Theological Treatises*. Translated by J. K. S. Reid. Philadelphia: Westminster, 1954.

———. *Calvin's Commentaries*, 22 vols. Grand Rapids: Baker, 2005

———. *Calvin's Ecclesiastical Advice*. Translated by Mary Beaty and Benjamin W. Farley. Louisville: Westminster John Knox Press, 1991.

———. *Institutes of the Christian Religion* (1536). Translated by Ford Lewis Battles. Grand Rapids: Eerdmans, 1995.

———. *Institutes of the Christian Religion* (1559). Translated by Henry Beveridge. Peabody, MA: Hendrickson, 2008.

———. *Ioannis Calvini opera quae supersunt omnia*. Edited by Guilielmus Baum, Eduardus Cunitz and Eduardus Reuss. 59 vols. New York: Johnson Reprint, 1964.

———. *Joannis Calvini Opera Selecta*. Edited by Petrus Barth. 5 vols. München: Kaiser, 1926.

———. *John Calvin: Writings on Pastoral Piety*. Edited by Elsie Anne McKee. New York: Paulist, 2002.

———. *Letters of John Calvin*. Edited by Jules Bonnet. 2 vols. Edinburgh: Thomas, 1860.

———. *Sermons on 2 Samuel*. Translated by Douglas Kelly. Edinburgh: Banner of Truth, 1992.

———. *Tracts Relating to the Reformation*. 3 vols. Translated by Henry Beveridge. Edinburgh: Calvin Translation Society, 1844.

Campione J. C., and A. L. Brown. "Memory and Metamemory Development in Educable Retarded Children." In *Perspectives on the Development of Memory and Cognition*, edited by R. Kail and J. Hagen, 367–406. Hillsdale, NJ: Lawrence Erlbaum, 1977.

Canlis, Julie. *Calvin's Ladder: A Spiritual Theology of Ascent and Ascension*. Grand Rapids: Eerdmans, 2010.

Carmeli, Varda, and Eli Carmeli. "Teaching Jewish Mentally Retarded Youngsters Holiday Awareness Through Symbols." In *Spirituality and Intellectual Disability: International Perspectives on the Effect of Culture and Religion on Healing Body, Mind, and Soul*, edited by William C. Gaventa, Jr. and David L. Coulter, 123–39. New York: Haworth, 2001.

Carson, D. A. *The Gospel According to John*. Grand Rapids: Eerdmans, 1991.

Carter, Erik W. "Exchanging Gifts: Faith Formation and People with Developmental Disabilities." In *Shaped by God: Twelve Essentials for Nurturing Faith in Children, Youth, and Adults*, edited by Robert J. Keely, 127–37. Grand Rapids: Faith Alive, 2010.

———. *Including People with Disabilities in Faith Communities: A Guide for Service Providers, Families, and Congregations*. Baltimore: Paul H. Brookes, 2007.

Casinos, David M. and Ivy Beckwith. *Children's Ministry in the Way of Jesus*. Downers Grove, IL: IVP Books, 2013.

Castleman, Robbie Fox. "Liturgy for a Lifetime: Faith Formation through Worship." In *Shaped by God: Twelve Essentials for Nurturing Faith in Children, Youth, and Adults*, edited by Robert J. Keely, 72–80. Grand Rapids: Faith Alive, 2010.

Cavalletti, Sofia. *The Religious Potential of the Child*. New York: Paulist, 1983.

Champagne, E. "Children's Inner Voice: Exploring Children's Contribution to Spirituality." In *Children's Voices, Children's Perspectives in Ethics, Theology and Religious Education*, edited by Annemie Dillen and Didier Pollefeyt, 373–396. Leuven, Belgium: Uitgeverij Peeters, 2010.

Chan, Simon. *Liturgical Theology: The Church as Worshiping Community*. Downers Grove, IL: IVP Academic, 2006.

———. *Spiritual Theology: A Systematic Study of the Christian Life*. Downers Grove, IL: IVP Academic, 1998.

Chang, Jongchul. "History of Christian Education in Korean Methodist Church." In *History of Christian Education in Korean Church*, edited by Intak Oh, 33–93. Seoul: Korean Presbyterian, 1999.

Chapell, Bryan. *Christ-Centered Worship: Letting the Gospel Shape Our Practice*. Grand Rapids: Baker, 2009.

Chauvet, Louis-Marie. *The Sacraments: The Word of God at the Mercy of the Body*. Collegeville, MN: Order of Saint Benedict, 2001.

Childs, Brevard S. *Memory and Tradition in Israel*. London: SCM, 1962.

Cho, H. J. "The History of Korean Special Education." http://www.chohongjoong.com/zboard/view.php?id=research01&page=1&sn1=&divpage=1&sn=off&ss=on&sc=on&select_arrange=headnum&desc=asc&no=18 (accessed November 12, 2013).

Christian Reformed Church in North America. *Acts of Synod 2000*. Grand Rapids: Board of Publications of the Christian Reformed Church, 2000.

———. *Acts of Synod 2013*. Grand Rapids: Board of Publications of the Christian Reformed Church, 2013.

———. *Church Order and Its Supplements 2012*. Grand Rapids: Christian Reformed Church, 2012.

———. "Liturgical Committee Report." In *Acts of Synod of the Christian Reformed Church*. Grand Rapids: Christian Reformed Church, 1968.

———. *Opening Doors to All God's People: A Disability-Resource Guide*. Grand Rapids: Breaking Barriers, 1993.

———. "Persons with Disabilities and Profession of Faith." In *Affirming Baptism and Forming Faith: Agenda for Synod 2011*. Grand Rapids: CRC, 2011.

Clapp, Rodney. *Tortured Wonders: Christian Spirituality for People, not Angels*. Grand Rapids: Brazos, 2004.

Coe, George Albert. *A Social Theory of Religious Education*. New York: Charles Scribner's Sons, 1917.

Cole, Peter. "Developmental Versus Difference: Approaches to Mental Retardation: A Theoretical Extension to the Present Debate." *American Journal on Mental Retardation* 102 (1998) 379–91.

Coles, Robert. *The Spiritual Life of Children*. Boston: Houghton Mifflin, 1990.

Collins, Randall. *Interaction Ritual Chains*. Princeton, NJ: Princeton University Press, 2004.

Connerton, Paul. *How Societies Remember*. Cambridge: Cambridge University Press, 1989.

Cooke, Bernard. *Formation of Faith*. Chicago: Loyola University Press, 1965.

Cooke, Bernard, and Gary Macy. *Christian Symbol and Ritual: An Introduction*. New York: Oxford University Press, 2005.

Covey, Herbert C. *Social Perceptions of People with Disabilities in History*. Springfield, IL: Charles Thomas, 1998.

Crain, William. *Theories of Development: Concepts and Applications*. Upper Saddle River, NJ: Pearson, 2004.

Crane, Lynda L. *Mental Retardation: A Community Integration Approach*. Belmont, CA: Wadsworth, 2002.

Crawford, Charles. "Infant Communion: Past Tradition and Present Practice." *Theological Studies* 31 (1970) 523–36.

Cromer, Richard F. "Differentiating Language and Cognition." In *Language Perspectives: Acquisition, Retardation and Intervention*, edited by Richard L. Schiefelbusch and Lyle L. Lloyd, 91–124. Austin, TX: Pro-Ed, 1988.

Currid, John D. *Deuteronomy*. Webster, NY: Evangelical, 2006.

d'Aquili, Eugene, and Andrew B. Newberg. *The Mystical Mind: Probing the Biology of Religious Experience*. Minneapolis: Fortress, 1999.

Dalby, J. M. M. "The End of Infant Communion." *Church Quarterly Review* 167.362 (1966) 59–71.

Dale, Edgar. *Audio-Visual Methods in Teaching*, 3rd ed. New York: Holt, 1969.

Damasio, Anthony. *Descartes' Error: Emotion, Reason, and the Human Brain*. New York: Putnam, 1994.

Davis, Thomas. *The Clearest Promises of God: The Development of Calvin's Eucharistic Teaching*. New York: AMS, 1995.

Dawson, Geraldine, and Julie Osterling. "Early Intervention in Autism." In *The Effectiveness of Early Intervention: Second Generation Research*, edited by Michael J. Guralnick, 307–26. Baltimore: Paul H. Brookes, 1997.

De Jong, James A. *Into His Presence: Perspectives on Reformed Worship*. Grand Rapids: Board of Publications of the Christian Reformed Church, 1985.

Derroitte, H. "Towards a Catechesis Where Children Are Not Accepted?" In *Children's Voices: Children's Perspectives in Ethics, Theology and Religious Education*, edited by Annemie Dillen and Didier Pollefeyt, 421–38. Leuven, Belgium: Uitgeverij Peeters, 2010.

Bibliography

Douglas, Mary. *Purity and Danger: An Analysis of Concepts of Pollution and Taboo.* New York: Routledge, 1966.

Doumergue, Emile. *Le Caractere de Calvin.* Paris: Ed. de Foi et vie, 1921.

Dowey, Edward A. *The Knowledge of God in Calvin's Theology.* Grand Rapids: Eerdmans, 1992.

Downing, June E. *Academic Instruction for Students with Moderate and Severe Intellectual Disabilities in Inclusive Classrooms.* Thousand Oaks, CA: Corwin, 2010.

Downs, Perry G. *Teaching for Spiritual Growth: An Introduction to Christian Education.* Grand Rapids: Zondervan, 1994.

Drew, Clifford J., and Michael L. Hardman. *Intellectual Disabilities Across the Lifespan.* Columbus, OH: Pearson, 2007.

Driver, Tom F. *Liberating Rites: Understanding the Transformative Power of Ritual.* Boulder, CO: Westview, 1998.

Dykstra, Craig. "Faith Development Issues and Religious Nurture." In *Changing Patterns of Religious Education,* edited by Marvin J. Taylor, 74–88. Nashville, TN: Abingdon, 1984.

———. *Vision and Character: A Christian Educator's Alternative to Kohlberg.* Eugene, OR: Wipf and Stock, 1981.

Dykstra, Craig, and Dorothy C. Bass. "A Theological Understanding of Christian Practice." In *Practicing Theology: Beliefs and Practices in Christian Life,* edited by Miroslav Volf and Dorothy C. Bass, 13–32. Grand Rapids: Eerdmans, 2002.

Dykstra, Craig, and Dorothy C. Bass. "Times of Yearning, Practices of Faith." In *Practicing Our Faith: A Way of Life for a Searching People,* edited by Dorothy C. Bass, 1–12. San Francisco: Jossey-Bass, 1997.

Edgerton, Robert B. *Mental Retardation.* Cambridge, MA: Harvard University Press, 1979.

Eiesland, Nancy L. *The Disabled God: Toward a Liberatory Theology of Disability.* Nashville, TN: Abingdon, 1994.

Ellis, Norman R., and Cynthia L. Dulaney. "Further Evidence for Cognitive Inertia of Persons with Mental Retardation." *American Journal on Mental Retardation* 95 (1991) 613–21.

Erickson, Craig Douglas. "Liturgical Participation and the Renewal of the Church." *Worship* 59 (1985) 231–43.

———. *Participating in Worship: History, Theory and Practice.* Louisville, KY: Westminster John Knox, 1989.

Erikson, Erik H. *Dimensions of New Identity.* New York: Norton, 1974.

———. *Identity: Youth and Crisis.* New York: Norton, 1968.

———. *Toys and Reasons.* New York: Norton, 1977.

Evangelical Lutheran Church in America, "A message on…People Living with Disabilities." http://download.elca.org/ELCA percent20Resource percent20Repository/People_with_DisabilitiesSM.pdf (accessed December 11, 2013).

———. "The Body of Christ and Mental Illness." http://download.elca.org/ELCA percent20Resource percent20Repository/Mental_IllnessSM.pdf. (accessed December 11, 2013).

———. "Mental Illness." http://www.elca.org/en/Faith/Faith-and-Society/Social-Messages/Mental-Illness (accessed December 11, 2013).

Evans, Daryl Paul. *The Lives of Mentally Retarded People.* Boulder, CO: Westview, 1983.

Faith Alive Christian Resources. "Disability Resources." http://www.faithaliveresources.org/Products/CategoryCenter/DMDR/disability-resources.aspx (accessed December 29, 2011).

Farley, Edward. "Theology and Practice outside the Clerical Paradigm." In *Practical Theology: The Emerging Field in Theology, Church, and World*, edited by Don. S. Browning, 21–41. San Francisco: Harper & Row, 1983.

Fee, Gordon D. *The First and Second Letters to the Thessalonians*. Grand Rapids: Eerdmans, 2009.

Flannery, Austin P., ed. *Documents of Vatican II*. Grand Rapids: Eerdmans, 1975.

Flynn, James R., and Keith F Widaman. "The Flynn Effect and the Shadow of the Past: Mental Retardation and the Indefensible and Indispensable Role of IQ." *International Review of Research in Mental Retardation* 35 (2008) 121–49.

Foley, Edward. "Introduction." In *Developmental Disabilities and Sacramental Access: New Paradigms for Sacramental Encounters*, edited by Edward Foley, 5–12. Collegeville, MN: Liturgical, 1994.

Foster, Charles R. "Intergenerational Religious Education." In *Changing Patterns of Religious Education*, edited by Marvin J. Taylor, 278–89. Nashville, TN: Abingdon, 1984.

———. *Teaching in the Community of Faith*. Nashville, TN: Abingdon, 1982.

Fowler, James. *Stages of Faith: The Psychology of Human Development and the Quest for Meaning*. San Francisco: Harper Collins, 1981.

Fowler, James W., and Mary Lynn Dell. "Stages of Faith and Identity: Birth to Teens." *Child and Adolescent Psychiatric Clinics* 13 (2004) 17–33.

Francis, Mark R. "Celebrating the Sacraments with Those with Developmental Disabilities: Sacramental/Liturgical Reflections." In *Developmental Disabilities and Sacramental Access: New Paradigms for Sacramental Encounters*, edited by Edward Foley, 73–93. Collegeville, MN: Liturgical, 1994.

Fulkerson, Mary McClintock. *Places of Redemption: Theology for a Worldly Church*. New York: Oxford University Press, 2007.

Gadamer, Hans-Georg. *Truth and Method*. New York: Continuum, 2011.

Gallant, Tim. *Feed My Lambs: Why the Lord's Table Should Be Restored to Covenant Children*. Grande Prairie, AB: Pactum Reformanda, 2002.

Gamble, Richard C. "Brevitas et facilitas: Toward an Understanding of Calvin's Hermeneutic." *Westminster Theological Journal* 47 (1985) 1–17.

Gangel, Kenneth O., and Warren S. Benson. *Christian Education: Its History and Philosophy*. Chicago: Moody, 1983.

Gardner, Howard E. *Extraordinary Minds: Portraits of Four Exceptional Individuals and an Examination of Our Own Extraordinariness*. New York: Basic Books, 1998.

———. *Frames of Mind: The Theory of Multiple Intelligences*. New York: Basic Books, 2011.

———. *Multiple Intelligences*. New York: Basic Books, 2006.

Gardner, Jane F. *Being a Roman Citizen*. New York: Routledge, 1993.

Geertz, Clifford. *The Interpretation of Cultures*. New York: Basic Books, 1973.

Gelineau, Joseph. "Reflections: Children and Symbols and Five Years after the Directory for Masses with Children." In *The Sacred Play of Children*, edited by Diane Apostolos-Cappadona, 25–30. New York: Seabury, 1983.

General Assembly of the Presbyterian Church in Korea (Kosin). *Constitution*. Seoul: General Assembly of Korean Presbyterian Church, 1992.

Bibliography

General Assembly of the Presbyterian Church in Korea (Hapdong). *Constitution*. Seoul: General Assembly of Korean Presbyterian Church, 2000.

General Assembly of the Presbyterian Church in Korea (Tonghap). *Constitution*. Seoul: General Assembly of Korean Presbyterian Church, 2012.

Gerrish, B. A. *Grace and Gratitude: The Eucharistic Theology of John Calvin*. Eugene, OR: Wipf and Stock, 2002.

Gesell, A. *The Child from Five to Ten*. New York: Harper and Brothers, 1947.

Giangreco, Michael. F. "Foundational Concepts and Practices for Educating Students with Severe Disabilities." In *Instruction of Students with Severe Disabilities*, edited by M. E. Snell and F. Brown, 1–27. Upper Saddle River, NJ: Pearson, 2006.

Gill, Jerry H. *The Tacit Mode: Michael Polanyi's Postmodern Philosophy*. Albany, NY: State University of New York Press, 2000.

Glassford, Darwin. "Fostering an Intergenerational Culture." In *The Church of All Ages*, edited by Howard Vanderwell, 71–88. Herndon, VA: Alban Institute, 2008.

Gluck, Mark A., Eduardo Mercado, and Catherine E. Myers, *Learning and Memory: From Brain to Behavior*. New York: Worth, 2008.

Gore, R. J. *Covenantal Worship: Reconsidering the Puritan Regulative Principle*. Phillipsburg, NJ: Presbyterian and Reformed, 2002.

Goswami, Usha. *Cognitive Development: The Learning Brain*. Oxford: Psychology Press, 1998.

Grass, Hans. *Die Abendmahlslehre bei Luther und Calvin*. Gütersloh: Bertelsmann, 1954.

Green, Joel B., ed. *In Search of the Soul: Four Views of the Mind-Body Problem*. Downers Grove, IL: InterVarsity, 2005.

Grimes, Ronald L. *Deeply into the Bone: Re-Inventing Rites of Passage*. Los Angeles: University of California Press, 2000.

Grossman, H. *Classification in Mental Retardation*. Washington, DC: American Association on Mental Retardation, 1983.

Groome, Thomas. *Educating for Life: A Spiritual Vision for Every Teacher and Parent*. New York: Crossroad, 2001.

Grün, Anselm. *Kinder Fragen nach Gott*. Hamburg: Rowohlt Verlag, 2011.

Guralnick, Michael J. "Effectiveness of Early Intervention for Vulnerable Children: A Developmental Perspective." *American Journal on Mental Retardation* 102 (1998) 319–45.

Haight, Roger. "The Point of Trinitarian Theology." *Toronto Journal of Theology* 4 (1988) 191–204.

Hall, Laura J. *Autism Spectrum Disorders: From Theory to Practice*. Boston: Pearson, 2013.

Hamlyn, D. W. *Experience and the Growth of Understanding*. London: Routledge, 2012.

Harper, John. *The Forms and Orders of Western Liturgy: From the Tenth to the Eighteenth Century*. Oxford: Clarendon, 1991.

Harrington, Mary Therese. "Affectivity and Symbol in the Process of Catechesis." In *Developmental Disabilities and Sacramental Access: New Paradigms for Sacramental Encounters*, edited by Edward Foley, 116–129. Collegeville, MN: Liturgical, 1994.

———. *A Place for All: Mental Retardation, Catechesis, and Liturgy*. Collegeville, MN: Liturgical, 1992

Hart, D. G., and John R. Muether. *With Reverence and Awe: Returning to the Basics of Reformed Worship*. Phillipsburg, NJ: P & R, 2002.

Haslam, Molly C. *A Constructive Theology of Intellectual Disability: Human Being as Mutuality and Response.* New York: Fordham University Press, 2012.

Hauerwas, Stanley M. "Christian Care of the Retarded." *Theology Today* 30 (1973) 130–37.

———. "The Church and the Mentally Handicapped: A Continuing Challenge to the Imagination." In *Dispatches from the Front: Theological Engagements with the Secular,* 177–86. Durham, NC: Duke University Press, 1994.

———. *A Community of Character: Toward a Constructive Christian Social Ethic.* Notre Dame: University of Notre Dame Press, 1981.

Hauerwas, Stanley M., and Charles Pinches. *Christians among the Virtues: Theological Conversations with Ancient and Modern Ethics.* Notre Dame, IN: University of Notre Dame Press, 1997.

Hay, David, and Rebecca Nye. *The Spirit of the Child.* London: Jessica Kingsley, 2006.

Heyer, Friedrich., ed. *Konfessionskunde.* Berlin: Walter de Gruyter, 1977.

Herzfeld, Noreen. "Human and Artificial Intelligence: A Theological Response." In *Human Identity at the Intersection of Science, Technology and Religion,* edited by Nancey Murphy and Christopher C. Knight, 117–30. Burlington, VT: Ashgate, 2010.

Herzog, Albert A. "Disability Advocacy in American Mainline Protestantism." In *Disability Advocacy among Religious Organizations: Histories and Reflections,* edited by Albert A. Herzog, 75–92. Binghamton, NY: Haworth Pastoral, 2006.

Hesselink, John. *Calvin's First Catechism: A Commentary.* Louisville, KY: Westminster John Knox, 1997.

Hickson, L. *Mental Retardation: Foundation of Educational Programming.* Boston: Allyn & Bacon, 1995.

Hielema, Syd. "Wide and Long and High and Deep: Biblical Foundations of Faith Formation." In *Shaped by God: Twelve Essentials for Nurturing Faith in Children, Youth, and Adults,* edited by Robert J. Keely, 9–22. Grand Rapids: Faith Alive, 2010.

Hodge, Charles. "The Mystical Presence: A Vindication of the Reformed or Calvinistic Doctrine of the Holy Eucharist." *The Biblical Repertory and Princeton Review* 20 (April 1848) 227–78.

———. "Presbyterian Liturgies." *The Biblical Repertory and Princeton Review* 27 (1855) 445–67.

———. *Systematic Theology,* 3 vols. Peabody, MA: Hendrickson, 2008.

Hoekema, Anthony A. *Created in God's Image.* Grand Rapids: Eerdmans, 1986.

Hoekendijk, J. C. *The Church Inside Out.* London: SCM, 1967.

Holeton, David. *Infant Communion—Then and Now.* New York: Grove, 1981.

Hollinger, Dennis P. *Head, Heart, Hands: Bringing Together Christian Thought, Passion and Action.* Downers Grove, IL: InterVarsity, 2005.

Holmes, Urban T. *Spirituality for Ministry.* Harrisburg, PA: Morehouse, 2002.

Honig, Anthonie. G. *Handboek van de Gereformeerde Dogmatiek.* Kampen: J. H. Kok, 1938.

Horton, Michael. *A Better Way.* Grand Rapids: Baker, 2002.

———. *The Christian Faith: A Systematic Theology for Pilgrims on the Way.* Grand Rapids: Zondervan, 2011

———. *Introducing Covenant Theology.* Grand Rapids: Baker, 2006.

Bibliography

Huels, John M. "Canonical Rights to the Sacraments." In *Developmental Disabilities and Sacramental Access: New Paradigms for Sacramental Encounters*, edited by Edward Foley, 94–115. Collegeville, MN: Liturgical, 1994.

Inhelder, Barbel. *The Diagnosis of Reasoning in the Mentally Retarded.* New York: John Day, 1968.

James, William. "The Experience of Activity." In *Essays in Radical Empiricism*, edited by Ralph Barton Perry, 65–77. Fairford, Gloucestershire: The Echo Library, 2010.

Jansen, John F. "Calvin on a Fixed Form of Worship—A Note in Textual Criticism." *Scottish Journal of Theology* 15 (1962) 282–87.

Jaspard, Jean-Marie. "Comprehension of Religious Rituals among Male and Female Mentally Handicapped Adults." The Sixth European Symposium for the Psychology of Religion, University of Lund (Sweden), June 1994.

Jeremias, J. *The Eucharistic Words.* London: Scribner, 1966.

Johnson, Maxwell E. *The Rites of Christian Initiation.* Collegeville, MN: Liturgical, 2007.

Joly, Martine. *L'Image et les signes: Approche semiologique de l'image fixe.* Paris: Nathan, 1994.

Joo, Seung-Joong and Kyeong Jin Kim, "The Reformed Tradition in Korea." In *The Oxford History of Christian Worship*, edited by Geoffrey Wainwright and Karen B. Westerfield Tucker, 484–91. New York: Oxford University Press, 2006.

Jordan, James B. *Sociology of the Church.* Eugene, OR: Wipf & Stock, 1999.

Kail, Robert. "General Slowing of Information-Processing by Persons with Mental Retardation." *American Journal on Mental Retardation* 97 (1992) 333–41.

Kalat, James W. *Biological Psychology*, 8th ed. Belmont, CA: Wadsworth/Thomson Learning, 2003.

Kane, Thomas A. "Drama, Liturgy, and Children." In *The Sacred Play of Children*, edited by Diane Apostolos-Cappadona, 93–98. New York: Seabury, 1983.

Kanner, Leo. *A History of the Care and Study of the Mentally Retarded.* Springfield, IL: Charles C. Thomas, 1964.

Kaufman, Gordon. *An Essay on Theological Method.* Atlanta: Scholars, 1995.

Kavanagh, Aidan. *On Liturgical Theology.* Collegeville, MN: Liturgical, 1984.

———. "Response: Primary Theology and Liturgical Acts." *Worship* 57 (1983): 309–24.

Keely, Robert J. *Helping Our Children Grow in Faith: How the Church Can Nurture the Spiritual Development of Kids.* Grand Rapids: Baker, 2008.

———. "Worship and Faith Development." In *The Church of All Ages*, edited by Howard Vanderwell, 35–53. Herndon, VA: The Alban Institute, 2008.

Keidel, Christian L. "Is the Lord's Supper for Children?" *Westminster Theological Journal* 37 (1975) 301–41.

Keller, Helen. *The World I Live In and Optimism: A Collection of Essays.* Mineola, NY: Dover, 2009.

Kim, Hae Yong. *Guidelines for Sacraments of the Cognitively Challenged.* Seoul: Hanjangyeon, 2009.

Kim, Kyeong-Jin. "The Context, Contour and Contents of Worship of the Korean Church." *Korea Presbyterian Journal of Theology* 44 (2012) 65–92

Kim, Seongtae, and Heajin Park. *A Comprehensive Survey of the Missionaries in Korea.* Seoul: Korean Christianity History Institutes, 1994.

Kingdon, Robert M. "Calvin and the Family: The Work of the Consistory in Geneva." In *Calvin's Work in Geneva*, edited by R. D. Gamble, 93–106. New York: Garland, 1992.

———. "Catechesis in Calvin's Geneva." In *Educating People of Faith: Exploring the History of Jewish and Christian Communities*, edited by John van Engen, 294–313. Grand Rapids: Eerdmans, 2004.

———. "Worship in Geneva Before and After the Reformation." In *Worship in Medieval and Early Modern Europe: Change and Continuity in Religious Practice*, edited by Karin Maag and John D. Witvliet, 41–60. Notre Dame, IN: University of Notre Dame Press, 2004.

Kokaska, Charles. "Disabled People in the Bible" *Rehabilitation Literature* 45 (1984) 20–21.

Korean Theological Seminary Faculty. "Church's Response on the Matter of Baptism for Cognitively Challenged." In *The 60th General Assembly Report*, 180–186. Seoul: Korean Presbyterian Church General Assembly, 2010.

Krych, Margaret A. *Teaching the Gospel Today: A Guide for Education in the Congregation*. Minneapolis: Augsburg, 1987.

Kumphuis, J. *In dienst van de vrede*. Groningen: De Vuurbaak 1980.

Kwong, A. K. T. "Memory Strategy Assessment with Adolescents with Mild Mental Disabilities." Ph.D. diss., University of Alberta, 1994.

L'Arche Internationale. "Charter of the Communities of L'Arche." http://www.larche.org/en/resources/official_documents/charter_of_the_communities_of_larche (accessed December 11, 2013).

LaCugna, Catherine M. *God for Us: The Trinity and Christian Life*. San Francisco: HarperOne, 1993.

Landy, Susan H., Heather B. Taylor, Cathy Guttentag, and Karen E. Smith. "Responsive Parenting: Closing the Learning Gap for Children with Early Developmental Problems." *International Review of Research in Mental Retardation* 36 (2008) 27–60.

Lanning, Ray. "Foundations of Reformed Worship" in *Living for God's Glory: An Introduction to Calvinism*, edited by Joel R. Beeke, 231–44. Sanford, FL: Reformation Trust, 2008.

Lathrop, Gordon W. *Holy Ground: A Liturgical Cosmology* Minneapolis: Fortress, 2009.

———. *Holy Things: A Liturgical Theology*. Minneapolis: Fortress, 1998.

Lawson, Kevin E. "Growing in Wisdom and Stature: Recent Research on Spirituality and Faith Formation." In *Shaped by God: Twelve Essentials for Nurturing Faith in Children, Youth, and Adults,* edited by Robert J. Keely, 139–51. Grand Rapids: Faith Alive, 2010.

Lecerf, Auguste. *An Introduction to Reformed Dogmatics*. Cambridge: James Clarke, 2002.

Lee, JaeKeun. "McCormick Seminary Graduates and the Shaping of Evangelical Presbyterian Churches in Korea, 1888–1939." *Korean Christianity and History* 35 (2011) 5–46.

Leith, John H. *Introduction to the Reformed Tradition: A Way of Being the Christian Community*. Atlanta: John Knox, 1977.

Letham, Robert. *The Lord's Supper: Eternal Word in Broken Bread*. Phillipsburg: P & R, 2001.

Levi-Strauss, Claude. "Mythe et oubli." In *Langue, discours, societe, pour Emile Benveniste*. Paris: Editions du Seuil, 1975.

Levine, Shellie. "Children's Cognition as the Foundation of Spirituality." *International Journal of Christian Spirituality* 4 (1999) 121–40.

Lillback, Peter A. *The Binding of God: Calvin's Role in the Development of Covenant Theology.* Grand Rapids: Baker, 2001.
Lindbeck, George A. *The Nature of Doctrine: Religion and Theology in a Postliberal Age.* Philadelphia: Westminster, 1984.
Loder, James E. *The Logic of the Spirit: Human Development in Theological Perspective.* San Francisco: Jossey-Bass, 1998.
———. *The Transforming Moment.* Colorado Springs: Helmers, 1989.
Loder, James E., and W. Jim Neidhardt. *The Knight's Move: The Relational Logic of the Spirit in Theology and Science.* Colorado Springs: Helmers, 1992.
Luther, Martin. *Luther's Works*, vol. 27, *Lectures on Galatians.* Translated by Jaroslav Pelikan and Richard Jungkuntz. Saint Louis: Concordia, 1964.
———. *Luther's Works*, vol. 3, *Word and Sacrament.* Translated by E. Theodore Bachmann and William A. Lambert. Philadelphia: Fortress, 1960.
———. *Luther's Works*, vol. 43, *Devotional Writings.* Translated by Martin H. Bertram. Philadelphia: Fortress, 1968.
———. *Luther's Works*, vol. 49, *Letters II.* Translated by Gottfried G. Krodel. Philadelphia: Fortress, 1972.
———. *Luther's Works*, vol. 54, *Table Talk.* Translated by Theodore G. Tappert. Philadelphia: Fortress, 1967.
Lynn, Robert W., and Elliott Wright. *The Big Little School: Two Hundred Years of the Sunday School.* Nashville, TN: Abingdon, 1971.
MacMillan, D. L., G. N. Siperstein, and J. S. Leffer. "Children with Mild Mental Retardation: A Challenge for Classification Practices." In *What is Mental Retardation?* edited by H. Switzky and S. Greenspan, 197–220. Washington, DC: American Association on Mental Retardation, 2002.
Maddix, Mark A. "Spiritual Formation and Christian Formation." In *Christian Formation: Integrating Theology and Human Development*, edited by James R. Estep and Jonathan H. Kim, 238–67. Nashville, TN: B & H Academic, 2010.
Marshall, I. Howard. *Last Supper and Lord's Supper.* Vancouver: Regent College, 1980.
Martimort, A.G. *The Church at Prayer, Vol. 1: Principles of the Liturgy*, translated by Matthew J. O'Connell. Collegeville, MN: Liturgical, 1987.
Mathison, Keith A. *Given for You: Reclaiming Calvin's Doctrine of the Lord's Supper.* Phillipsburg, NJ: P & R, 2002.
Matthaei, Sondra Higgins. "Rethinking Faith Formation." *The Religious Education Journal* 99 (2004) 56–70.
Maxwell, William D. *A History of Christian Worship: An Outline of Its Development and Forms.* Grand Rapids: Baker, 1936.
May, Scottie, Beth Posterski, Catherine Stonehouse, and Linda Cannell. *Children Matter: Celebrating Their Place in the Church, Family, and Community.* Grand Rapids: Eerdmans, 2005.
McKee, Elsie Anne. "Context, Contours, Contents: Towards a Description of the Classical Reformed Teaching on Worship." *The Princeton Seminary Bulletin* 16 (1995) 172–202.
———. *John Calvin: Writings on Pastoral Piety.* New York: Paulist, 2001.
McKim, LindaJo H. "Reflection on Liturgy and Worship in the Reformed Tradition." In *Major Themes in the Reformed Tradition*, edited by Donald K. Mckim, 305–317. Eugene, OR: Wipf and Stock, 1998.

Mead, George Herbert. *Mind, Self, and Society from the Standpoint of a Social Behaviorist*, edited by Charles W. Morris. Chicago: University of Chicago Press, 1962.

Mercer, Joyce Ann. *Welcoming Children: A Practical Theology of Childhood*. St Louis: Chalice, 2005.

Merleau-Ponty, Maurice. *Child Psychology and Pedagogy: The Sorbonne Lectures 1949-1952*. Translated by Talia Welsh. Evanston, IL: Northwestern University Press, 2010.

———. "Eye and Mind." In *Basic Writings*, edited by Thomas Baldwin, 290–324. New York: Routledge, 2004.

———. *Phenomenologie de la perception*. Paris: Gallimard, 1945.

———. *Phenomenology of Perception*. Translated by Colin Smith. New York: Routledge, 2002.

Micks, M. H. *The Joy of Worship*. Philadelphia: Westminster, 1982.

Migliore, Daniel L. *Faith Seeking Understanding: An Introduction to Christian Theology*. Grand Rapids: Eerdmans, 1991.

Miles, M. "Martin Luther and Childhood Disability in 16th Century Germany: What Did He Write? What Did He Say?" *Journal of Religion, Disability and Health* 5 (2001) 5–36.

Moltmann, Jürgen. *God in Creation: A New Theology of Creation and the Spirit of God*. Minneapolis: Fortress, 1993.

———. *The Church in the Power of the Spirit: A Contribution to Messianic Ecclesiology*. London: SCM, 1977.

Moltmann-Wendel, Elisabeth. *I Am My Body: A Theology of Embodiment*. New York: Continuum, 1994.

Moon, Hwarang. "What the Korean Presbyterian Church Can Learn from Contemporary Debates about Infant Communion among Reformed Christians in North America." ThM diss., Calvin Theological Seminary, 2009.

———. "When is it Appropriate for Children to Participate in the Lord's Supper? A Perspective from Developmental Theory," *Christian Education Journal*, 10 (Spring 2013) 30–47.

Moore-Keish, Martha L. *Do This in Remembrance of Me: A Ritual Approach to Reformed Eucharistic Theology*. Grand Rapids: Eerdmans, 2008.

Moore, Mary Elizabeth Mullino. *Teaching from the Heart*. Harrisburg, PA: Trinity, 1998.

Morrill, Bruce T. *Divine Worship and Human Healing: Liturgical Theology at the Margins of Life and Death*. Collegeville, MN: Liturgical, 2009.

Muir, Edward. *Ritual in Early Modern Europe*. New York: Cambridge University Press, 1997.

Muller, Richard A. *The Unaccommodated Calvin*. New York: Oxford University Press, 2000.

Muller-Fahrenholz, Geiko, ed. *And Do Not Hinder Them: An Ecumenical Plea for the Admission of Children to the Eucharist*. Geneva: World Council of Churches, 1982.

Mussen, P. H., ed. *Handbook of Child Psychology*. New York: John Wiley, 1983.

Myers, David. *Social Psychology*. New York: McGraw Hill, 2002.

Nelson, C. Ellis. "Ten Righteous People." In *A Colloquy on Christian Education*, edited by John Westerhoff, 45–50. Philadelphia: United Church Press, 1972.

Nevin, John Williamson. *The Mystical Presence and Other Writings on the Eucharist*. Edited by Bard Thompson and George H. Bricker. Philadelphia: United Church Press, 1966.

———. *The Mystical Presence: A Vindication of the Reformed or Calvinistic Doctrine of the Holy Eucharist*. Philadelphia: J. B. Lippincott, 1846.

Nichols, James Hastings. *Corporate Worship in the Reformed Tradition*. Philadelphia: Westminster, 1968.

Noble, W. A. "Some Personal Reminiscences of 35 Years of Sunday School Work in Korea." *The Korea Mission Field* 5 (1929) 93–97.

Noll, Mark A. "What Can the Korean Church Learn from the History of American Evangelism?" *Christian Thought* 48 (2004) 244–59.

Nouwen, Henri J. M. *Adam: God's Beloved*. New York: Orbis Books, 1997.

Old, Hughes Oliphant. "Calvin's Theology of Worship." In *Give Praise to God: A Vision for Reforming Worship*, edited by Phillip Graham Ryken, Derek W. H. Thomas, and J. Ligon Duncan III, 412–35. Phillipsburg, NJ: P & R, 2003.

———. *The Patristic Roots of Reformed Worship*. Zürich: Theologischer Verlag, 1975.

Ormrod, Jeanne Ellis. *Human Learning*, 5th edition. Columbus, OH: Pearson, 2008.

Orthodox Presbyterian Church. *The Book of Church Order*. Willow Grove, PA: Committee on Christian Education of the Orthodox Presbyterian Church, 2011.

———. "The Book of Church Order." http://www.opc.org/order.html (accessed December 2011).

Otto, Rudolf. *The Idea of the Holy*. New York: Oxford University Press, 1923.

Ozment, Steven. *When Fathers Ruled: Family Life in Reformation Europe*. Cambridge, MA: Harvard University Press, 1983.

Pailin, David A. *A Gentle Touch: From a Theology of Handicap to a Theology of Human Being*. London: SPCK, 1992.

Parmley, Ingram, and Tresco Shannon. "Ministry and Persons with Developmental Disabilities." *Worship* 66.1 (1992) 10–24

Park, Seong-Won. *Worship in the Presbyterian Church in Korea: Its History and Implications*. New York: Peter Lang, 2001.

Pascal, Blaise. *Pensees and Other Writings*. Translated by Honor Levi. New York: Oxford University Press, 2008.

Pathways to Promise Ministry & Mental Illness. "Faith Group Statements on Mental Illness." http://www.pathways2promise.org/pdf/resolutionsoffaithgroups.pdf (accessed August 31, 2013).

Paulsell, Stephanie. "Honoring the Body." In *Practicing our Faith: A Way of Life for a Searching People*, edited by Dorothy C. Bass, 13–27. San Francisco: Jossey-Bass, 2010.

The People of the United Methodist Church. "The Church and People with Mental, Physical, and/or Psychological Disabilities." http://www.umc.org/site/apps/nlnet/content2.aspx?c=lwL4KnN1LtH&b=4951419&ct=7489959 (accessed December 28, 2013).

Peter, Rodolphe. "Calvin and Liturgy, According to the Institutes." In *John Calvin's Institutes, His Opus Magnum*, edited by B. van der Walt, 239–65. Potchefstroom: Institute for Reformational Studies, 1986.

———. "The Geneva Primer, or Calvin's Elementary Catechism." In *Calvin Studies*, edited by John H. Leith, 135–61. Davidson, NC: Colloquium on Calvin Studies, 1990.

Peterson, David. *Engaging with God: A Biblical Theology of Worship*. Downers Grove, IL: IVP Academic, 1992.

Phillips, John L. *Piaget's Theory: A Primer*. San Francisco: W.H. Freeman, 1981.

Piaget, Jean. *Child and Reality: Problems of Genetic Psychology*. New York: Grossman, 1973.

———. "Piaget's Theory." In *Handbook of Child Psychology*, edited by P. H. Mussen, 703–32. New York: John Wiley, 1983.

———. *The Construction of Reality in the Child*. Translated by Margaret Cook. New York: Basic Books, 1954.

———. *The Moral Judgment of the Child*. Translated by Marjorie Gabain. New York: Free Press, 1997.

Piaget, Jean, and Barbel Inhelder. *The Psychology of the Child*. Translated by Helen Weaver. New York: Basic Books, 1969.

Pickett-Cooper, Patricia K. "In My Own Words, a Study of Faith as Articulated by Adults with Developmental Disabilities." PhD diss., Oregon State University, 2010.

Pitkin, Barbara. "The Heritage of the Lord: Children in the Theology of John Calvin." In *The Child in Christian Thought*, edited by Marcia J. Bunge, 160–93. Grand Rapids: Eerdmans, 2001.

Pivarnik, R. Gabriel. *Toward a Trinitarian Theology of Liturgical Participation*. Collegeville, MN: Liturgical, 2012.

Plato. *Phaedrus*. Translated by Christopher Row. London: Penguin, 2005.

Pöhlmann, Horst Georg. *Abriss der Dogmatik*. Gutersloh: Gutersloher Verlagshaus, 1973.

Polanyi, Michael. *Knowing and Being*. London: Routledge and K. Paul, 1969.

———. *Personal Knowledge: Toward a Post-Critical Philosophy*. Chicago: University of Chicago Press, 1962.

———. *Science, Faith and Society*. Chicago: University of Chicago Press, 1964.

———. *The Tacit Dimension*. Garden City, NY: Anchor, 1967.

Polanyi, Michael, and Harry Prosch. *Meaning*. Chicago: University of Chicago Press, 1975.

Poston, D. J., and A. P. Turnbull. "Role of Spirituality and Religion in Family Quality of Life for Families of Children with Disabilities." *Education and Training in Developmental Disabilities* 39 (2004) 95–108.

Presbyterian Church in America. *The Book of Church Order*. Lawrenceville, GA: The Office of the Stated Clerk of the General Assembly of the Presbyterian Church in America, 2012.

Presbyterian Church in the United States of America, *Minutes of the 200th General Assembly, Part 1*." Louisville, KY: Office of the General Assembly, 1988.

———. "2011 Disability Inclusion Resource Packet." http://www.pcusa.org/resource/2011-disability-inclusion-resource-packet/ (accessed July 20, 2013).

———. "Comfort My People: A Policy Statement on Serious Mental Illness." http://www.pcusa.org/resource/comfort-my-people-policy-statement-serious-mental-/ (accessed November 12, 2013).

———. *Book of Order, Part II*. Louisville, KY: The Office of the General Assembly, 2011.

Presbyterian Health, Education, and Welfare Association. "Inclusion from the Inside Out: Welcoming God's Children of All Abilities." http://www.phewacommunity.org/images/disability-inclusion-packet-2011.pdf (accessed December 11, 2014).

Rappaport, Roy A. *Ritual and Religion in the Making of Humanity*. Cambridge: Cambridge University Press; 1999.

Ratzinger, Joseph. *Der Geist der Liturgie: Eine Einfuhrung*. Freiburg: Herder, 2006.

Rayburn, Robert G. *O Come, Let Us Worship: Corporate Worship in the Evangelical Church.* Eugene, OR: Wipf & Stock, 1980.

Reformed Church in America. "Breaking Barriers." https://www.rca.org/sslpage.aspx?pid=7239 (accessed December 29, 2011).

———. "What the Church Can Learn by Welcoming Persons with Disabilities." https://www.rca.org/page.aspx?pid=4994 (accessed December 29, 2011).

Reid, Barbara. "The Whole Broken Body of Christ: New Testament Reflections on Access to the Holy through Jesus." In *Developmental Disabilities and Sacramental Access: New Paradigms for Sacramental Encounters,* 33–52. Collegeville: Liturgical, 1994.

Reinders, Hans S. *Receiving the Gift of Friendship: Profound Disability, Theological Anthropology, and Ethics.* Grand Rapids: Eerdmans, 2008.

Reisz, H. Frederick. "Infant Communion: A Matter of Christian Unity." *Word & World* 8 (1988) 63–65.

Reymond, Robert L. *A New Systematic Theology of the Christian Faith.* Nashville, TN: Thomas Nelson, 1998.

Rice, Howard L. *Reformed Spirituality.* Nashville, TN: John Knox, 1991.

Richter, Don C. "Embodied Wisdom: Faith Formation through Faith Practices." In *Shaped by God: Twelve Essentials for Nurturing Faith in Children, Youth, and Adults,* edited by Robert J. Keely, 23–35. Grand Rapids: Faith Alive, 2010.

Ritchie, James H. *Always in Rehearsal: The Practice of Worship and the Presence of Children.* Nashville, TN: Discipleship Resources, 2005.

Rizzuto, Ana-Maria. *The Birth of the Living God: A Psychoanalytic Study.* Chicago: University of Chicago Press, 1979.

Robertson, O. Palmer. *The Christ of the Covenants.* Grand Rapids: Baker, 1980.

Robinson, Edward. *The Original Vision: A Study of the Religious Experience of Childhood.* New York: Seabury, 1983.

Rojahn, Johannes, and Lisa J. Meier. "Epidemiology of Mental Illness and Maladaptive Behavior in Intellectual Disabilities." *International Review of Research in Mental Retardation* 38 (2009) 239–87.

Rorem, Paul E. "The Consensus Tigurinus (1549): Did Calvin Compromise?" In *Calvinus Sacrae Scripturae Professor: Calvin as Confessor of Holy Scripture,* edited by Wilhelm H. Neuser, 72–90. Grand Rapids: Eerdmans, 1994.

Rosenberg, Sheldon, and Leonard Abbeduto. *Language and Communication in Mental Retardation: Development, Processes, and Intervention.* Hillsdale, NJ: Lawrence Erlbaum, 1993.

Ryu, Dae Young. "The Origin and Characteristics of Evangelical Protestantism in Korea at the Turn of the Twentieth Century." *Church History* 77.2 (2008) 371–99.

Ryu, Sun Young. "Special Education and Social Services in Korea: Past, Present, and Future." *International Review of Research in Mental Retardation* 38 (2009) 125–46.

Ruthrof, Horst. *The Body in Language.* London: Cassell, 2000.

Saliers, Don E. *Music and Theology.* Nashville, TN: Abingdon, 2007.

———. *Worship and Spirituality.* Akron, OH: OSL, 1996.

———. *Worship as Theology: Foretaste of Glory Divine.* Nashville, TN: Abingdon, 1994.

Schaefer, Mary M. "What is Liturgical Worship?" In *Liturgy and Music: Lifetime Learning,* edited by Robin A. Leaver and Joyce Ann Zimmerman, 3–18. Collegeville, MN: Liturgical, 1998.

Scheerenberger, R. C. *A History of Mental Retardation*. Baltimore: Paul H. Brookes, 1983.

Schilder, Klass. *Heidelbergsche Catechismus*, 2 vols. Goes: Oosterbaan, 1949.

Schillebeeckx, Edward. *Christ the Sacrament of the Encounter with God*. Lanham, MD: A. Sheed & Ward, 1987.

Schmemann, Alexander. *For the Life of the World: Sacraments and Orthodoxy*. Crestwood, NY: St. Vladimir's Seminary Press, 2002.

Schweitzer, Friedrich. *Das Recht des Kindes auf Religion*. Gütersloher: Verlagshaus, 2000.

———. *Lebensgeschichte und Religion*. München: Gutersloher Verlagshaus, 2007.

Scranton, M. F. "Woman's Work in Korea." *The Korean Repository* (1896) 2–9.

Searle, Mark. "Ritual." In *Foundations in Ritual Studies*, edited by Paul Bradshaw and John Melloh, 9–16. Grand Rapids: Baker, 2007.

Segler, Franklin M. *Christian Worship: Understanding, Preparing for, and Practicing*. Revised by Randall Bradley. Nashville, TN: Broadman, 1996.

Selderhuis, Herman J. *Calvin's Theology of the Psalms*. Grand Rapids: Baker, 2007.

Selway, Deborah, and Adrian F. Ashman. "Disability, Religion and Health: A Literature Review in Search of the Spiritual Dimensions of Disability." *Disability & Society* 13 (1998) 429–39.

Senn, Frank C. *Christian Liturgy: Catholic and Evangelical*. Minneapolis: Fortress, 1997.

———. *Introduction to Christian Liturgy*. Minneapolis: Fortress, 2012.

———. *New Creation*. Minneapolis: Fortress, 2000.

———. *The People's Work: A Social History of the Liturgy*. Minneapolis: Fortress, 2006.

Shepherd, Massey H. *The Worship of the Church*. New York: Seabury, 1952.

Shogren, K. A., and M. S. Rye. "Religion and Individuals with Intellectual Disabilities." *Journal of Religion, Disability & Health* 9 (2005) 29–53.

Shrader, Wesley. "Our Troubled Sunday Schools." *Life*, February 1957.

Siegler, Robert S., and Martha Wagner Alibali. *Children's Thinking*. Upper Saddle River, NJ: Prentice Hall, 2005.

Smith, James K. A. *Desiring the Kingdom: Worship, Worldview, and Cultural Formation*. Ada, MI: Baker, 2009.

———. *Imagining the Kingdom: How Worship Works*. Grand Rapids: Baker, 2013.

———. *Letters to a Young Calvinist: An Invitation to the Reformed Tradition*. Grand Rapids: Brazos, 2010.

———. *Who's Afraid of Post Modernism? Taking Derrida, Lyotard, and Foucault to Church*. Grand Rapids: Baker, 2006.

Smith, Jonathan Z. *To Take Place: Toward Theory in Ritual*. Chicago: University of Chicago Press, 1992.

Smith, Wilfred Cantwell. *The Meaning and End of Religion*. Minneapolis: Fortress, 1991.

Sohn, Won Young. "A Study on the Early Sunday School Education in Korea." *Journal of Christian Religious Education* 18 (2008) 153–78.

Solms, Mark, and Oliver Turnbull. *The Brain and the Inner World: An Introduction to the Neuroscience of Subjective Experience*. New York: Other, 2013.

Sousa, David A. *How the Special Needs Brain Learns*. Thousand Oaks, CA: Corwin, 2006.

Spelke E. S., and E. L. Newport. "Nativism, Empiricism, and the Development of Knowledge." In *Handbook of Child Psychology, Volume 1: Theoretical Models of Human Development*, edited by R. M. Lerner, 275–340. New York: Wiley, 1998.

Bibliography

Spieling, Karen E. *Infant Baptism in Reformation Geneva: The Shaping of a Community, 1536–1564.* Philadelphia: Westminster John Knox, 2009.

St. Clair, Michael. *Human Relationships and the Experience of God.* Eugene, OR: Wipf & Stock, 2004.

Steinmetz, David C. "John Calvin on Isaiah 6: A Problem in the History of Exegesis." *Interpretation* 36 (1982) 156–70.

———. "Luther and Formation in Faith." In *Educating People of Faith,* edited by Jon Van Engen, 253–269. Grand Rapids: Eerdmans, 2004.

Stern, Daniel N. *The First Relationship: Infant and Mother.* Cambridge, MA: Harvard University Press, 2002.

———. *The Interpersonal World of the Infant.* New York: Basic Books, 1985.

Stonehouse, Catherine, and Scottie May. *Listening to Children on the Spiritual Journey.* Grand Rapids: Baker, 2010.

Stookey, Laurence H. "Personal and Community Faith in Relation to Baptism and Other Rites of Christian Initiation." *Review and Expositor* 77 (1980) 71–81.

———. *Baptism: Christ's Act in the Church.* Nashville, TN: Abingdon, 1982.

Strathmann, H. "Leitourgia." In *Theological Dictionary of the New Testament,* vol. 4, edited by Gerhard Kittel, translated by Geoffrey W. Bromiley, 215–22. Grand Rapids: Eerdmans, 1967.

Swift, Fletcher H. *Education in Ancient Israel: From Earliest Times to 70 A. D.* Chicago: Open Court, 1919.

Swinton, John. *Critical Reflections of Stanley Hauerwas' Theology of Disability: Disabling Society, Enabling Theology.* New York: Routledge, 2005.

———. "Friendship in Community: Creating a Space for Love." In *Spiritual Dimensions of Pastoral Care,* edited by David Willows and John Swinton, 102–06. London: Jessica Kingsley, 2000.

———. *From Bedlam to Shalom: Towards a Practical Theology of Human Nature, Interpersonal Relationships, and Mental Health Care.* New York: Peter Lang, 2000.

———. *Resurrecting the Person: Friendship and the Care of People with Mental Health Problems.* Nashville, TN: Abingdon, 2000.

Swinton, John, and Harriet Mowat. *Practical Theology and Qualitative Research.* London: SCM, 2006.

Tarasar, Constance. "Taste and See: Orthodox Children at Worship." In *The Sacred Play of Children,* edited by Diane Apostolos-Cappadona, 43–54. New York: Seabury, 1983.

Taylor, Charles. *Modern Social Imaginaries.* Durham: Duke University Press, 2004.

Taylor, Ronald L., Stephen B. Richards, and Michael P. Brady. *Mental Retardation: Historical Perspectives, Current Practices, and Future Directions.* Boston: Allyn & Bacon, 2004.

The Arc Q&A: Introduction to Mental Retardation. Silver Spring, MD: The Arc, 2004.

Theißen, Gerd. *Die Religion der ersten Christen: Eine Theorie des Urchristentums.* München: Gutersloher, 2000.

Thomas, Virginia. "Children at Worship: A Presbyterian Perspective." In *The Sacred Play of Children,* edited by Diane Apostolos-Cappadona, 122–28. New York: Seabury, 1983.

Thompson, Bard. *Liturgies of the Western Church.* Philadelphia: Fortress, 1980.

Thompson, Nicholas. *Eucharistic Sacrifice and Patristic Tradition in the Theology of Martin Bucer 1534–1546.* Leiden: Brill, 2005.

Tibbatts, Wendy L. "Our Brother's Keeper: The Individual in Caring Community and the Mentally Handicapped." *Christian Education Journal* X (1990) 99–106.

Tomporowski, P. D., and V. Tinsley. "Effects of Target Probability and Memory Demands on the Vigilance of Adults with and without Mental Retardation." *American Journal on Mental Retardation* 98 (1994) 688–703.

Torrance, James B. "Some Theological Grounds for Admitting Children to the Lord's Table." *Reformed Review* 40 (1987) 200–05.

———. *Worship, Community and the Triune God of Grace*. Downers Grove, IL: IVP Academic, 1996.

Torrance, Thomas F. *Belief in Science and in Christian Life: The Relevance of Michael Polanyi's Thought for Christian Faith and Life*. Edinburgh: Handsel, 1980.

———. *Calvin's Doctrine of Man*. London: Lutterworth, 1949.

———. *Theology in Reconciliation*. Grand Rapids: Eerdmans, 1975.

Tylenda, Barbara, Jacqueline Beckett, and Rowland P. Barrett. "Assessing Mental Retardation Using Standardized Intelligence Tests." *International Review of Research in Mental Retardation* 34 (2007) 27–97.

Ulanov, Ann, and Barry Ulanov. *Religion and the Unconscious*. Louisville, KY: Westminster John Knox, 1985.

United States Department of Labor. "Americans with Disabilities Act." http://www.dol.gov/dol/topic/disability/ada.htm (accessed August 9, 2013).

van de Poll, G. J. *Martin Bucer's Liturgical Idea*. Assen: Van Gorgum, 1954.

van Gennep, Arnold. *The Rites of Passages*. New York: Psychology, 2004.

van Peursen, C. A. *Body, Soul, Spirit: A Survey of the Body-Mind Problem*. Translated by Hubert H. Hoskins. London: Oxford University Press, 1966.

Van Til, Cornelius. "Faith: Faith and Our Program." In *Foundations of Christian Education: Address to Christian Teachers*, edited by Dennis E. Johnson, 82–101. Phillipsburg, NJ: P & R, 1990.

van 't Spijker, Willem. *The Church's Book of Comfort*. Grand Rapids: Reformation Heritage, 2009.

Vanderwell, Howard. "Biblical Values to Shape the Congregation." In *The Church of All Ages*, edited by Howard Vanderwell, 17–33. Herndon, VA: Alban Institute, 2008.

———. "A New Issue for a New Day." In *The Church of All Ages*, edited by Howard Vanderwell, 1–15. Herndon, VA: Alban Institute, 2008.

Vanderwell, Howard and Norma de Waal Malefyt. "Worship as Covenant Renewal." http://worship.calvin.edu/resources/resource-library/worship-as-covenant-renewal-bible-study-/ (accessed Feb 13, 2013).

Vanier, Jean. *Becoming Human*. New York: Paulist, 1998.

Venema, Cornelis P. "New Testament Evidence Regarding Paedocommunion." *The Outlook* 57 (2007) 23–28.

———. "Paedocommunion: Should Covenant Children Be Admitted to the Lord's Table? An Introduction." *The Outlook* 55 (2005) 25–30.

Virji-Babul, N., and D. Weeks. "Perception, Cognition, and Action: New Perspectives on Down's Syndrome." *International Review of Research in Mental Retardation* 38 (2009) 147–70.

Vogel, J., E. A. Polloway, and J. D. Smith. "Inclusion of People with Mental Retardation and Other Developmental Disabilities in Communities of Faith." *Mental Retardation* 44 (2006) 100–11.

Volf, Miroslav. *After Our Likeness: The Church as the Image of the Trinity.* Grand Rapids: Eerdmans, 1998.

———. "Theology for a Way of Life." In *Practicing Theology*, 245–63. Grand Rapids: Eerdemans, 2002.

von Allmen, Jean-Jacques. *Celebrer le Salut: Doctrine et Pratique du Culte Chretien.* Geneve: Labor et Fides, 1984.

von Rad, Gerhard. *Genesis: A Commentary.* London: SCM, 1972.

Vygotsky, L. S. *The Fundamentals of Defectology.* In *The Collected Works of L. S. Vygotsky.* Vol. 2, edited by Robert W. Rieber and Aaron S. Carton, translated by Jane E. Knox and Carol B. Stevens. New York: Plenum, 1993.

———. *The History of the Development of Higher Mental Functions.* Vol. 4. In *The Collected Works of L. S. Vygotsky.* Translated by M. J. Hall. Edited by Robert W. Rieber. Translated by Marie J. Hall. New York: Plenum, 1997.

———. *Mind in Society: The Development of Higher Psychological Process*, edited by Michael Cole. Cambridge, MA: Harvard University Press, 1978.

Wadell, Paul J. "Pondering the Anomaly of God's Love: Ethical Reflections on Access to the Sacraments." In *Developmental Disabilities and Sacramental Access: New Paradigms for Sacramental Encounters*, 53–72. Collegeville, MN: Liturgical, 1994.

Wainwright, Geoffrey. *Doxology: The Praise of God in Worship, Doctrine and Life.* New York: Oxford University Press, 1980.

Walker, Williston. *A History of the Christian Church.* New York: Scribner, 1959.

Wandel, Lee Palmer. *The Eucharist in the Reformation: Incarnation and Liturgy.* Cambridge: Cambridge University Press, 2006.

———. "Zwingli and Reformed Practice" In *Educating People of Faith*, edited by John Van Engen, 270–93. Grand Rapids: Eerdmans, 2004.

Wangerin, Walter. *The Orphean Passages.* Grand Rapids: Zondervan, 1996.

Watanabe, Nobuo. "Calvin's Second Catechism: Its Predecessors and Its Environment." In *Calvinus Sacrae Scripturae Professor: Calvin as Confessor of the Holy Spirit*, edited by Wilhelm. H. Neuser, 224–32. Grand Rapids: Eerdmans, 1994.

Webb-Mitchell, Brett. *Beyond Accessibility: Toward Full Inclusion of People with Disabilities in Faith Communities.* New York: Church, 2010.

———. *Christly Gestures: Learning to Be Members of the Body of Christ.* Grand Rapids: Eerdmans, 2003.

———. *Dancing with Disabilities: Opening the Church to All God's Children.* Eugene, OR: Wipf & Stock, 2008.

———. *God Plays Piano, Too: The Spiritual Lives of Disabled Children.* New York: Crossroad, 1993.

———. *Unexpected Guests at God's Banquet: Welcoming People with Disabilities into the Church.* New York: Crossroad, 1994.

Webber, Robert E. *Ancient-Future Evangelism.* Grand Rapids: Baker, 2003.

———. *Ancient-Future Worship: Proclaiming and Enacting God's Narrative.* Grand Rapids: Baker, 2008.

———. *Worship Old and New.* Grand Rapids: Zondervan, 1994.

Webster, John. *Confessing God.* London: T & T Clark, 2005.

Webster, R. S. "Personal Identity: Moving Beyond Essence." *International Journal of Children's Spirituality* 10 (2005) 5–16.

Wehmeyer, Michael L. "Self-Determination and the Empowerment of People with Disabilities." *American Rehabilitation* 28 (2004) 22–29.

Weil, Louis. "Growth in Faith through Liturgical Worship." In *Handbook of Faith*, edited by James Michael Lee, 203–20. Birmingham, AL: Religious Education, 1990.

———. *A Theology of Worship*. Lanham, MD: A Cowley, 2002.

Weima, Jeffrey A. D. "Children at the Lord's Supper and the Key Text of 1 Corinthians 11:17–34." *Calvin Theological Seminary Forum* (2007) 7–8.

Weisz, John. R. "Cultural-Familial Mental Retardation: A Developmental Approach on Cognitive Performance and Helpless Behavior." In *Issues in the Developmental Approach to Mental Retardation*, edited by R. M. Hodapp, J. A. Burack, and E. Ziegler, 137–68. Cambridge: University of Cambridge Press, 1990.

Wendel, François. *Calvin: The Origins and Development of His Religious Thought*. Translated by Philip Mairet. New York: Harper & Row, 1963.

Westerhoff, John H. "What is Religious Socialization?" In *Generation to Generation*, edited by John H. Westerhoff and Gwen Kennedy Neville, 37–49. Philadelphia: Pilgrim, 1974.

———. *A Faithful Church: Issues in the History of Catechesis*. Wilton, CT: Morehouse-Barlow, 1981.

———. "A Socialization Model." In *A Colloquy on Christian Education*, edited by John H. Westerhoff, III, 80–90. Philadelphia: Pilgrim, 1972.

———. *Bringing up Children in the Christian Faith*. Minneapolis: Winston, 1980.

———. *Inner Growth, Outer Change: An Educational Guide to Church Renewal*. New York: Seabury, 1979.

———. "Introduction." In *The Original Vision: A Study of the Religious Experience of Childhood*, edited by Edward Robinson, ix–xiii. New York: Seabury, 1983.

———. *Will Our Children Have Faith?* New York: Morehouse, 2000.

Westerhoff, John H., and Gwen Kennedy Neville, *Generation to Generation*. Philadelphia: Pilgrim, 1974.

Westerhoff, John H., and William Willimon. *Liturgy and Learning throughout the Life Cycle*. New York: Seabury, 1980.

Westermann, Claus. *Genesis 1–11: A Commentary*. Translated by John J. Scullion. Minneapolis: Augsburg, 1984.

White, James F. *Introduction to Christian Worship: Third Edition, Revised and Expanded*. Nashville, TN: Abingdon, 2000.

———. *Protestant Worship: Traditions in Transition*. Louisville, KY: Westminster John Knox, 1989.

———. *Sacraments as God's Self-Giving*. Nashville, TN: Abingdon, 2003.

William Harmless. *Augustine and the Catechumenate*. Collegeville, MN: Liturgical, 1995.

Williamson, G. I. *The Westminster Shorter Catechism*. Phillipsburg, NJ: P & R, 2003.

Winkler, Eberhard. *Praktisch Theologische Elementar*. NeukirchenVluyn: Neukirchener-Verlag, 1997.

Winzer, Margret A. *The History of Special Education*. Washington, DC: Gallaudet, 1993.

Witvliet, John D. *Worship Seeking Understanding: Windows into Christian Practice*. Grand Rapids: Baker, 2003.

Wolff, H. Walter. "Wissen um Gott bei Hosea als Urform von Theologie." In *dem Gesammelte Studien zum Alten Testament*, 182–205. München: Chr. Keiser Verlag, 1964.

Wolterstorff, Nicholas. "The Reformed Liturgy." In *Major Themes in the Reformed Tradition*, edited by Donald K. McKim, 273–304. Eugene, OR: Wipf & Stock, 1998.

———. *Until Justice and Peace Embrace*. Grand Rapids: Eerdmans, 1983.
Woudstra, Marten H. *The Book of Joshua*. Grand Rapids: Eerdmans, 1981.
Yong, Amos. *The Bible, Disability, and the Church: A New Vision of the People of God*. Grand Rapids: Eerdmans, 2011.
———. *Theology and Down Syndrome: Reimagining Disability in Late Modernity*. Waco, TX: Baylor University Press, 2007.
Yongsu, Ko. "Crisis and Task of Korean Christian Education." *Jangshinnondan* 13 (1997) 345–75.
Yongwon, Kang. "The History of Christian Education in Korea." In *History of Christian Education*, edited by Intahk Oh, 201–39. Seoul: The Korean Society for the Study of Christian Religious Education, 2008.
Youngjae, Kim. *Church and Worship*. Suwon, Korea: Hapdong Theological Seminary Press, 2008.
Yust, Karen Marie. *Real Kids, Real Faith: Practices for Nurturing Children's Spiritual Lives*. San Francisco: Jossey-Bass, 2004.
———. "A World Apart: Autism Spectrum Disorders." In *The Church Leader's Counseling Resource Book: A Guide to Mental Health and Social Problems*, edited by Cynthia Franklin and Rowena Fong, 68–79. New York: Oxford University Press, 2011.
Yust, Karen Marie and E. Byron Anderson, *Taught by God: Teaching and Spiritual Formation*. St. Louis: Chalice, 2006.
Zachman, Randall C. *John Calvin as Teacher, Pastor, and Theologian*. Grand Rapids: Baker, 2006.
Zeaman, D., and B. J. House. "The Role of Attention in Retardate Discrimination Learning." In *Handbook of Mental Deficiency*, edited by N.R. Ellis, 159–223. New York: McGraw-Hill, 1963.
Zigler, Edward. "Developmental Versus Difference Theories of Mental Retardation and the Problem of Motivation." *American Journal of Mental Deficiency*, 73 (1969) 536–56.
———. "The Individual with Mental Retardation as a Whole Person." In *Personality Development in Individuals with Mental Retardation*, edited by Edward Zigler and Diane Bennett-Gates, 1–16. Cambridge: Cambridge University Press, 1999.
Zizioulas, John D. "The Contribution of Cappadocia to Christian Thought." In *Sinasos in Cappadocia*, edited by Frosso Pimenides and Stelios Roades, 23–37. Greece: Agra, 1986.
———. *Being as Communion*. New York: St. Vladimir's Seminary Press, 2004.

Index

accommodation, 87, 133
Act for the Promotion of Special Education for the Handicapped (Korea), 117
Allen, Holly, 197
Allmen, Jean-Jacques von, 1
Americans with Disabilities Act (US), 100–101
American Sunday School Union, 98
Anderson, E. Byron, 19
Anderson, Herbert, 170
Aquinas, Thomas, 102, xv, 103–4, 158, 202, 210
Aristotle, 72, 99, 158, 199, 202
Arnheim, Rudolf, 66
assimilation, 87, 133
Assmann, Aleida, 88, 89
Atkins, Peter, 11, 80, 83, 87, 88
Augustine, xv, 102–3
autism spectrum, 136, 145
awareness, types of, 71

Baillie, Donald M., 28–29
baptism, 34, 104. *See also* infant baptism
    for cognitively challenged, 104, 106, 110, 118–19
    and profession of faith, 109
baptismal covenant, 173
Barr, Martin, 101
Barrett, Rowland P., 137
Bass, Dorothy, 61, 77

Bavinck, Herman, xvii, 2, 58, 143–44, 175
Beale, Gregory, 101
Beckett, Jacqueline, 137
Beckwith, Ivy, 108, 124, 206
Beeke, Joel, 38–39, 41, 42
Belcher, Kimberly, 8, 14–15
beliefs, preoccupation with, 73
Bell, Catherine, xv, 12
belonging, importance of, 190–91
Bergson, Henri, 68, 84
Berkhof, Hendrikus, 173
Berkouwer, G. C., 159
Bernardin, Joseph, 200
Berryman, Jerome, 128, 142
Bissonnier, Henri, 138–39, 147, 156
bodiliness, affirmation of, xiv
body
    centrality of, 62–63
    experience inscribed in, 149
    as learning tool, 149
    relation with the soul, 59
    resurrection of, xiv
    as tool for remembrance, 84–87
body/spirit dualism, 2, 56, 57–58, 209
Book of Church Order (PCA), 115
Borg, Marcus, 73–74
Boulton, Matthew Myer, 49, 50–51
Bourdieu, Pierre, 64, 67
Browning, Don, xxiii, 77
Bruce, F. F., 101
Bruner, Jerome, 88–89, 135, 136

Bucer, Martin, x, 13–14, 32n56, 53–54

calmness, related to holiness, xvii, 107, 123, 190
Calvin, John, x, xi, 158, 209, 211
    on ceremony, 31–34
    on children's communion, 165
    exegetical principles of, 29
    on faith, xiii, xvi
    on faith formation, 38–51
    on image of God, 160
    including Decalogue in public worship, 10, 53–54
    inclusiveness of, 37
    influence of, 23
    insisting on need for knowledge of God, 30
    on kneeling, 15–16
    on knowledge, xiv
    on liturgy, xiii, 24–38
    on participation with Christ, 41–44
    on piety, 40–41
    pneumatology of, 186–87
    on prayer, 25, 26–27
    on public worship, 10, 30–31, 53–54
    on the sacraments, xviii–xix, 25–26, 28–29, 49–51, 52, 73
    sacramental theology of, 174–88
    on singing the Psalms, 53
    theology of, God's Word central to, 178–79
    on worship and faith formation, 51–55
    on worship form and content, 35
    worship theology of, 28–30, 54–55
Calvinism, posterity of, 35–36
Carmeli, Eli, 69, 140, 154
Carmeli, Verda, 69, 140
catechisms, x, 25–26, 46–51
Catholic Church, liturgy of, 13
Catholic Church in America National Apostolate with Mentally Retarded Persons (NAMRP), 111
Catholics, view of Protestants' sacramental theology, 175
ceremony, 31–34
Chan, Simon, 6, 21, 91

Chappel, Brian, 4
Chauvet, Louis-Marie, 75
children
    abstract thinking by, 135
    baptism for, 104, 106
    believing in God, 152
    benefits for, of church participation, 189–194, 196
    cognitive abilities of, 71–72, 123–24
    cognitive development of, 132–35
    cognitively challenged, 126–27
    in communion with the Trinity, 166
    developing understanding, 142
    early education for, 144–45
    experience and faith development in, 146–50
    faith of, 45–46
    faith formation of, 151–52, 170
    family's responsibility for faith of, 48–49
    image of God and, 124–25, 158–62
    judged by adult criteria, 154, 161
    in Korean churches, 116–17
    learning processes for, 130–35
    need for belonging, 190–91
    in North American churches, 107–9
    participating in the sacraments, 97, 115–16, 151, 164–65, 176, 187–88
    participating in worship, xvii–xviii, 97, 162–63
    personhood of, in the faith community, 162
    religious development of, xvi–xvii
    religious life of, 128–29
    religious thinking of, 210
Childs, Brevard, 83
Christ, communion with, 42
Christian Church (Disciples of Christ), 111
Christian identity, 75–76, 167
Christian Reformed Church (CRC), 97, 108–12, 116
church
    benefits for, with children and cognitively challenged participating, 194–207

formation of, everyone necessary for, 205
Clapp, Rodney, 58, 61–62
cognitive disabilities, terms for, ix n1
cognitively challenged
  adapting to ordinary life, 138
  artistic expression of, 138–39
  attitudes toward, changes in, 100–101
  baptism for, 104, 106, 110, 118–19
  benefits for, of church participation, 189–194, 196
  capable of knowledge, 71–72
  church's attitude toward, 101–6
  cognitive abilities of, 123–24
  cognitive development of, 134
  in communion with the Trinity, 166
  in community of believers, 171–72
  communication by, 139–40
  developing understanding, 142
  early attitudes toward, 99–100
  early education for, 144–45
  embracing into church life, 172
  experience and, 146–50
  expressing themselves, 155–57
  faith development in, 146–54
  faith expressed by, 156–57
  image of God and, 158–62
  judged by adult criteria, 154
  in Korea, 116–17
  in Korean churches, 117–20
  learning by, 135–42
  learning processes for, 130–31
  made in God's image, 121
  misunderstanding of, 100
  in North American churches, 106–15
  nurturing of, in church settings, 141–42
  participating in the liturgy, xvii–xviii, 97, 156–57, 162–63
  participating in the sacraments, 97, 104–6, 115–16, 151, 164–65, 176, 187–88
  personhood of, in the faith community, 162
  presenting gifts of God's spirit, 198
  rarely mentioned in church documents, xv
  rarely seen in public worship, 114–15
  religious knowledge of, xvi–xvii
  religious life of, 129
  religious thinking of, 210
  repetitive experiences for, 145–46
  spirituality in, 154
Collins, Randall, 93
communal memory, 80, 81–82
communal remembrance, 87–89
communion, 165
community, experience of, 142
confession, reexamining, 172
confessions of faith, 14, 20, 173
confirmation, 104
Connerton, Paul, xv, 15, 65, 80, 81, 82
Consensus Tigurinus (Calvin), 179–80, 183
consubstantiation, 181
Cooke, Bernard, 78–79
covenant, xviii, 91, 116, 161, 165
  continuity between old and new, 174
  grace and, 173
  inclusive nature of, 173
  infant baptism and, 44–46
  renewal of, 83
covenant community
  participation in, 170–73
  perfecting of, 203–7
Crane, Lynda L., 130, 140
cultural development, 137

D'Aquili, Eugene, 65–67
De catechizandis rudibus (Augustine), 102
De Jong, James, 78–79
Descartes' Error (Damasio), 150
development
  of the cognitively challenged, 135–42
  experience and, 146–50
disabilities, types of, ix n1
Disabled Persons Welfare Act (Korea), 117
discrimination, social, 192–93

Division of Handicapped Children and Youth (US), 100
dogmatics, xix
Down's syndrome, 156–57
Downs, Perry, 135, 146, 147, 149–50
doxology, 125
Dykstra, Craig, 61, 77, 148

Education of All Handicapped Children Act (US), 100
embodiment
  faith formation and, 56–62
  liturgy and, 56–62
  memory and, 89–90
  practice and, 61
epistemology, personal, 70
Erickson, Craig, 16
Erikson, Erik, 134
eugenics, 100
Evangelical Lutheran Church in America (ELCA), 111, 112–13
ex opera operato, 175, 186
excommunication, 52–53
experience
  communication improved with, 189
  faith and, 150
  faith formation and, 142–44, 146–50
  inscribed in the body, 149
  joining the human body and senses, 64
  learning and, 63–66, 70
  need of, for children and cognitively challenged, 124
  perception and, 145–46
  understanding and, 142–46

faith. *See also* faith formation
  as belief, 73–74
  Calvin's definition of, 39–40
  children's, 45–46
  cognitive knowledge and, ix–xii
  communal dimension of, 204
  conceptualized by worship, 157
  contents of, 157
  definition of, 57, 125
  development of, 201, 211–12
  embodiment of, 60
  experience and, 150
  expressed by cognitively challenged, 156–57
  formed through liturgy, xix–xxii
  gaining, through practice and participation, 50
  grace and, 125–26
  intergenerational transfer of, xviii
  knowledge and, 40, 73–79
  liturgy fortifying, 9
  practice of, 70
  stages of, 152–53
faith formation
  balance in, 76–77
  Calvin on, 38–51
  ceremony and, 33
  for children, 47–48
  definition of, 21
  embodiment and, 56–62
  experience and, 142–44, 147
  infant baptism and, 44–46
  intellect and, 159
  knowledge-centered model of, 208
  liturgy and, 51–55
  through liturgy and ritual, 19–22
  relationship and, 192
  repetition and, 26–27, 147–48
  worship and, 51–55
families, welcomed into church, 193–95
fellowship, learned in the church, 146
Flynn, James, 126, 127
focal awareness, 71
fore-understanding, 143
friendship, in the faith community, 197–200
Friendship Series, 110
Fulkerson, Mary, 139, 201

Gadamer, Hans-Georg, xxiii, 82–83, 85, 143
Gamble, Richard, 29
Gardner, Howard, 127, 135, 144, 147
Geertz, Clifford, 84
Geneva Church
  liturgy of, 55
  rituals in, 34–35

worship practices in, 38
Gerrish, B. A., 41, 45, 129
gesture, 15
Glassford, Darwin, 107–8
God
   image of, 124–25, 158–62, 210
   knowledge of, xi–xii, 30
   liturgy as encounter with, 8
   relationship with, 166–70
   sovereignty of, 178
   time for meeting, varying, 153
grace, 21, 42, 44, 51, 122
   faith and, 125–26
   God's sacrifice and, 174
   and image of God, 161
   requiring human response, 173
   sacrament and, 177
Grass, Hans, 183
Grimes, Ronald, xv, 62

habit memory, 82
habitus, xiii, xxi, 68, 78–80, 89–90
Hapdong denomination (KPC), 118, 119
Harrington, Mary, 71–72, 171
Hauerwas, Stanley, 200, 202, 204
Hay, David, 129, 152
Herzfeld, Noreen, 150
Hodge, Charles, 13, 179, 183–85, 211
holiday awareness, 69
Hollinger, Dennis, 76
Holy Spirit
   aiding in transformation, 95
   faith and, xxii, 21, 39–40
   freedom of, 186
   grace and, 162, 177
   presence of, 187
   relationship with, 163
   sovereignty of, 182
   work of, 163–65
Horton, Michael, 4, 173–74, 187
hospitality, xviii–xix
humans. *See also* body
   bodies of, affirming, 58, 59
   bodily nature of, 1–2
   brains of, 65, 66
   created to correspond to God, 159
   forming cognitive systems, 64
   memory of, 63
   nature of, 1–2, 36–37
   needing communion, 167
   in relationship with God, 166–70
   ritual and, 14
identity, formation of, 87–90
imitation, 82–83, 132
indwelling, 71
infant baptism, 210
   faith formation and, 44–46
   requiring catechetical instruction, 46–51
Inhelder, Barbel, 130, 131–32
Institutes of the Christian Religion (Calvin), xi, xiii–xiv, 23, 31, 73, , 179, 180–81, 209
intelligence
   faith formation and, 159
   not proportionate to religious ability, 156
   religious ability and, 156, 157
   types of, 127–28
intercessory prayer, 71
interdependence, 206
intergenerational worship, 195–97, 211
IQ scores, 126–27

Jesus
   incarnation of, 1, 2, 58, 59–60, 86
   resurrection of, 58
Johnson, Susan, 170
justification, 42

Keely, Robert, 150, 163
Keller, Helen, 64–65, 66
Kennedy, John F., 100
Kim, Shannon, 126
Kingdon, Robert, 34, 45, 47, 48–49, 52
kneeling, 15–16, 19, 72
knowledge. *See also* ritual knowledge; tacit knowledge
   acquired through imitation, 132
   experience-based, xi–xii
   faith and, 73–79
   importance of, for Calvin, 40–41
   perception and, 63–66

knowledge *(continued)*
   types of, 40–41
Korea, generational gap in worship in, 195
Korean churches
   children in, 119–20
   cognitively challenged in, treatment of, 117–20
   North American churches' influence on, 97–98
Korean Handicapped Ministry Institute, 118
Korean Presbyterian Church, xv, 97, 118–20
Kosin Church, 118–20

L'Arche community, 142, 154, 198
LaCugna, Catherine M., 125
language, 64
Lathrop, Gordon, 9, 10, 86
learning
   children's process for, 130–35
   of the cognitively challenged, 130–31, 135–42
   definition of, 62
   developmental approach to, 130–31
   experience and, 63–66, 70
   occurring through the body, 62
   repetition and, 66–69
Leith, John, 29, 38
Letham, Robert, 184–85
Levi-Strauss, Claude, 93
Lindbeck, George A., 159
liturgical worship. *See also* liturgy
   goal of, 76
   participation in, 168
   rhythm of, 67
liturgy. *See also* liturgical worship
   bodily action of, 2
   Calvin on, 24–38
   central elements of, 9–10
   character of, 7–10
   characteristics of, 12–13
   embodiment and, 56–62
   as encounter with God, 8
   ethos of, 92
   faith formation and, 19–22, 51–55
   formative function of, xi, xiii, xix–xxii
   forming identity, 87–90
   fortifying faith, 9
   functions of, 2–3
   goal of, 90
   including children and cognitively challenged in, xiii
   including two God-human interchanges, 2–3
   increased attention to, x
   meaning of, 3–7
   memory and, 11, 80–84
   as method for understanding faith, 70
   participation in, 20–21, 91–93
   power of, 10–11, 208
   as public worship, 31
   reorienting locally, 9–10
   ritual and, xiv, 11–22
   start of, 1–2
   symbolism of, 86–87
   as tool for helping human weakness, 37–38
   transformation and, 90–95
   as verb, 21–22
Loder, James, 163, 168
logic, theology and, xxi–xxii
Lord's Supper. *See also* sacraments
   children included in, 115–16, 192–93
   children and cognitively challenged excluded from, 192
   Christ's presence at, 182
   cognitively challenged included in, 115–16
   holy place of, 187
   overcoming differences among people, 164
   participation in, 81
   and profession of faith, 109
   weekly celebration of, 49–50
Luther, Martin, xv, 102, 105–6, 178, 181, 210
Lutheran Church Missouri Synod, 111, 113
Lutherans, theology of, 182

Index

marriage, 34
Martimort, A. G., 3, 7
materiality, goodness of, 60
matter, as tool for remembrance, 84–87
May, Scottie, 132, 153, 210
McKee, Elsie, 40n101, 53
Mead, George Herbert, 63
memory
    of the cognitively challenged, 137
    communal, 80, 81–82
    liturgy and, 11, 80–84
    perception and, 63
    repetition and, 83
    ritual practice and, 79–90
mental retardation, ix n1
Merleau-Ponty, Maurice, 62–63
metaphoric logic, 129
Micron's Shorter Catechism, 102, 106
Migliore, Daniel, 76
Moltmann, Jürgen, 58, 164
Moore-Keish, Martha L., 8, 15
multiple intelligences, 127–28, 135

NAMRP. *See* Catholic Church in America National Apostolate with Mentally Retarded Persons
Nelson, Ellis, 171
Nevin, John, 184–85, 211
Newberg, Andrew B., 65–67
Noll, Mark, 97–98
nonverbal factors, 64, 66
North American churches, xv
    children in, 107–9
    cognitively challenged in, 106, 109–15
Nouwen, Henri, 155, 198, 202–3
Nye, Rebecca, 129, 152

On Liturgical Theology (Kavanagh), xix
ordination, 104
Orthodox Presbyterian Church (OPC), 108–9, 116
orthodoxy, 73–75
Otto, Rudolf, 74–75

parenting style, 144

parents, educational duties of, x
participation, theology of, 41–44
Pascal, Blaise, 68
Patton, James, 126
perception, 65–66, 145–46
performativity, 82
perichoresis, 166
personhood, 167, 199
Phaedrus (Plato), 89
phronesis, 72, 120
physical health, 191
Piaget, Jean, 87, 131–34, 135, 141
pietas, 40n101
piety, 30, 40–41
Plato, 89, 99, 158
Pohlmann, Horst, 74
Polanyi, Michael, xii–xiii, 70–71
posture, 15
practical comprehension, 68
practical theology, 72
practice
    bodily, 61–62
    wisdom in, 78
prayer
    Calvin on, 25, 26–27
    form in, 25
    intercessory, 71
    public venue for, 27. *See also* public worship
preaching, emphasis on, 90
Presbyterian Church in America (PCA), 108–9, 115, 116
Presbyterian Church in the United States, 111
Presbyterian Church in the United States of America (PCUSA), 97, 108–9, 110–11, 115
Protestant Church, losing liturgical tradition, 208
Protestants, view of Catholics' sacramental theology, 175
Psalms, the, 53
public worship, 173, 190, 192, 197, 209, 212

Rappaport, Roy, xv, 19–21, 93
Rayburn, Robert, 4
reconciliation, 34

Reformation, context for, 28
Reformed churches, x
    liturgy of, 6, 7
    ritual and, 13-17
    simplifying Catholic liturgy, 13
    symbols in worship of, 84
Reformed Church in America (RCA), 97, 108-9
Reinders, Hans, 168-69, 199-200, 202, 205-6
religious ability, intelligence and, 156, 157
religious concepts, cognitive ability and, 124-29
religious experience
    capacity for, 151-52
    effect of, 126
remembrance, 80
reparation, 34
repetition
    gaining knowledge through, 132
    learning and, 66-69
res, Calvin's use of, 181-83, 187
retardation, degrees of, 137-38
Richter, Don, 70
right knowing, 74
rites, regularity of, 93
ritual, xiv-xv
    in Christianity, 17
    definition of, 11-12
    dimensions of, 12
    faith formation and, 19-22
    function of, 17-18
    liturgy and, 11-22
    negative responses to, 16-17
    in the Old Testament, 16-17
    phronesis as, 72
    in worship, 69-73
ritualism, 16
ritualization, steps of, 134-35
ritual knowing, xiv-xv, 65-69
ritual practice, memory and, 79-90
Robinson, Edward, 128
Roman Catholic Church, x
    liturgy of, 5, 7
    reliance of, on ceremony, 34
    theology of, 182
Rorem, Paul, 180

Rosenberg, Sheldon, 139
Ruthrof, Horst, 64-65

sacramental theology, 103-4, 174
sacraments
    Aquinas on, 103-4
    Calvin on, 25-26, 28-29, 49-51, 52, 176-85
    for children, 104-6
    for cognitively disabled, 104-6
    and communal confession and practice, 203
    facilitating understanding, 84-85
    inclusive nature of, 151
    objectivity and subjectivity of, 211
    objectivity or subjectivity of, 174-77
    participation in, xiii
    showing God's generosity, 173
    subjectivity of, xviii-xix
Sacrosanctum Concilium (The Constitution on the Sacred Liturgy), 5-6
Saliers, Don, xxii, 67, 81, 91
salvation, 51, 166, 205
sanctification, 42, 178
Schillebeeckx, Edward, 175
self-determination, 191
Senn, Frank, 9, 11
Smith, James K., x-xi, xiii, xv, 59-60, 80, 88, 92, 94
Smith, Jonathan, 13
Smith, Wilfred, 90
socialization, xviii, 170
social memory, 82
social skills development, 191-92
Solms, Mark, 63
Southern Presbyterian Church in the USA, 98
spirituality
    Christian, 59
    cognitively challenged people and, 154
    fundamental nature of, 152
    growth of, 201
    in serving the church, 200-3
split-brain people, 65
spiritual worship, 62

Index

sterilization, 100
Stern, Daniel, xvi, 131
Stookey, Laurence, 165, 175, 203–4
subconscious, 65–66
subsidiary awareness, 71
Sullivan, Annie, 64–65
Sunday school, 98–99, 107–8, 115, 119, 195, 197
superstition, 36–37
Swinton, John, 120, 121–22, 142–43, 172, 198–99
symbols, 15, 178–79
   recognition of, 69
   as tool for remembrance, 84–87

Table Talk, 105
tacit knowledge, xii, 71, 78
Tarasar, Constance, 171
tardocide, 99
Ten Commandments, in the liturgy, 10, 53–54, 81
Thaumaturges, Nicholas, 101
Theißen, Gerd, 93
theology
   liturgical, xix–xxi, 60
   practical, 72
   sacramental, 103–4, 174
   Western, xxi
Tonghap denomination (KPC), 119–20
Tongsung kido, 19–20
Torrance, James, 95, 161, 162, 171
transformation, through liturgy, 90–95
transubstantiation, 181
Trinity
   doctrine of, 166
   experience of, 43
   humans in communion with, 166
   relationship with, 170

unconscious, formation of, 88
United Church of Christ, 111
United Methodist Church (UMC), 111, 113

Van de Poll, G. J., 53–54
Vanier, Jean, 142, 189
Volf, Miroslav, 69, 77, 167
Vygotsky, L. S., 136–37, 140–41, 196–97

Wainwright, Geoffrey, 24
Wandel, Lee, xiii–xiv, 26, 49–50, 186
Webber, Robert, 17, 81
Webb-Mitchell, Brett, xv, 67, 72, 106–7, 120–21, 138, 154, 155, 157, 164–65, 205, 206, 210
Weil, Louis, 76, 80, 91
Weima, Jeffrey A. D., 192–93
Wendel, Francois, 179–80
Westerhoff, John, xvii–xviii, 129, 152, 170–71
Westermann, Claus, 159
Westminster Shorter Catechism, 7
White, James, 54–55, 175
Widaman, Keith, 126
Witvliet, John, x–xi, 23, 24, 27
Wolterstorff, Nicholas, x–xi, 4
World Council of Churches, x, 148
worship, 3–4. *See also* liturgy
   faith formation and, xxii, 51–55
   formative power of, 148
   God's power shown through, 146
   participation in, xiii, 50
   practice of, 70
   public, 30–31
   repetition in, 67–68
   rituals in, 69–73
   sensory experience of, 67
   spiritual, 62

Yong, Amos, 120, 121, 156, 159, 163–64, 169, 198
Yust, Karen Marie, 57, 173, 125–26, 191, 210

Zizioulas, John D., 164, 166–67
zone of proximal development, 140, 196–97
Zwingli, Huldrych, x, 178, 183

www.ingramcontent.com/pod-product-compliance
Lightning Source LLC
Chambersburg PA
CBHW050436240426
43661CB00055B/2400